COOKING LIGHT

® Landoll, Inc.
Ashland, Ohio 44805
© 1995 Coombe Books Ltd.

Table of Contents

Quick & Easy Cooking

Low Calorie Cooking

Pasta Cooking

Sugar Free Cooking

The Chicken Cookbook

Vitamin Rich Cooking

Fish & Seafood Cooking

Low Cholesterol Cooking

QUICK & EASY
COOKING

Introduction

Many people who do not have much time and energy to spend shopping or preparing meals have resorted to buying 'fast food' in the form of ready-prepared meals and take-aways. Unfortunately, as well as being an expensive way to eat, it does not necessarily guarantee an adequate supply of vitamins, minerals and fibre. For these very reasons, there has been something of a resurgence of home-cooking with an emphasis on quick and easy meals. With this in mind it is essential to know how to prepare food quickly and, just as importantly, what ingredients to use for the minimum of effort. Certain foods such as pasta, salads, fish, shellfish and eggs, are perfectly suited to quick cooking, but it is often the choice of meat which people find difficult. The various cuts best suited to quick cooking are as follows:

Beef - steak and minute steak, mince
Veal - escalopes, calves' liver
Pork - tenderloin (sliced into medallions), mince, steaks, chops, escalopes, liver
Lamb - noisettes, cutlets, leg chops, neck fillet, liver, kidney
Poultry - breast, escalopes, mince, liver
Game - duck breast, venison steak

Obviously, the method of cooking is all important, and you will find that in *Quick and Easy Cooking* there is less baking in the oven and more grilling, pan- and stir-frying and sautéeing. These short methods of cooking are very effective with the cuts of meat and fish already mentioned. Organisation and making the most of the time that you have available is all important. For cooks in a hurry the freezer can be most advantageous, as many people find it easier to do a large amount of cooking when they have the time, freeze it, and buy accompaniments such as fresh fruit and vegetables as required.

When short of time, entertaining can pose a problem. Planning is the key to success here and ease of preparation paramount. Choose one or two dishes, such as a starter (try Quick Liver Paté, Fennel and Orange Croustade or Stuffed Eggs) and a dessert, (such as Crepes, Strawberry Cloud, or Chocolate Brandy Mousse) that can be prepared in advance, even the day before. Dishes that can be part prepared and then frozen are also a boon, but remember to allow sufficient thawing time in your schedule. The main course should be something easy but effective, such as Trout with Chive Sauce, Chicken with Cherries, or Veal Scallopine with Prosciutto. This allows you the maximum time with guests, with the minimum of fuss and effort.

As you can see, successful quick and easy cooking may require a bit of thought at first and perhaps some change to your normal cooking style, but once undertaken this new way of cooking will soon become second nature and the term 'fast food' will have a new meaning in your household.

Contents

SPINACH AND APPLE SOUP

The two main flavours complement each other perfectly in this hearty soup.

SERVES 4

30g/1oz butter or margarine
1 small onion, chopped
30g/1oz flour
570ml/1 pint vegetable stock
450g/1lb spinach, shredded
225g/8oz apple purée
280ml/½ pint milk
Salt and freshly ground black pepper
Pinch of nutmeg
Lemon juice
Natural yogurt
A little parsley, finely chopped

1. Melt the butter in a large saucepan and sauté the onion until soft.

2. Add the flour and cook to a pale straw colour.

3. Add the stock slowly, stirring well, and simmer for 10 minutes.

4. Add the spinach and cook until tender.

5. Cool slightly and mix in the apple purée.

6. Place all the ingredients in a liquidiser and blend until smooth.

7. Return to the pan and reheat slowly together with the milk.

8. Add the salt and pepper, nutmeg and lemon juice to taste.

9. Serve in individual bowls with the yogurt swirled on the top and garnished with chopped parsley.

TIME: Preparation takes 15 minutes, cooking takes 15 minutes.

COOK'S TIP: The apple purée can be omitted if not available but it adds an unusual flavour to the soup.

VARIATIONS: If there is no vegetable water available for the stock, a stock cube can be mixed with 570ml/1 pint of boiling water instead.

EASY LENTIL SOUP

A good old-fashioned soup which is sure to please all the family.

SERVES 4-6

225g/8oz split red lentils
30g/1oz butter or margarine
1 medium onion, finely chopped
2 celery stalks, finely diced
2 carrots, finely diced
Grated rind of 1 lemon
1150ml/2 pints light vegetable stock
Salt and freshly ground black pepper

1. Pick over the lentils and remove any stones. Rinse well.

2. Heat the butter or margarine in a pan and sauté the onion for 2-3 minutes.

3. Add the diced celery and carrots and let the vegetables sweat for 5-10 minutes.

4. Stir in the lentils, add the lemon rind, stock and salt and pepper to taste.

5. Bring to the boil, reduce the heat and simmer for 15-20 minutes until the vegetables are tender.

6. Roughly blend the soup in a liquidiser; it should not be too smooth.

7. Check the seasoning and reheat gently.

TIME: Preparation takes about 10 minutes, cooking takes 15-20 minutes.
SERVING IDEAS: Sprinkle with cheese and serve with hot toast.
TO FREEZE: Freeze for up to 3 months.

MISO SOUP

This delicious soup of Japanese origin makes a nice change for a starter.

SERVES 2

1 small onion, grated
2cm/¾-inch fresh root ginger, peeled and
    finely chopped
1 clove garlic, crushed
1 tbsp sesame oil
1 carrot, finely sliced
¼ small cauliflower, divided into florets
1150ml/2 pints water
1 large tbsp arame (Japanese seaweed)
30g/1oz peas (fresh or frozen)
2 tbsps shoyu (Japanese soy sauce)
1 tbsp miso (soya bean paste)
Black pepper to taste
2 spring onions, finely chopped

1. Sauté the onion, ginger and garlic in the sesame oil for a few minutes.

2. Add the carrot and cauliflower and gently sweat the vegetables for 5 minutes.

3. Add the water, arame, peas and shoyu. Cook for 15-20 minutes or until the vegetables are soft.

4. Blend the miso to a paste with a little of the soup liquid and add to the soup, but do not allow to boil.

5. Season with freshly ground black pepper to taste.

6. Serve garnished with chopped spring onions.

TIME: Preparation takes 15 minutes, cooking takes 20 minutes.

SERVING IDEAS: Serve with hot garlic bread.

VARIATIONS: Substitute other vegetables such as mooli, turnip, swede, mange tout or green beans, but remember that this soup is mainly a broth with a few floating vegetables.

COOK'S TIP: Arame, shoyu and miso are available from Japanese grocers and some health food specialists.

CROUTON STUDDED CRISPY PRAWN BALLS

These crispy, crouton coated prawn balls make an excellent starter or snack.

SERVES 4

4 slices white bread
225g/8oz white fish fillets
225g/8oz shelled prawns
2 tsps salt
Pepper to taste
2 egg whites
2 slices fresh root ginger
2 tbsp cornflour
Oil for deep frying

1. Remove crusts from the bread. Cut each slice into small crouton-sized cubes. Spread out on a large baking tray and dry in a hot oven until slightly browned.

2. Chop the fish and prawns very finely. Mix together with the salt, pepper, egg white, finely chopped ginger, and cornflour. Blend well.

3. Shape the mixture into 5cm/2-inch balls, and roll over the croutons to coat.

4. Heat the oil in a deep fryer. Add the crouton studded prawn balls one by one. Turn with a perforated spoon until evenly browned, this takes about 2 minutes. Remove and drain.

5. Return to the oil and cook for a further 1 minute. Drain well on kitchen paper.

TIME: Preparation takes about 15 minutes and cooking takes 3 minutes per batch.

COOK'S TIP: Fry the prawn balls in batches if necessary.

SERVING IDEAS: Serve with a good quality soy sauce, ketchup or chilli sauce as dips.

EGGS BAKED IN TARRAGON CREAM

Extremely quick and easy to make, this is a very tasty way of cooking eggs for either a quick snack or a starter.

SERVES 4

---

1 knob of butter
4 large eggs
1 tbsp chopped fresh tarragon
Salt and pepper
60ml/4 tbsps cream

---

1. Butter 4 individual ovenproof ramekins, and break an egg into each one.

2. In a small bowl, stir the chopped tarragon and salt and pepper into the cream and mix well.

3. Spoon 1 tbsp of the cream mixture onto each egg.

4. Put the ramekins onto a baking sheet and cook in a preheated oven, 180°C/350°F/Gas Mark 4 for about 6-8 minutes, until set. Serve immediately.

TIME: Preparation takes about 5 minutes, and cooking takes up to 8 minutes.

PREPARATION: When cooking the eggs, check them during the cooking time to see how hard they have become. If you cook them for 8 minutes, they will be very set. If you require a softer yolk, cook them for a shorter time.

SERVING IDEAS: Serve piping hot with buttered toast or crusty French bread.

FENNEL AND ORANGE CROUSTADE

A delicious mixture which is simple to prepare and suitable to serve at a dinner party.

SERVES 4

4 × 2.5cm/1-inch thick slices wholemeal
  bread
Oil for deep frying
2 fennel bulbs (reserve any fronds)
4 oranges
1 tbsp olive oil
Pinch salt
Chopped fresh mint for garnishing

1. Trim the crusts off the bread and cut into 7.5cm/3-inch squares.

2. Hollow out the middles, leaving evenly shaped cases.

3. Heat the oil in a deep fat fryer or large saucepan, and deep fry the bread until golden brown.

4. Drain the bread well on absorbent kitchen paper, and leave to cool.

5. Trim the fennel bulbs and slice thinly. Place in a mixing bowl.

6. Remove all the peel and pith from the oranges. Cut flesh into segments – do this over the mixing bowl to catch the juice.

7. Mix the orange segments with the fennel.

8. Add the olive oil and salt and mix together thoroughly.

9. Just before serving, divide the fennel and orange mixture evenly between the bread cases and garnish with fresh mint and fennel fronds.

TIME: Preparation takes 15 minutes, cooking takes 5 minutes.

VARIATIONS: Serve the salad on individual plates sprinkled with croutons.

COOK'S TIP: The salad can be made in advance and refrigerated until required, but do not fill the cases until just before serving.

SMOKED SALMON ROLLS WITH PRAWN FILLING

This simply delicious starter will ensure guests feel spoiled without too much effort from the cook.

SERVES 4

225g/8oz frozen or fresh shelled, cooked prawns
2 tbsps mayonnaise
1 tbsp whipped cream
2 tbsps tomato purée
Squeeze lemon juice
8 slices of smoked salmon, about 30g/1oz each
Lemon wedges, sliced cucumber and tomato for garnish

1. Defrost the prawns and drain, if using frozen prawns.

2. Mix the mayonnaise, cream, tomato purée and lemon juice in a bowl and fold in the prawns.

3. Divide the mixture between the 8 slices of smoked salmon, placing it on top in a wedge shape and rolling the salmon around it in a cone shape. Allow two for each person.

4. Garnish with lemon wedges and sliced cucumber and tomato. Serve with thinly sliced soda bread and butter.

TIME: Preparation takes 15 minutes.

SERVING IDEAS: Serve on its own as a starter, or with bread and salad for a light lunch or supper.

STUFFED EGGS

Stuffed eggs makes an attractive, and deliciously different, party appetiser.

MAKES 36

18 small eggs, or quail eggs
60g/2oz unsalted butter
1 clove garlic, crushed
90g/3oz cooked, peeled prawns, finely
    chopped
½ tsp finely chopped fresh basil
Freshly ground black pepper, to taste

1. Cook the eggs in boiling water for 5 minutes. Drain, and plunge them immediately into cold water.

2. Allow the eggs to cool completely, then remove the shells. Rinse and drain.

3. Cut each egg in half lengthways and carefully remove the yolks.

4. Put the yolks into a large bowl and beat in the butter and garlic. Mix well. This, and the next step, could be carried out in a food processor.

5. Add the prawns, basil and pepper to the creamed egg yolk mixture. Beat thoroughly until a soft consistency results.

6. Fill each egg white half with a little of the prepared mixture, piling it attractively into the cavity left by the egg yolk.

7. Refrigerate until required.

TIME: Preparation takes 15 minutes, cooking takes 5 minutes.

VARIATIONS: Use flaked white crab meat instead of the prawns. For a more exotic dish, use quail eggs instead of hens' eggs.

SERVING IDEAS: Serve the filled egg halves on a plate which has been garnished with frisée lettuce leaves, and tiny pieces of red pepper.

QUICK LIVER PÂTÉ

*Liver sausage is lightly seasoned and smoked, and is available with either a
smooth or coarse consistancy.
It makes an "instant" pâté.*

SERVES 4

300g/11oz German liver sausage
60g/2oz melted butter, preferably unsalted
2 tbsps brandy (optional)
1 clove garlic, crushed
Salt and pepper
Salad, cress and black olives for garnish

1. Place the sausage in a bowl with the butter, brandy, if using, garlic, salt and pepper and beat until smooth. Alternatively, use a food processor.

2. Pour the mixture into a piping bag fitted with a rosette nozzle.

3. Choose a large serving dish or individual plates and pipe out several swirls of pâté. Garnish with sliced or whole black olives, salad and cress.

TIME: Preparation takes about 15 minutes.

COOK'S TIP: Always squeeze out the mixture from the top of the piping bag down to the nozzle. If the bag is held in the middle, the mixture will soften and melt or it will burst out of the top.

SERVING IDEAS: Serve with hot toast fingers or thin slices of buttered rye bread. Instead of piping the pâté, serve in individual pots.

MUSHROOMS IN SOUR CREAM

This very old recipe originally called for freshly gathered forest mushrooms.

SERVES 4-6

450g/1lb button mushrooms, quartered
30g/1oz butter or margarine
6 spring onions, thinly sliced
1 tbsp flour
1 tbsp lemon juice
2 tbsps chopped fresh dill or 1 tbsp dried
    dill
Pinch salt and pepper
90ml/3 fl oz sour cream
Paprika

1. Rinse the mushrooms and pat dry well. Trim the stalks level with the caps before quartering. Melt the butter in a frying pan and add the mushrooms and onions. Sauté for about 1 minute and stir in the flour.

2. Add the lemon juice and all the remaining ingredients, except the sour cream and paprika, and cook slowly for about 1 minute.

3. Stir in the sour cream and adjust the seasoning. Heat through for about 1 minute. Spoon into individual serving dishes or on top of buttered toast. Sprinkle with paprika and serve immediately.

TIME: Preparation takes about 20 minutes, cooking takes about 5-7 minutes.

WATCHPOINT: Sour cream will curdle if boiled, although the addition of flour to the sauce will help to stabilise it somewhat.

SERVING IDEAS: Use as a side dish or a starter with meat, poultry or game. Prepare double quantity and serve with a salad and bread as a light lunch.

MUSSELS IN GINGER-CUMIN SAUCE

This delicious combination of seafood, wine and spices makes for a mouthwatering start to a meal.

SERVES 4

1kg/2¼lbs mussels in their shells, scraped
2 shallots, chopped
1 bay leaf
90ml/3 fl oz white wine
30g/1oz butter
1 small piece ginger, grated
½ tsp cumin
¼ tsp turmeric
½ green chilli, seeded and chopped
Juice of ½ lime
140ml/¼ pint cream
Salt and pepper
2 tbsps chopped parsley

1. Discard any mussels that are open or have cracked shells.

2. Put mussels into a large, deep pan and sprinkle over half the shallot. Add the bay leaf and wine.

3. Cover the pan and bring to the boil, shaking the pan. Cook for about 3 minutes or until the mussels have opened. Set aside and keep covered.

4. Melt the butter in a saucepan and add the remaining chopped shallot. Soften for 2 minutes and add the ginger, cumin, turmeric and chilli.

5. Add the lime juice and strain on the cooking liquid from the mussels. Bring to the boil, stirring occasionally and allow to boil to reduce by half.

6. Pour on the cream and reboil to reduce slightly and thicken.

7. Divide the mussels between 4 serving bowls and pour on the sauce.

8. Sprinkle parsley over each serving.

TIME: Preparation takes 20 minutes and cooking takes about 15 minutes.

SERVING IDEAS: Serve with wholemeal French bread.

COOK'S TIP: Double the ingredients to serve 4 as a main course.

PASTA SHELLS WITH SEAFOOD

This speedy meal is excellent for informal entertaining.

SERVES 4

60g/2oz butter or margarine
2 cloves garlic, crushed
75ml/5 tbsps dry white wine
280ml/½ pint single cream
1 tbsp cornflour
2 tbsps water
1 tbsp lemon juice
Salt and pepper
275g/10oz pasta shells
450g/1lb prawns, shelled and de-veined
120g/4oz scallops, cleaned and sliced
1 tbsp chopped parsley

1. Melt the butter in a pan. Add the garlic, and cook for 1 minute. Add the wine and cream, bring back to the boil, and cook for 2 minutes.

2. Mix the cornflour with the water, and pour into the sauce. Stir until boiling. Add the lemon juice and salt and pepper to taste.

3. Meanwhile, cook the pasta in plenty of boiling, salted water, for about 10 minutes, until tender. Drain, shaking to remove excess water.

4. Add the prawns and scallops to the sauce and cook for 3 minutes.

5. Pour the sauce over the pasta shells, toss, and garnish with parsley before serving.

TIME: Preparation takes 5 minutes, cooking takes 15 minutes.

BUYING GUIDE: When buying fresh prawns ensure they are firm and brightly coloured.

TURKEY MARSALA

Marsala is a dessert wine from Sicily which also complements turkey, veal or chicken surprisingly well. It is traditional, but sherry will serve as a substitute if Marsala is unavailable.

SERVES 4

4 turkey escalopes or breast fillets
60g/2oz butter or margarine
1 clove garlic
4 anchovy fillets, soaked in milk
4 slices Mozzarella cheese
Capers
2 tsps chopped marjoram
1 tbsp chopped parsley
3 tbsps Marsala
140ml/¼ pint double cream
Salt and pepper

1. If using the turkey breasts, flatten between two sheets of greaseproof paper with a meat mallet or rolling pin.

2. Melt butter in a frying pan and, when foaming, add the garlic and the turkey. Cook for a few minutes on each side until lightly browned. Remove them from the pan.

3. Drain the anchovy fillets and rinse them well. Dry on kitchen paper. Put a slice of cheese on top of each turkey fillet and arrange the anchovies and capers on top of each. Sprinkle with the chopped herbs and return the turkey to the pan.

4. Cook the turkey a further 5 minutes over moderate heat, until the turkey is cooked through, and the cheese has melted. Remove to a serving dish and keep warm.

5. Return the pan to the heat and add the Marsala to deglaze, then reduce the heat. Add the cream and whisk in well. Lower the heat and simmer gently, uncovered, for a few minutes to thicken the sauce. Season the sauce with salt and pepper and spoon over the turkey fillets to serve.

TIME: Preparation takes about 25 minutes and cooking about 15 minutes.

WATCHPOINT: Turkey breast fillets are very lean so can dry out easily if over-cooked.

SERVING IDEAS: Accompany the Turkey Marsala with new potatoes and lightly cooked courgettes.

TROUT WITH CHIVE SAUCE

Chive sauce really complements trout and turns a simple dish into a speedy meal fit for a special occasion.

SERVES 4

---

4 even-sized rainbow trout, gutted and fins trimmed
Flour mixed with salt and pepper for dredging
45g/1½oz butter, melted
2 tbsps white wine
280ml/½ pint double cream
1 small bunch chives, snipped
Salt and pepper

---

1. Dredge the trout with the seasoned flour and place on a lightly greased baking sheet. Spoon the melted butter over the fish.

2. Bake in a 200°C/400°F/Gas Mark 6 oven for about 10 minutes, basting frequently with the butter. Cook until the skin is crisp. Check the fish on the underside close to the bone. If the fish is not cooked through, lower the oven temperature to 160°C/325°F/Gas Mark 3 for a further 5 minutes.

3. Pour the wine into a small saucepan and bring to the boil. Boil to reduce by half. Pour on the cream and bring back to the boil. Allow to boil rapidly until the cream thickens slightly. Stir in the snipped chives, reserving some to sprinkle on top, if wished.

4. When the fish are browned remove to a serving dish and spoon over some of the sauce. Sprinkle with the reserved chives and serve the rest of the sauce separately.

TIME: Preparation takes 15 minutes and cooking takes 15-20 minutes.

VARIATIONS: Use this sauce with other fish such as salmon steaks.

SERVING IDEAS: Serve with boiled new potatoes and broccoli.

COD CURRY

The fragrant spices used in this recipe are now readily available at most supermarkets.

SERVES 4

1 large onion, chopped
3 tbsps vegetable oil
2.5cm/1-inch piece cinnamon stick
1 bay leaf
1 tsp ginger paste
1 tsp garlic paste
1 tsp chilli powder
1 tsp ground cumin
1 tsp ground coriander
¼ tsp ground turmeric
140ml/¼ pint natural yogurt
    or 225g/8oz can tomatoes, chopped
1-2 fresh green chillies, chopped
2 sprigs fresh coriander leaves, chopped
1lb cod cutlets, or fillets, cut into 5cm/2-
    inch pieces
1 tsp salt

1. In a large heavy-based saucepan, sauté the onion in the oil until golden brown. Add the cinnamon, bay leaf and the ginger and garlic pastes and cook for 1 minute.

2. Add the ground spices and cook for a further minute, then stir in *either* the yogurt, *or* the canned tomatoes and the chopped chillies and coriander leaves.

3. Only if you have used yogurt, stir in 140ml/¼ pint water and simmer the mixture for 2-3 minutes. Do not add any water if you have used the canned tomatoes.

4. Stir the cod into the sauce, and add the salt. Cover the pan and simmer for 15-18 minutes before serving.

TIME: Preparation takes about 15 minutes, and cooking takes about 20 minutes.

COOK'S TIP: Great care should be taken when preparing fresh chillies. Always wash hands thoroughly afterwards, and avoid getting any juice in the eyes or mouth. Rinse with copious amounts of clear water if this happens. For a milder curry, remove the seeds.

SERVING IDEAS: Serve with boiled rice and a cucumber salad.

BARBECUED PRAWNS

It's the sauce rather than the cooking method that gives the dish its name.
It's spicy, zippy and hot.

SERVES 2

450g/1lb large prawns, cooked and
    unpeeled
120g/4oz unsalted butter
1 tsp each white, black and cayenne
    pepper
Pinch salt
1 tsp each chopped fresh thyme, rosemary
    and marjoram
1 clove garlic, crushed
1 tsp Worcestershire sauce
140ml/¼ pint fish stock
60ml/4 tbsps dry white wine
Cooked rice, to serve

1. Remove the eyes and the legs from the prawns.

2. Melt the butter in a large frying pan and add the white pepper, black pepper, cayenne pepper, salt, herbs and garlic. Add the prawns and toss over heat for a few minutes until heated through. Remove the prawns and set them aside and keep warm.

3. Add the Worcestershire sauce, stock and wine to the ingredients in the pan. Bring to the boil and cook for about 3 minutes to reduce. Add salt to taste.

4. Arrange the prawns on a bed of rice and pour over the sauce to serve.

TIME: Preparation takes about 15 minutes and cooking takes about 5 minutes.

PREPARATION: Because the prawns are precooked, cook them very briefly again, just to heat through. Use uncooked, unpeeled prawns if possible. Cook these until they curl and turn pink.

SERVING IDEAS: The prawns may also be served cold. If serving cold, prepare the sauce with 90ml/6 tbsps oil instead of the butter.

LIVER VENEZIANA

As the name indicates, this recipe originated in Venice. The lemon juice offsets the rich taste of liver in this very famous Italian dish.

SERVES 4-6

Risotto

45g/1½oz butter or margarine
1 large onion, chopped
250g/9oz Italian (risotto) rice
60ml/4 tbsps dry white wine
570ml/1 pint chicken stock
¼ tsp saffron
Salt and pepper
2 tbsps grated fresh Parmesan cheese

Liver

450g/1lb calves' or lambs' liver
Flour for dredging
30g/1oz butter or margarine
2 tbsps oil
3 onions, thinly sliced
Juice of ½ a lemon
Salt and pepper
1 tbsp chopped parsley

1. Melt the butter for the risotto in a large frying pan, add the onion and cook until soft but not coloured, over gentle heat.

2. Add the rice and cook for about a minute until the rice looks transparent.

3. Add the wine, stock, saffron and seasoning. Stir well and bring to the boil. Lower the heat and cook gently for about 20 minutes, stirring frequently, until the liquid has been absorbed.

4. Meanwhile, heat the butter or margarine and 1 tbsp oil in a large frying pan, and cook the onions until golden.

5. Trim the liver and cut into strips. Toss in a sieve with the flour to coat.

6. Remove the onions from the pan to a plate. Add more oil if necessary, raise the heat under the pan and add the liver. Cook, stirring constantly, for about 2 minutes.

7. Return the onions and add the lemon juice and parsley. Cook a further 2 minutes or until the liver is tender. Season with salt and pepper and serve with the risotto.

8. To finish the risotto, add the cheese and salt and pepper to taste when the liquid has been absorbed, and toss to melt the cheese.

TIME: Risotto takes about 30 minutes to prepare and cook. Liver takes about 4 minutes to cook.

WATCHPOINT: Liver needs only brief cooking or it will toughen.

PREPARATION: Tossing the liver and flour together in a sieve coats each piece of meat more evenly than can be done by hand.

COOK'S TIP: If wished add 60ml/4 tbsps stock to the recipe for a little more sauce.

SMOKED SALMON ROMA

This quick dish has a fresh, light tasting sauce, perfect for summer eating.
A simple green salad goes well.

SERVES 4

1 small onion, chopped
A little butter and oil for frying
2 courgettes, cut into sticks
Small bunch fresh dill, chopped
225ml/8 fl oz single cream mixed with
    2 tbsps of soured cream
Salt and black pepper
120g/4oz smoked salmon, cut into strips
225g/8oz fine ribbon pasta (linguine)
Lemon and dill to decorate

1. Fry the onion in a little butter and oil until soft.

2. Add the courgettes and sauté for a few minutes. Do not overcook, they should remain crisp.

3. Add the chopped dill and the cream mixture, and gently heat through.

4. Season to taste and fold in the salmon strips. Keep warm.

5. Cook the pasta as directed on packet; drain.

6. Put the pasta in an oval dish and pour the sauce into the centre. Decorate with lemon wedges and dill.

TIME: Preparation and cooking takes about 25 minutes.

VARIATIONS: Use different shapes of pasta such as bows, or whatever you have to hand.

OVEN BAKED SPAGHETTI

A convenient way to cook this favourite mid-week meal.

SERVES 4

225g/8oz wholewheat spaghetti, cooked
2 × 400g/14oz tins tomatoes, roughly
  chopped
1 large onion, grated
1 tsp oregano
Seasoning
120g/4oz Cheddar cheese
2 tbsps grated Parmesan cheese

1. Grease four individual ovenproof dishes and place a quarter of the spaghetti in each one.

2. Pour the tomatoes over the top.

3. Add the onion, sprinkle with oregano and season well.

4. Slice the cheese finely and arrange over the top of the spaghetti mixture.

5. Sprinkle with Parmesan and bake at 180°C/350°F/Gas Mark 4 for 20-25 minutes.

TIME: Preparation takes 10 minutes, cooking takes 20-25 minutes.

SERVING IDEAS: Serve with garlic bread.

WATCHPOINT: When cooking spaghetti remember to add a few drops of oil to the boiling water to stop it sticking together.

COOK'S TIP: Oven Baked Spaghetti may be cooked in one large casserole if required, but add 10 minutes to the cooking time.

PRAWNS AND GINGER

Quick and easy to prepare, this dish is really delicious and also very nutritious.

SERVES 6

2 tbsps oil
675g/1½lbs peeled prawns
2.5cm/1-inch piece fresh root ginger,
    peeled and finely chopped
2 cloves of garlic, peeled and finely
    chopped
2-3 spring onions, chopped
1 leek, white part only, cut into strips
120g/4oz peas, shelled
175g/6oz bean sprouts
2 tbsps dark soy sauce
1 tsp sugar
Pinch salt

1. Heat the oil in a wok and stir-fry the prawns for 2-3 minutes. Set the prawns aside.

2. Reheat the oil and add the ginger and garlic. Stir quickly, then add the onions, leek and peas. Stir-fry for 2-3 minutes.

3. Add the bean sprouts and prawns to the cooked vegetables. Stir in the soy sauce, sugar and salt, and cook for 2 minutes. Serve immediately.

TIME: Preparation takes about 10 minutes, and cooking takes about 7-9 minutes.

PREPARATION: The vegetables can be prepared in advance and kept in airtight plastic boxes in the refrigerator for up to 6 hours before needed.

SERVING IDEAS: Serve this on its own with rice or pasta, or as part of an authentic Chinese meal.

SPAGHETTI MARINARA

A delightful mix of seafood makes this dish special enough for any occasion, and it's quick and easy too!

SERVES 4

45g/1½oz can anchovy fillets
75ml/5 tbsps water
75ml/5 tbsps dry white wine
1 bay leaf
4 peppercorns
225g/8oz scallops, cleaned and sliced
2 tbsps olive oil
2 cloves garlic, crushed
1 tsp basil
1 x 400g/14oz can plum tomatoes, seeded
    and chopped
1 tbsp tomato purée
275g/10oz spaghetti
450g/1lb cooked prawns, shelled and
    de-veined
1 tbsp chopped parsley
Salt and pepper

1. Drain anchovies and cut into small pieces.

2. Place water, wine, bay leaf and peppercorns in a pan. Heat to a slow boil. Add scallops and cook for 2 minutes. Remove and drain.

3. Heat the oil, add garlic and basil, and cook for 30 seconds. Add tomatoes, anchovies and tomato purée. Stir until combined. Cook for 10 minutes.

4. Meanwhile, cook the spaghetti in a large pan of boiling, salted water for 10 minutes, or until tender but still firm. Drain.

5. Add seafood to sauce, and cook a further 1 minute, to heat through. Add parsley and stir through. Season with salt and pepper to taste. Toss gently.

6. Pour sauce over spaghetti and serve immediately, sprinkled with parsley.

TIME: Preparation takes 10 minutes, cooking takes 20 minutes.

VARIATIONS: Substitute the prawns and scallops with the fresh seafood 'cocktails' now available in many supermarkets.

HAM AND GREEN PEPPER OMELETTE

Served with salad and crusty French bread, this makes a tasty lunch or supper dish.

MAKES 1

3 eggs
2 tbsps milk
Freshly ground black pepper
1 tbsp vegetable oil
30g/1oz chopped green pepper
2 tomatoes, skinned, seeded and roughly chopped
60g/2oz lean ham, cut into small dice

1. Break the eggs into a bowl and beat in the milk and pepper.

2. Heat the oil in an omelette pan and cook the green pepper until it is just soft.

3. Stir in the tomatoes and the ham. Heat through for 1 minute.

4. Pour the egg mixture into the frying pan over the vegetables. Stir the mixture briskly with a wooden spoon, until it begins to cook.

5. As the egg begins to set, lift it slightly and tilt the pan to allow the uncooked egg to flow underneath.

6. When the egg on top is still slightly creamy, fold the omelette in half and slip it onto a serving plate. Serve immediately.

TIME: Preparation takes about 15 minutes, cooking takes 5 minutes.

COOK'S TIP: To skin tomatoes easily, cut a small cross into the skin and drop them into boiling water for about 10 seconds, then plunge into cold water. This loosens the skin.

VARIATIONS: Use any selection of your favourite vegetables to vary this delicious dish.

RICH PAN-FRIED STEAKS

Thin steaks are quickly fried and then cooked in a savoury brown sauce.

SERVES 4

4-8 pieces frying steak, depending on size
1 tbsp oil
1 tbsp butter or margarine
1 tbsp flour
6 spring onions
1 clove garlic, crushed
1 tsp chopped thyme
2 tsps chopped parsley
3 tomatoes, skinned, seeded and chopped
280ml/½ pint beef stock
Dash of Tabasco
Salt and pepper

1. Place the meat between 2 sheets of greaseproof or waxed paper and pound with a rolling pin or a meat mallet to flatten slightly.

2. Heat the oil in a large frying pan and brown the meat quickly, a few pieces at a time. Set the meat aside.

3. Melt the butter or margarine in the frying pan and add the flour. Cut the white part off the spring onions and chop it finely. Add to the flour and butter, reserving the green tops for later use.

4. Add the garlic to the pan and cook the mixture slowly, stirring frequently until it is a dark golden brown. Add the herbs, tomatoes, stock, Tabasco and salt and pepper to taste, and bring to the boil. Cook for about 5 minutes to thicken and then add the steaks. Cook to heat the meat through.

5. Chop the green tops of the spring onions and sprinkle over the steaks to garnish.

TIME: Preparation takes about 20 minutes and cooking takes about 20 minutes.

SERVING IDEAS: Serve with rice or potatoes. Add a green vegetable or salad.

VARIATIONS: Add chopped red or green pepper to the sauce.

SAUTÉED LEMON PORK

A perfect way to prepare this tender cut of pork. Butchers will bat out the meat for you.

SERVES 4

8 small pork escalopes or steaks, batted out
    until thin
Flour for dredging
Salt and pepper
30g/1oz butter or margarine
1 green pepper, thinly sliced
90ml/6 tbsps dry white wine or sherry
1 tbsp lemon juice
175ml/6 fl oz chicken stock
1 lemon, peeled and thinly sliced

1. Dredge pork with a mixture of flour, salt and pepper. Shake off the excess.

2. Melt the butter or margarine in a large frying pan and brown the pork, a few pieces at a time. Remove the meat and keep it warm.

3. Cook the peppers briefly and set aside with the pork.

4. Pour the wine or sherry and lemon juice into the pan to deglaze. Add the stock and bring to the boil. Boil for 5 minutes to reduce. Add the pork and peppers and cook for 15 minutes over gentle heat. Add the lemon slices and heat through before serving.

TIME: Preparation takes about 25 minutes and cooking takes about 20-25 minutes.

PREPARATION: Cut off all the rind and pith of the lemon, using a sharp knife, before slicing the flesh.

VARIATIONS: Use red pepper instead of green pepper and add chopped spring onions.

MACARONI CHEESE WITH ANCHOVIES

Anchovies add extra flavour to this much loved homely dish.

SERVES 4

60g/2oz can anchovy fillets
225g/8oz macaroni
60g/2oz butter or margarine
60g/2oz flour
570ml/1 pint milk
½ tsp dry mustard
175g/6oz Gruyère or Cheddar cheese,
    grated
Salt and pepper

1. Drain the anchovies, and set enough aside to slice to make a thin lattice over the dish. Chop the rest finely.

2. Cook the macaroni in plenty of boiling, salted water for 10 minutes, or until tender but still firm. Rinse in hot water and drain well.

3. Meanwhile, melt the butter in a pan. Stir in the flour and cook for 1 minute.

4. Remove from the heat, and gradually stir in the milk. Return to the heat and bring to the boil. Simmer for 3 minutes, stirring occasionally.

5. Stir in the mustard, anchovies, and half the cheese. Season with salt and pepper to taste. Stir in the macaroni, and pour into an ovenproof dish.

6. Sprinkle the remaining cheese over the top, and make a latticework with the remaining anchovies. Brown under a hot grill. Serve immediately.

TIME: Preparation takes 5 minutes, cooking takes 15 minutes.

SERVING IDEAS: Serve this hearty dish with crusty bread and a mixed green salad.

CHICKEN WITH CHERRIES

Canned cherries make an easy sauce that really dresses up chicken.

SERVES 6

Oil
6 chicken breasts, skinned and boned
1 sprig fresh rosemary
Grated rind and juice of ½ a lemon
140ml/¼ pint red wine
Salt and pepper
450g/1lb canned black cherries, pitted
2 tsps cornflour

1. Heat about 60ml/4 tbsps oil in a frying pan over moderate heat. Place in the chicken breasts, skinned side down first. Cook until just lightly browned. Turn over and cook the second side about 2 minutes.

2. Remove any oil remaining in the pan and add the rosemary, lemon rind, wine and salt and pepper. Bring to the boil and then lower the heat.

3. Add the cherries and their juice. Cook, covered, for 15 minutes or until the chicken is tender. Remove the chicken and cherries and keep them warm. Discard the rosemary.

4. Mix the cornflour and lemon juice. Add several spoonfuls of the hot sauce to the cornflour mixture. Return the mixture to the frying pan and bring to the boil, stirring constantly, until thickened and cleared.

5. Pour the sauce over the chicken and cherries. Heat through and serve.

TIME: Preparation takes about 10 minutes and cooking takes about 20 minutes.

PREPARATION: Serve the chicken dish on the day that it is cooked – it does not keep well.

SERVING IDEAS: Serve with plain boiled rice. Accompany with a green vegetable such as lightly steamed mange tout.

VEAL SCALOPPINE WITH PROSCIUTTO AND CHEESE

Veal is the meat used most often in Italian cooking. Good veal is tender and quick cooking, but expensive. Save this recipe for your next dinner party!

SERVES 4

8 veal escalopes
30g/1oz butter or margarine
1 clove garlic, crushed
8 slices prosciutto ham
3 tbsps sherry
140ml/¼ pint beef stock
1 sprig rosemary
8 slices Mozzarella cheese
Salt and pepper

1. Pound the veal escalopes out thinly between two pieces of greaseproof paper with a meat mallet or a rolling pin.

2. Melt the butter or margarine in a frying pan and add the veal and garlic. Cook until the veal is lightly browned on both sides.

3. Place a piece of prosciutto on top of each piece of veal and add the sherry, stock and sprig of rosemary to the pan. Cover the pan and cook the veal for about 10 minutes over gentle heat or until tender and cooked through.

4. Remove the meat to a warmed heatproof serving dish and top each piece of veal with a slice of cheese.

5. Bring the cooking liquid from the veal to the boil, season and allow to boil rapidly to reduce slightly.

6. Meanwhile, grill the veal to melt and brown the cheese. Remove the sprig of rosemary from the sauce and pour the sauce around the meat to serve.

TIME: Preparation takes about 15 minutes, cooking takes 15-20 minutes.

VARIATIONS: White wine may be substituted for the sherry, if wished, and 1 tsp of tomato purée may be added to the sauce. Use chicken, turkey or pork instead of the veal.

CRUNCHY COD

Cod provides the perfect base for a crunchy, slightly spicy topping.

SERVES 4

4 even-sized cod fillets
Salt and pepper
90g/3oz butter, melted
90g/3oz dry breadcrumbs
1 tsp dry mustard
1 tsp finely chopped onion
Dash Worcestershire sauce and Tabasco
2 tbsps lemon juice
1 tbsp finely chopped parsley

1. Season the fish fillets with salt and pepper and place them on a grill pan. Brush with some of the butter and grill for about 5 minutes.

2. Combine the remaining butter with the breadcrumbs, mustard, onion, Worcestershire sauce, Tabasco, lemon juice and parsley.

3. Spoon the mixture carefully on top of each fish fillet, covering it completely. Press down lightly to pack the crumbs into place. Grill for a further 5-7 minutes, or until the top is lightly browned and the fish flakes.

TIME: Preparation takes about 15 minutes and cooking takes about 12 minutes.

PREPARATION: If wished, the fish may also be baked in the oven at 180°C/350°F/Gas Mark 4. Cover the fish with foil for the first 5 minutes of baking time, uncover and top with the breadcrumb mixture. Bake for a further 10-12 minutes.

VARIATIONS: The breadcrumb topping may be used on other fish such as haddock, halibut or sole.

BROCCOLI AND CAULIFLOWER SALAD

Serve this simple salad with crackers.

SERVES 4

1 red pepper
300g/10oz broccoli
300g/10oz cauliflower
1 tbsp roasted almond flakes

Dressing
60ml/4 tbsps Greek yogurt
2 tbsps lemon juice
2 tbsps olive oil
Salt and pepper
Pinch of nutmeg

1. Cut the pepper into matchstick pieces.

2. Wash and trim the broccoli and cauliflower and break into small florets.

3. Place the pepper, broccoli and cauliflower in a mixing bowl.

4. Combine the yogurt, lemon juice, olive oil, seasoning and nutmeg in a screw top jar and shake well.

5. Spoon the dressing over the salad and mix together well.

6. Divide the mixture between 4 individual serving plates and garnish with the almond flakes.

TIME: Preparation takes 10 minutes.

VARIATIONS: Omit the nutmeg from the dressing and add a few freshly chopped herbs.

COOK'S TIP: If preparing this salad in advance, don't garnish with the almonds until serving time.

KENSINGTON SALAD

This salad has plenty of crunch to it and a lovely tangy dressing.

SERVES 2-3

3 large mushrooms, thinly sliced
1 medium eating apple, cut into chunks and
    coated with lemon juice
2 celery sticks, cut into matchsticks
30g/1oz walnut pieces
1 bunch watercress

Dressing
1 tbsp mayonnaise
1 tbsp thick yogurt
½ tsp herb mustard
A little lemon juice
Salt and pepper

1. Place the mushrooms, apple, celery and walnuts in a bowl.

2. Combine all the ingredients for the dressing and mix gently with the vegetables.

3. Arrange the watercress on a flat dish or platter and mound the salad mixture on the top.

TIME: Preparation takes about 10 minutes.

VARIATIONS: A medium bulb of fennel, finely sliced, could be used in place of the celery.

SERVING IDEAS: Decorate the top of this salad with a line of sliced strawberries or kiwi fruit.

GREEK COUNTRY SALAD

Lettuce is cut finely for salads in Greece. In fact, the finer the shreds of lettuce the better the salad is considered to be.

SERVES 4

2 tbsps olive oil
1 tbsp lemon juice
Salt and ground black pepper
1 clove garlic, crushed
1 cos lettuce, well washed
3 tomatoes, sliced
90g/3oz black olives
120g/4oz feta cheese, diced
½ red pepper, sliced
6 peperonata
Fresh or dried oregano

1. Whisk the oil, lemon juice, salt and pepper and garlic together until well emulsified. A blender or food processor may be used for this.

2. Stack up 5 or 6 lettuce leaves and shred them finely with a sharp knife.

3. Place the lettuce in the bottom of a serving dish and arrange the other ingredients on top. Spoon over the dressing and sprinkle on the oregano.

TIME: Preparation takes about 10-15 minutes.

BUYING GUIDE: Peperonata are small whole peppers preserved in brine. They can be bought bottled in delicatessens and some supermarkets.

VARIATIONS: Substitute green pepper for red pepper if wished. Other varieties of lettuce may also be used.

GREEN AND GOLD SUNFLOWER SALAD

This colourful salad makes a spectacular and delicious addition to a summer meal.

SERVES 4

3 tbsps sunflower oil
1 tbsp lemon juice
Salt and pepper
2 large ripe avocados
8 ripe apricots
140ml/¼ pint natural yogurt
2 tsps honey
Grated rind of 1 lemon
2 tsps chopped fresh parsley
1 small webb lettuce, washed and separated
    into leaves
60g/2oz toasted sunflower seeds

1. Put the oil and lemon juice into a small bowl with the salt and pepper. Mix together well.

2. Cut the avocados in half and remove the stones. Peel them, cut into slices and mix these into the oil and lemon juice dressing very carefully, taking care not to break them.

3. Cut the apricots in half and remove the stones. If the apricots are large, cut them in half again. Add them to the avocados in the dressing.

4. In another bowl, mix together the yogurt, honey, lemon rind and parsley.

5. Put the lettuce leaves onto individual salad plates and arrange the avocado and apricots on top in a sunflower design.

6. Spoon a little of the yogurt mixture over the salad, and sprinkle with sunflower seeds. Pour any remaining yogurt dressing into a small jug and serve separately.

TIME: Preparation takes about 15 minutes.

VARIATIONS: Use segments of ruby grapefruit in place of the apricots.

SERVING IDEAS: Serve as an unusual first course, or as an accompaniment to a chicken or fish dish.

RICE AND NUT SALAD

This refreshing salad is high in protein from the rice, nuts and beans, so it could be eaten as a vegetarian main course.

SERVES 4

2 tbsps olive oil

2 tbsps lemon juice

Freshly ground sea salt and black pepper

120g/4oz sultanas

60g/2oz currants

275g/10oz cooked brown rice, well drained

90g/3oz blanched almonds, chopped

60g/2oz cashew nuts, chopped

60g/2oz shelled walnuts, chopped

425g/15oz can peach slices in natural juice, drained and chopped

¼ cucumber, cubed

120g/4oz cooked red kidney beans

A few pitted black olives

1. Put the olive oil, lemon juice and salt and pepper into a screw top jar. Shake vigorously, until the mixture has thickened.

2. Put the sultanas and the currants into a small bowl, and cover with boiling water. Allow to stand for 10 minutes, before draining the fruit.

3. Mix together the rice, nuts, soaked fruit, peaches, cucumber, kidney beans and olives in a large mixing bowl.

4. Pour the dressing over the salad, and mix together thoroughly, to ensure all the ingredients are evenly coated.

TIME: Preparation will take about 15 minutes.

PREPARATION: If you would like to create a slightly unusual flavour, soak the sultanas and currants in hot jasmine tea, instead of water.

VARIATIONS: Use a 425g/15oz can apricot halves in natural juice, in place of the can of peaches.

SERVING IDEAS: Serve the salad on a bed of crisp lettuce, or endive, chopped.

CREAMY SWEETCORN AND PEPPERS

Sweetcorn is essential to this recipe, but other vegetables can be added, too. Choose your favourites or use what you have to hand.

SERVES 6

60ml/4 tbsps oil
30g/1oz butter
2 medium onions, finely chopped
1 clove garlic, crushed
1 medium green pepper, cut into small dice
6 tomatoes, skinned, seeded and diced
225g/8oz frozen corn kernels
280ml/½ pint chicken or vegetable stock
Pinch salt
60ml/4 tbsps double cream
Pinch of paprika

1. Heat the oil in a large casserole and add the butter. When foaming, add the onions and garlic and cook, stirring frequently, for about 5 minutes or until both are soft and transparent but not browned.

2. Add the green pepper, tomatoes, corn and stock. Bring to the boil over high heat.

3. Reduce the heat, partially cover the casserole and allow to cook slowly for about 10 minutes, or until the corn is tender. Add salt and stir in the cream. Heat through, sprinkle with paprika and serve immediately.

TIME: Preparation takes about 25 minutes. Cooking takes about 10 minutes.

VARIATIONS: Use canned tomatoes, coarsely chopped.

COOK'S TIP: Sweetcorn toughens if cooked at too high a temperature for too long, or if boiled too rapidly.

STRAWBERRY CLOUD

It takes no time at all to make this delightful summer dessert.

SERVES 4-6

450g/1lb strawberries
1 × 275g/10oz pack silken tofu
Juice of ½ lemon
2 tbsps soft brown sugar
Few drops vanilla essence

1. Wash and hull the strawberries. Leave a few on one side to decorate.

2. Drain the tofu and put into the liquidiser together with the strawberries, lemon juice and sugar.

3. Liquidise until smooth.

4. Add vanilla essence to taste and mix well.

5. Divide the mixture between 4-6 individual serving dishes and decorate with the reserved strawberries.

6. Chill until required.

TIME: Preparation takes 5-8 minutes.

SERVING IDEAS: For a special occasion, pipe whipped cream around the edges of the serving dishes.

VARIATIONS: Other fruits such as apples or peaches may be used instead but they will not produce such a colourful dessert.

COOK'S TIP: Substitute cream cheese for tofu if wished and add lemon juice to taste.

BROWN SUGAR BANANAS

Bananas in a rich brown sugar sauce make a delectable dessert.

SERVES 4

4 ripe bananas, peeled
Lemon juice
120g/4oz butter
120g/4oz soft brown sugar, light or dark
Pinch ground cinnamon and nutmeg
140ml/¼ pint orange juice
60ml/4 tbsps white or dark rum
Juice of ½ lemon
140ml/¼ pint whipped cream
2 tbsps chopped pecans

1. Cut the bananas in half lengthwise and sprinkle with lemon juice on all sides.

2. Melt the butter in a large frying pan and add the sugar, cinnamon, nutmeg and orange juice. Stir over gentle heat until the sugar dissolves into a syrup.

3. Add the banana halves and cook gently for about 3 minutes, basting the bananas often with syrup, but not turning them.

4. Once the bananas are heated through, warm the rum in a small saucepan and ignite with a match. Pour the flaming rum over the bananas and shake the pan gently until the flames die down naturally. Place 2 banana halves on each serving plate and top with some of the whipped cream. Sprinkle with pecans and serve immediately.

TIME: Preparation takes about 15 minutes and cooking takes about 5 minutes for the sugar and butter syrup and 3-4 minutes for the bananas.

SERVING IDEAS: The bananas may be served with vanilla ice cream instead of whipped cream, if wished.

COOK'S TIP: Sprinkling the cut surfaces of the banana with lemon juice keeps them from turning brown and also offsets the sweetness of the sauce.

SWEET ALMOND PUDDING

A delicious variation on a traditional pudding; ground rice was never like this at school!

SERVES 4

180g/6oz blanched almonds
430ml/¾ pint water
180g/6oz sugar
3 tbsps ground rice
140ml/¼ pint milk

1. Blend the blanched almonds and the water in a liquidiser or food processor, until the almonds are well chopped.

2. Put the almond liquid into a medium-sized saucepan and bring this mixture to the boil over a gentle heat.

3. Add the sugar and stir until it has completely dissolved.

4. Blend together the rice and the milk in a jug.

5. Add the rice mixture slowly to the simmering sugar and almond mixture, stirring continuously, until the pudding thickens.

6. Remove the rice pudding from the heat and pour into individual serving dishes.

TIME: Preparation takes about 5 minutes, and cooking takes 6-7 minutes.

VARIATIONS: Lightly toast some flaked or chopped almonds and sprinkle these over the top of the pudding to serve.

SERVING IDEAS: Serve this pudding cold with fresh or stewed fruit.

OATLET COOKIES

A delicious mix of oats, seeds and syrup make these cookies extra special.

MAKES 10 COOKIES

120g/4oz porridge oats
120g/4oz plain flour
90g/3oz sunflower seeds
30g/1oz sesame seeds
½ tsp mixed spice
120g/4oz margarine
1 tbsp brown sugar
1 tsp golden syrup or molasses
½ tsp baking powder
1 tbsp boiling water
225g/8oz chocolate drops

1. Mix the oats, flour, sunflower seeds, sesame seeds and spice together.

2. Melt the margarine, sugar and golden syrup or molasses over a gentle heat.

3. Add the baking powder and water to the syrup mixture and stir well.

4. Pour over dry ingredients and mix.

5. Place spoonfuls of the mixture, well apart, onto a greased baking tray and bake for 10 minutes at 190°C/375°F/Gas Mark 5.

6. Allow to cool on the tray.

7. Melt the chocolate drops in a bowl over hot water and place teaspoonsful of the melted chocolate on top of the cookies. Leave to set. Store in an airtight tin.

TIME: Preparation takes 15 minutes, cooking takes 10 minutes.

VARIATIONS: Ground ginger can be used in place of the mixed spice.

COOK'S TIP: A block of chocolate may be used in place of the chocolate drops.

SHORTBREAD BISCUITS

Sandwich these biscuits together with raspberry jam for children's birthday parties.

MAKES ABOUT 18

150g/5oz plain flour
75g/2½oz light muscovado sugar, finely ground
120g/4oz soft margarine
½ tsp vanilla essence

1. Sieve the flour and sugar together and rub in the margarine.

2. Add the vanilla essence and bind the mixture together.

3. Form into small balls and place on a baking tray a few inches apart.

4. With the back of a fork, press the balls down making a criss-cross pattern.

5. Bake at 190°C/375°F/Gas Mark 5 for about 10-15 minutes until golden brown in colour.

6. Cool on a wire rack.

TIME: Preparation takes 10 minutes, cooking takes 10-15 minutes.

VARIATIONS: Add a tablespoon of currants to make fruit biscuits. Omit the vanilla essence and substitute almond essence to make almond biscuits.

COOK'S TIP: Store these biscuits in an airtight container.

YOGURT SCONES

These scones make a delicious alternative to the more usual plain scones.

MAKES 10 SCONES

60g/2oz butter
225g/8oz wholemeal self-raising flour
30g/1oz demerara sugar
60g/2oz raisins
Natural yogurt to mix

1. Rub the butter into the flour and sugar.

2. Add the raisins and mix well.

3. Slowly stir in enough yogurt to mix to a fairly stiff dough.

4. Turn the mixture onto a floured board and knead lightly.

5. Roll out the dough to about 2cm/¾-inch thick and cut into 5cm/2-inch rounds.

6. Place on a lightly greased baking tray and bake, near the top of the oven, at 220°C/425°F/Gas Mark 7 for 14-16 minutes.

7. Remove from the tray and cool on a wire rack. Serve warm.

TIME: Preparation takes 10 minutes, cooking takes 14-16 minutes.

VARIATIONS: Use chopped dried apricots instead of raisins.

SERVING IDEAS: Serve with jam and cream.

Quick & Easy
Notes

_____

_____

_____

_____

_____

_____

_____

_____

_____

_____

_____

_____

_____

_____

_____

_____

_____

_____

_____

_____

Quick & Easy
Notes

LOW CALORIE COOKING

Introduction

Keeping a check on your weight is probably one of the best ways to improve your general health. By eating a nutritionally balanced, calorie-controlled diet you will be helping your body to become fitter and to function more efficiently. Being overweight increases the chances of high blood pressure, thrombosis and heart attack, it makes keeping fit more difficult and often leaves people with low self-esteem. This is not to suggest that we should all be "model-girl slim." Watching your weight simply means sustaining a healthy weight for your height and age.

Whether you are on a weight-reducing diet or are simply trying to sustain your present weight, it is important to balance the food you consume against the benefits obtained from it. A chocolate milkshake will provide you with a few important nutrients, but it will not provide you with sufficient amounts of fiber, vitamins or protein for one meal, nor will it educate you to rely upon a well balanced and regular diet.

Calorie counting is in fact an ideal way of checking, on a daily basis, that you are consuming the correct amount of calories to stay at your present weight. If the amount of calories being consumed does not exceed the amount of calories being expended, a constant body weight will be maintained. In this respect the significance of regular exercise cannot be ignored – the more active you are the easier weight control becomes. There are no fast solutions to maintaining a healthy weight, a nutritionally balanced, calorie-controlled diet in conjunction with regular exercise is the healthiest and most natural answer.

These recipes have been compiled to help you plan a regular pattern of eating which is both low in calories and high in enjoyment. All the recipes are calorie counted so all you have to do is set a realistic daily allowance and decide which of the easily prepared meals to include in your menu.

SERVES 4

44 kilocalories per serving

CARROT SOUP

Carrots make a most delicious soup which is both filling and extremely low in calories.

1lb carrots
1 medium-sized onion
1 medium-sized turnip
2 cloves garlic, minced
3 cups water or vegetable stock
¾ tsp dried thyme
¾ tsp ground nutmeg
Salt and ground white pepper to taste
Toasted sunflower seeds, slivered almonds and pistachio nuts, mixed together for garnish

1. Peel the carrots and cut them into thick slices.

2. Peel and roughly chop the onion and turnip.

3. Put the vegetables, garlic and water or stock, into a large saucepan and bring to the boil. Cover the pan, reduce the heat and simmer for 20 minutes.

4. Add all the seasonings and simmer for a further 5 minutes.

5. Remove the soup from the heat and allow to cool for 15 minutes.

6. Using a liquidizer or food processor, blend the soup until it is thick and smooth.

7. Reheat the soup as required, garnishing with the seeds and nuts before serving.

Step 2 Using a sharp knife, roughly chop the peeled onions and turnip.

Step 1 Cut the carrots into thick slices, approximately ½-inch thick.

Step 6 Purée the soup in a liquidizer or food processor, until it is thick and smooth.

Cook's Notes

Time
Preparation takes about 12 minutes, cooking takes 25-30 minutes.

Cook's Tip
Make the recipe in double quantities and freeze half for a future date.

Variation
Use ¼ tsp cayenne pepper in place of the nutmeg in this recipe.

SERVES 4

115 kilocalories per serving

MELON AND PROSCIUTTO

This typically Italian appetizer is wonderful served well chilled on warm summer days.

1 large ripe melon, either Galia or Honeydew
16 thin slices prosciutto ham
French flat leaf parsley to garnish

Step 1 Using a spoon, scoop out and discard the seeds and fibrous core of the melon.

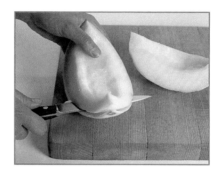

Step 2 Carefully remove the rind from the quartered melon, using a sharp knife.

Step 4 Roll a slice of prosciutto ham around each thin slice of melon.

1. Cut the melon in half lengthwise. Using a spoon, scoop out and discard all the seeds and fibers.

2. Cut the melon into quarters and carefully peel away the skin using a sharp knife.

3. Cut each quarter into 4 thin slices.

4. Wrap each slice of melon in a slice of the prosciutto ham, and arrange on a serving dish. Chill well and garnish with parsley before serving.

Cook's Notes

Time
Preparation takes 15 minutes.

Cook's Tip
Use this recipe, along with other items such as olives, stuffed eggs and sliced salami, as Italian antipasta for a buffet party.

Variation
Serve the slices of prosciutto ham in rolls, accompanied by quartered fresh figs in place of the melon.

SERVES 20
334 kilocalories per serving
SPICED BEEF

Spiced beef makes an attractive addition to a buffet or cold table and only a small serving is necessary for each guest. If you do not wish to cook a piece of meat this size, simply reduce the recipe by half.

6lb piece brisket, silverside, or topside of beef
3 bay leaves
1¼ tsps powdered mace
6 cloves
1¼ tsps black peppercorns
1¼ tsps allspice
2 large cloves garlic
2½ tbsps molasses
2½ tbsps brown sugar
1lb cooking salt
2¼ tsps saltpetre

1. Trim the excess fat from the piece of beef and make sure that it is well tied with string, so that it will keep its shape during the spicing.

2. Break the bay leaves into small pieces, and mix with the powdered mace.

3. Put the cloves, peppercorns and allspice into a mortar and crush them to a fine powder with a pestle.

4. Chop the garlic and add this to the crushed spices in the mortar, along with 1 tsp of the salt. Blend this to a paste, using the pestle.

5. Put the bay leaves, mace, ground spices, garlic, black treacle, brown sugar, cooking salt and the saltpetre in a very large bowl, and mix them together thoroughly.

6. Place the beef in a bowl, and rub all the surfaces thoroughly with the spicing mixture. Cover the bowl and set aside.

7. Repeat this process every day for 1 week, turning the meat and rubbing in the spices each day. Keep the meat in a cool place, or refrigerator, during this time.

8. To cook, cover the joint of beef with water in a very large saucepan. Bring the water to the boil, cover and simmer slowly for 6 hours. Allow the meat to cool in the cooking liquid.

9. Remove the cooled meat from the liquid, remove the string and place in a tight fitting dish or large loaf pan.

10. Put a plate on top of the piece of beef and weigh it down with balance scale weights or bags of sugar. Leave the beef to press in a cool place overnight.

11. To serve, slice the beef very thinly and serve cold on a bed of lettuce.

Step 6 Rub the surface of the beef evenly with some of the spicing mixture, making sure that all surface areas are well coated.

Step 8 Put the beef in a large pan and pour over enough water to cover.

Cook's Notes

Time
Preparation takes 1 week, cooking time takes approximately 6 hours.

Cook's Tip
Saltpetre can be purchased from any chemist.

Watchpoint
Make sure the beef in kept in a cool place whilst the spicing takes effect.

SERVES 4
24 kilocalories per serving

ORANGE, GRAPEFRUIT AND MINT SALAD

Fresh citrus fruits are complemented beautifully by the fragrant flavor of fresh mint. Serve chilled for an ideal low calorie appetizer.

2 grapefruits
3 oranges
Liquid sweetener to taste (optional)
8 sprigs of mint

1. Using a serrated knife, cut away the peel and the white pith from the grapefruit and the oranges.

2. Carefully cut inside the skin of each segment to remove each section of flesh.

3. Squeeze the membranes over a bowl to extract all the juice. Sweeten the juice with the liquid sweetener, if required.

4. Arrange the orange and the grapefruit segments in alternating colors on 4 individual serving dishes.

5. Using a sharp knife, chop 4 springs of the mint very finely. Stir the chopped mint into the fruit juice.

6. Carefully spoon the juice over the arranged fruit segments and chill thoroughly.

7. Garnish with a sprig of mint before serving.

Step 1 Using a serrated knife, cut away the peel from the grapefruits and the oranges, making sure that you remove all the white pith as you cut.

Step 2 Carefully cut inside the skin of each segment to remove each section of flesh, trying to keep each piece as intact as possible.

Cook's Notes

Time
Preparation takes about 20 minutes, plus chiling time.

Cook's Tip
This appetizer can be prepared up to a day in advance.

Preparation
Make sure all the white pith is removed from the fruit, as it produces a bitter flavor.

Variation
Use ruby grapefruits and blood oranges, when available, in place of the normal types of fruit for a colorful variation. Use borage leaves in place of the mint, and garnish with a few of the blue flowers.

SERVES 4

41 kilocalories per serving

INDIAN TOMATO SOUP

This highly fragrant and spicy tomato soup makes an interesting
low calorie appetizer.

½lb tomatoes
1 medium-sized onion
2½ tbsps vegetable oil
1 green chili, seeded and finely chopped
3 cloves garlic, minced
1¼ tbsps tomato paste
4½ cups water, or vegetable stock
4-6 green curry leaves, or ¾ tsp curry powder
Freshly ground sea salt to taste
Coriander leaves and green chilies for garnish

1. Cut a small cross in the skin of each tomato and plunge them into boiling water for 30-40 seconds.

2. Remove the tomatoes and carefully peel away the loosened skin with a sharp knife.

3. Remove the green core from the tomatoes and roughly chop the flesh.

4. Peel the onion and chop it into small pieces using a sharp knife.

5. Heat the oil in a large saucepan and gently sauté the onion, chopped chili and garlic for 3-4 minutes until it is soft, but not browned.

6. Stir in the chopped tomatoes and cook for 5 minutes, stirring often to prevent the vegetables from burning.

7. Blend the tomato paste with the water and pour this into the onions and tomatoes. Add the curry leaves or powder, season with the salt and simmer for 5-7 minutes.

8. Remove the soup from the heat and stir in the coriander leaves and the chili halves.

9. Pour the soup into 4-6 serving bowls and serve piping hot, discarding the chili garnish before eating.

Step 2 Remove the tomatoes from the boiling water and carefully peel away the loosened skin.

Step 3 Cut away and discard the hard green core from the tomatoes, and chop the flesh roughly with a sharp knife.

Cook's Notes

 Time
Preparation takes about 15 minutes, cooking takes 17-18 minutes.

 Watchpoint
Great care must be taken when preparing fresh chilies. Try not to get the juice into your eyes or mouth. If this should happen, rinse with lots of cold water.

Freezing
This soup freezes well, but should be frozen before adding the garnish.

SERVES 4

113 kilocalories per serving

"BURNT" PEPPER SALAD

Burning peppers under a hot broiler is a traditional way of preparing this sweet vegetable which enhances, rather than impairs, its subtle flavor.

3 large colored peppers, e.g. red, green and yellow
5 tbsps olive oil
1 clove garlic, finely chopped
8 basil leaves, roughly chopped
3 sprigs of fresh marjoram, roughly chopped
2½ tbsps fresh pickled capers
2½ tbsps white wine vinegar

1. Cut the peppers in half lengthwise. Remove and discard the core and seeds.

Step 2 Press the pepper halves down on a flat surface with the palm of your hands to flatten them completely.

2. Lay the peppers, cut side down, on a flat surface and flatten them out by pressing down with the palm of your hand.

3. Preheat the broiler to hot. Arrange the peppers on a broiler pan and brush with 1¼ tbsps of the olive oil.

4. Broil the peppers until the skins are well charred. Wrap them in a clean towel and leave for 15 minutes.

5. Unwrap the peppers and peel off the charred and

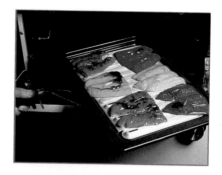

Step 4 Char the skin of the peppers under a hot broiler, turning them around, if necessary, to burn evenly.

Step 5 Wrap the charred peppers in a cloth to retain the moisture and lift the charred skins away from the pepper flesh.

loosened skin.

6. Cut the peppers into thick strips and arrange them onto a serving dish.

7. Scatter over the chopped garlic, basil leaves, marjoram and capers.

8. Mix together the remaining olive oil and the vinegar, and pour over the peppers. Refrigerate for at least 1 hour before serving.

Cook's Notes

Time
Preparation takes about 30 minutes, plus 1 hour chiling time.

Variation
For a special occasion use nasturtium flower buds instead of the capers.

Preparation
The skins of the peppers must be very well charred on the outside before wrapping them in the towel, otherwise their skin will not peel away properly.

Cook's Tip
If you do not wish to broil the peppers, pierce the whole pepper with a fork and hold them over a gas flame to char the skin.

SERVES 2
252 kilocalories per serving

FRESH TOMATO OMELET

Omelets can make substantial low calorie lunches or light meals and can be varied by using different fillings. This recipe uses lots of tasty fresh tomatoes, which can be eaten in abundance on a calorie controlled diet.

1lb fresh tomatoes
Salt and freshly ground black pepper
4 eggs
5 tbsps water
¾ tsp fresh chopped basil
2½ tbsps olive or vegetable oil
¾ tsp fresh chopped oregano or basil to garnish

1. Cut a small cross into the skins of each tomato and plunge them into boiling water. Leave for 30 seconds, then remove them with a draining spoon.

2. Using a sharp knife carefully peel away the tomato skins and discard them.

3. Cut the tomatoes in half and remove and discard the seeds, juice and any tough core.

4. Cut the tomato flesh into thin strips.

5. Break the eggs into a bowl and beat in the water and chopped herbs. Season with salt and pepper and continue beating until the egg mixture is frothy.

6. Heat the oil in a large frying pan or skillet, then pour in the egg mixture.

7. Using a spatula, stir the egg mixture around the skillet for about 2-3 minutes, or until the eggs are beginning to set.

8. Spread the tomato strips over the partially cooked eggs, and continue cooking without stirring until the eggs have completely set and the tomatoes are just warmed through.

9. Sprinkle with the additional chopped basil before serving.

Step 2 Carefully peel away and discard the tomato skins from the blanched fruit, using a sharp knife.

Step 3 Remove the seeds and juice from the halved tomatoes with a teaspoon.

Step 5 Beat the eggs, water and herbs together thoroughly, until they are frothy.

Cook's Notes

Time
Preparation takes about 25 minutes, cooking takes about 5 minutes.

Variation
Add 1 clove of minced garlic to the egg mixture, if desired.

Serving Idea
Cut the omelet into wedges and serve straight from the frying pan.

SERVES 4

83 kilocalories per serving

VEGETABLE KEBABS

A colorful and flavorsome way to serve delicious fresh vegetables as part of a low calorie diet.

1 large eggplant
Salt
1 large green pepper
4 zucchini
12-14 cherry tomatoes, red or yellow
12-14 pickling onions
12-14 button mushrooms
5 tbsps olive oil
2½ tbsps lemon juice
¾ tsp salt
¾ tsp freshly ground black pepper

1. Cut the eggplant in half and dice it into 1-inch pieces.

2. Put the eggplant pieces into a large bowl, and sprinkle liberally with salt. Stir well and allow to stand for 30 minutes to degorge.

3. Rinse the eggplant pieces thoroughly in a colander under cold water, to remove all traces of salt.

4. Cut the green pepper in half. Remove and discard the core and seeds. Cut the pepper flesh into 1-inch pieces with a sharp knife.

5. Slice the zucchini diagonally into pieces approximately 1-inch thick.

6. Remove the tough cores form the cherry tomatoes and peel the onions. Rinse the mushrooms under cold water to remove any bits of soil, but do not peel.

7. Put all the prepared vegetables into a large bowl and pour in the remaining ingredients. Mix well to coat evenly, cover with plastic wrap and allow to stand for about 30 minutes, stirring the vegetables once or twice to ensure they remain evenly coated.

8. Thread the vegetables alternately onto skewers and arrange them on a broiler pan.

9. Brush the kebabs with the marinade and broil for 3-4 minutes, turning frequently and basting with the marinade until they are evenly browned. Serve piping hot.

Step 5 Cut the zucchini diagonally into 1-inch pieces.

Step 8 Thread the prepared and marinated vegetables alternately onto kebab skewers, keeping an even number of vegetable pieces on each skewer.

Cook's Notes

Time
Preparation takes about 30 minutes. Cooking takes about 10 minutes, plus time for the vegetables to marinate.

Preparation
It is important to degorge the eggplant before cooking, as this removes the bitterness from the flavor and some of the moisture as well.

Variation
Use any combination of your favorite vegetables in this recipe.

SERVES 6

213 kilocalories per serving

DOLMAS

Delicious individual parcels of rice, herbs, nuts and fruit, make a very different low calorie lunch or supper dish.

12 large cabbage leaves, washed
1 cup long grain rice
8 green onions
1¼ tbsps fresh chopped basil
1¼ tbsps fresh chopped mint
1¼ tbsps fresh chopped parsley
½ cup pine nuts
⅓ cup currants
Salt and freshly ground black pepper
5 tbsps olive oil
Juice 1 lemon
⅔ cup unset natural yogurt
¼lb cucumber

Step 5 Pile tablespoons of the filling onto the blanched leaves, pressing it gently into sausage shapes in the center of the leaves.

1. Using a sharp knife trim away any tough stems from the cabbage leaves.

2. Put the leaves into boiling water for about 30 seconds. Remove them using a slotted spoon and drain thoroughly before laying them out flat on a work surface.

3. Put the rice into a saucepan along with enough boiling water to just cover. Cook for 15-20 minutes, or until the rice is soft and the liquid almost completely absorbed. Rinse the rice in cold water to remove any starchiness.

4. Cut the green onions into thin diagonal slices. Put the rice and the chopped onions into a large bowl along with all the remaining ingredients, except 2½ tbsps olive oil, the yogurt and cucumber. Mix the rice mixture thoroughly to blend evenly.

5. Place about 2 tbsps of the rice filling onto each blanched cabbage leaf, pressing it gently into a sausage shape.

6. Fold the sides of the leaves over to partially cover the stuffing, and then roll up, jelly roll fashion, to completely envelop the filling.

7. Place the rolls seam side down in a large baking dish. Brush with the remaining olive oil. Pour hot water around the cabbage leaves until it comes about halfway up their sides.

8. Cover the baking dish with aluminum foil, pressing it gently onto the surface of the leaves to keep them in place. Bake in a preheated oven 375°F for 30-40 minutes.

9. Peel the cucumber and cut it lengthwise into quarters. Remove the pips and discard. Chop the cucumber flesh and half of the peel into very small pieces.

10. Mix the chopped cucumber into the yogurt and chill until required.

11. Drain the dolmas from the cooking liquid and arrange on a serving plate with a little of the cucumber sauce spooned over.

Cook's Notes

Time
Preparation takes about 30 minutes, cooking takes 40 minutes.

Serving Idea
Serve the dolmas either hot or cold.

Preparation
Dolmas can be prepared a day in advance and allowed to stand in their liquid in the refrigerator. They can be reheated just before serving if required.

Variation
Use any other ingredients you particularly like in the filling along with the rice. Use vine leaves instead of cabbage leaves in this recipe.

SERVES 6
156 kilocalories per serving

EGGPLANT BAKE

Eggplants are wonderfully filling vegetables with very few calories – the ideal ingredient in a calorie controlled diet.

2 large or 3 medium-sized eggplants
2½ tsps salt
⅔ cup malt vinegar
2½ tbsps vegetable oil
2 large onions, peeled and sliced into rings
2 green chilies, seeded and finely chopped
2 cups peeled plum tomatoes, chopped
¾ tsp chili powder
1¼ tsps minced garlic
¾ tsp ground turmeric
8 tomatoes, sliced
1⅓ cups natural unset yogurt
1¼ tsps freshly ground black pepper
1 cup Cheddar cheese, finely grated

1. Cut the eggplants into ¼-inch thick slices. Arrange the slices in a shallow dish and sprinkle with 1½ tsps of the salt. Pour over the malt vinegar, cover the dish and marinate for 30 minutes.

2. Drain the eggplant well, discarding the marinade liquid.

3. Heat the vegetable oil in a frying pan and gently fry the onion rings until they are golden brown.

4. Add the chilies, the remaining salt, chopped tomatoes, chili powder, garlic and turmeric. Mix well and simmer for 5-7 minutes until thick and well blended.

5. Remove the sauce from the heat and cool slightly. Blend to a smooth purée using a liquidizer or food processor.

6. Arrange half of the eggplant slices in the base of a lightly greased shallow ovenproof dish.

7. Spoon half of the tomato sauce over the eggplant slices. Cover the tomato sauce with the remaining eggplant, and then top this with the remaining tomato sauce and sliced tomatoes.

8. Mix together the yogurt, the freshly ground black pepper and the Cheddar cheese. Pour this mixture over the tomato slices.

9. Preheat an oven to 375°F, and cook the eggplant bake for 20-30 minutes, or until the cheese topping bubbles and turns golden brown. Serve hot straight from the oven.

Step 4 Fry the chilies, tomatoes and seasoning with the golden onion rings until they are softened and juice flows.

Step 7 Spoon half the tomato sauce over the eggplant slices in the gratin dish.

Cook's Notes

Time
Preparation takes about 30 minutes, cooking takes 40 minutes.

Preparation
Make sure that the eggplants are well drained when they are removed from the marinade. Press them into a colander using the back of your hand, to remove all excess vinegar. Do not rinse, as the vinegar gives a tangy flavor to the dish.

Cook's Tip
Use a low calorie cheese in place of the Cheddar cheese to reduce the calorie content further.

SERVES 4
54 kilocalories per serving

OKRA CASSEROLE

Okra has an interesting texture and a mild flavor which combines well with tomatoes to make this delicious Mediterranean-style casserole.

2½ tbsps olive oil
1 small onion
½lb fresh okra
6 ripe tomatoes
Juice of ½ lemon
Salt and freshly ground black pepper
2½ tbsps fresh chopped parsley

---

1. Peel the onions and cut them in half lengthwise. Use a sharp knife to cut them across in slices.

2. Heat the oil in a large saucepan and cook the onion until it is soft and transparent, but not browned.

3. Remove just the stems from the okra, but leave on the pointed tail. Take care not to cut off the very top of the okra.

4. Add the okra to the onions and cook gently for 10 minutes, stirring occasionally.

5. Cut a small cross into the skins of the tomatoes, and plunge them into boiling water for 30 seconds.

6. Drain the tomatoes and carefully peel away and discard the loosened skins. Chop the peeled fruit roughly.

7. Add the tomatoes, lemon juice, seasoning and parsley to the okra, and continue to cook for about 5 more minutes, or until the tomatoes are just heated through.

8. Spoon into a serving dish and serve hot or cold.

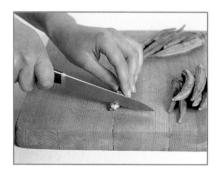

Step 3 Trim just the stems from the top of the okra, but take care not to remove the whole top, or the pointed tails.

Step 1 Place the halved peeled onions cut side downwards, and use a sharp knife to cut across into thin slices.

Step 6 Carefully peel the skins away from the blanched tomatoes, using a sharp knife.

Cook's Notes

Time
Preparation takes 15 minutes, cooking takes approximately 15 minutes.

Variation
Green beans can be used in place of the okra.

Cook's Tip
If you cannot get fresh okra, use canned okra in its place, but drain and rinse this before use and cut the cooking time in half.

Watchpoint
If too much liquid is left at the end of cooking, remove the vegetables with a slotted spoon and boil the liquid quickly to reduce the sauce.

SERVES 6

234 kilocalories per serving

PASTA WITH FRESH TOMATO AND BASIL SAUCE

Pasta is a good item to include on a low calorie diet, as it is very filling and can be served with any variety of low calorie sauces.

1 small onion, finely chopped
1lb fresh tomatoes
2½ tbsps tomato paste
1 orange
2 cloves garlic, minced
Salt and freshly ground black pepper
⅔ cup red wine
⅔ cup chicken stock
2½ tbsps coarsely chopped basil
1¾ cups whole-wheat pasta

1. Peel and finely chop the onion.

2. Cut a small cross in the skins of the tomatoes and plunge them into boiling water for 30 seconds. Remove the blanched tomatoes from the water and carefully peel away the loosened skin.

3. Cut the tomatoes into quarters, and remove and discard the pips. Chop the tomato flesh roughly, and put this, the onion and the tomato paste into a large saucepan.

4. Heat the onion and tomatoes over a gentle heat, stirring continuously until the tomatoes soften and begin to lose their juice.

5. Finely grate the rind from the orange. Cut the orange in half and squeeze out the juice.

6. Put the orange, rind and juice into a large saucepan along with all the remaining ingredients, and bring to the boil.

Step 1 To chop an onion finely, pierce the peeled onion with a fork and use this to hold the vegetable steady whilst you chop with a sharp knife.

Step 3 Cut the tomatoes into quarters and remove and discard the seeds.

7. Continue to boil until the sauce has reduced and thickened and the vegetables are soft.

8. Whilst the sauce is cooking, put the pasta into another saucepan with enough boiling water to cover. Season with a little salt and cook for 10-15 minutes, or until the pasta is soft.

9. Drain the pasta in a colander, and stir it into the hot sauce. Serve at once with a salad.

Cook's Notes

Time
Preparation takes 15-20 minutes, cooking takes 10-15 minutes.

Variation
Add ½ cup thinly sliced mushrooms to the sauce, if liked.

Freezing
This sauce will freeze very well for up to 3 months.

SERVES 6

153 kilocalories per serving

VEGETABLE AND OLIVE CASSEROLE

The addition of vinegar and capers gives this refreshing vegetable dish a sharp twist to its flavor.

1 eggplant
Salt
⅔ cup olive, or vegetable oil
1 onion, peeled and thinly sliced
2 red peppers, seeded and chopped
2 sticks of celery, sliced thickly
1lb canned plum tomatoes
2½ tbsps red wine vinegar
1¼ tbsps sugar
1 clove garlic, minced
12 black olives, pitted
1¼ tbsps capers
Salt and freshly ground black pepper

1. Cut the eggplant in half lengthwise and score the cut surface deeply, in a lattice fashion, with the point of a sharp knife.

2. Sprinkle the cut surface of the eggplant liberally with salt, and leave to stand for 30 minutes.

3. Rinse the eggplants thoroughly under running water, then pat dry and cut it into 1-inch cubes.

4. Heat the oil in a large sauté pan and add the onion, peppers and celery. Cook gently for about 5 minutes, stirring occasionally until the vegetables have softened but not browned.

5. Add the eggplant to the pan and mix well to coat thoroughly with the oil. Continue cooking gently for 5 minutes.

6. Chop the plum tomatoes and then press them through a nylon sieve, using the back of a wooden spoon to press out all the juice and pulp, leaving the seeds and pith in the sieve.

7. Add the sieved tomatoes to the vegetables in the sauté pan, along with the remaining ingredients, except for the olives and capers. Cover and simmer for 5 minutes.

8. Cut the olives into quarters and add these to the simmering vegetables, along with the capers.

9. Continue cooking gently, uncovered, for a further 15 minutes, or until most of the liquid has evaporated and the sauce has thickened and reduced.

Step 1 Score the cut surface of the eggplants in a lattice pattern, using the point of a sharp knife.

Step 9 Simmer the casserole, uncovered, over a low heat until the juice has thickened and reduced.

Cook's Notes

Time
Preparation takes 30 minutes, plus 30 minutes for the eggplants to degorge. Cooking takes approximately 25 minutes.

Preparation
Scoring and salting the eggplant will remove any bitter taste and toughness from the vegetable. Be very sure, however, to rinse all the salt off the eggplant before cooking, or this will affect the flavor of the dish.

Cook's Tip
This recipe may be prepared 2-3 days in advance and kept covered in a refrigerator.

Serving Idea
This recipe is delicious served cold as a salad, or hot with rice and pitta bread.

SERVES 6

21 kilocalories per serving

SALADE PAYSANNE

This homely salad can be made with any selection of fresh vegetables you have to hand. So whether its winter or summer, there's no excuse for not serving a delicious fresh salad.

4 green onions
½ cucumber
3 carrots
6 large tomatoes
10 button mushrooms
3 stems celery
1 green pepper, seeded and chopped
15-20 tiny cauliflower flowerets
15-20 radishes, quartered
1 tbsp chopped watercress, or mustard and cress
2 sprigs fresh green coriander leaf, or chopped parsley
¾ tsp salt
¾ tsp freshly ground black pepper
2½ tbsps cider vinegar
1¼ tbsps lemon juice
5 tbsps olive or vegetable oil
Pinch mustard powder
Liquid sweetener to taste
8 lettuce leaves for garnish

Step 3 Cut the carrot into thin pieces, slicing diagonally with a sharp knife.

Step 9 Whisk all the dressing ingredients together using a fork or eggbeater whisk, until the mixture becomes thick and cloudy.

1. Trim the green onions and slice them diagonally into thin slices.

2. Peel the cucumber and quarter it lengthwise. Use a sharp knife to remove the soft, seedy center, discard this, and dice the remaining flesh.

3. Peel and carrots and slice them thinly, cutting the carrots diagonally with a sharp knife.

4. Cut a small cross into the skins of each tomato, and plunge into boiling water for 30 seconds. Remove the tomatoes and carefully peel away the blanched skin from the fruit. Quarter the peeled tomatoes and cut away the tough green stalk.

5. Thinly slice the mushrooms and sticks of celery.

6. Cut the pepper in half lengthwise and remove all the seeds and the white pith. Discard this, and chop the flesh.

7. Break the cauliflower flowerets into small pieces, and quarter the radishes.

8. Roughly chop the watercress, or mustard and cress, along with the coriander leaves or parsley.

9. For the dressing mix together all the remaining ingredients, except for the lettuce leaves. Whisk thoroughly using a fork, or eggbeater, until the mixture becomes thick and cloudy.

10. Arrange the lettuce leaves on a serving dish, and pile the prepared vegetables on top.

11. Just before serving, spoon a little of the dressing over the salad and serve the remainder separately in a small jug.

Cook's Notes

Time
Preparation takes about 20 minutes.

Variation
Use any combination of your own favorite vegetables in this recipe.

Serving Idea
Serve with cheese or chicken for a light lunch.

SERVES 4

87 kilocalories per serving

BLACK OLIVE AND CAULIFLOWER SALAD

The exciting flavors of the Mediterranean combine in this recipe to produce a refreshingly different salad.

⅔ cup black olives
1 large cauliflower
1 large Spanish onion
5 tbsps olive oil
⅔ cup water
Juice ½ lemon
3½ tbsps tomato paste
Salt and freshly ground black pepper
2½ tbsps fresh chopped parsley

4. Heat the oil in a large sauté pan and gently cook the cauliflower for 2 minutes. Remove the cauliflower to a plate, and cook the onion in the same pan, in the same way.

5. Return the cauliflower to the pan and add the water and the lemon juice. Bring to the boil, reduce the heat and simmer until tender, adding a little more water should the mixture begin to boil dry.

6. Using a slotted spoon, remove the cauliflower from the sauté pan, reserving the juices.

Step 1 To loosen the stones before pitting, roll the olives firmly on a flat surface using the palm of your hand.

Step 3 Slice the onion into rings by piercing the peeled vegetable with a fork to hold it steady whilst you slice.

1. Roll the olives firmly on a flat surface with the palm of your hands to loosen the stones. Remove the stones using a cherry pitter or the tip of a potato peeler. Chop the olives roughly and set aside.

2. Trim the leaves from the cauliflower and break it into small flowerets.

3. Peel the onion and slice it into rings.

7. Add the tomato paste to the liquid and boil rapidly to reduce.

8. Stir the olives into the pan and heat through.

9. Arrange the cauliflower flowerets on a serving dish, and spoon the olive sauce over the top. Chill well.

10. Sprinkle with the chopped parsley just before serving.

Cook's Notes

Time
Preparation takes about 20 minutes, cooking takes approximately 20 minutes, plus chiling time.

Cook's Tip
Add a bay leaf to the cauliflower during the cooking to reduce the strong smell.

Variation
Use green olives instead of black.

SERVES 4

99 kilocalories per serving

STIR-FRIED SALAD

Stir fries are served hot, but the ingredients are cooked so quickly that they retain all of their crunchiness.

1 onion
2 large leeks
5 tbsps olive oil
2 cloves garlic, minced
½lb snow peas, topped and tailed
¼lb bean sprouts, or lentil sprouts
Salt and freshly ground black pepper
1 tbsp fresh chopped coriander leaf

1. Peel the onion and cut it into thin rings.

Step 1 Pierce the onion with a fork to hold it steady whilst you slice it into thin rings.

2. Trim the leeks and cut down the length of one side. Open the leek out and wash it thoroughly under running water.

3. Cut the leek into three pieces, then thinly slice each piece lengthwise into thin strips.

4. Heat the oil in a large wok or frying pan, and add the onions and garlic. Cook for 2 minutes, stirring all the time until the onions have softened but not browned.

5. Add the snow peas and sliced leeks to the wok and continue stir-frying for 4 minutes.

6. Add the remaining ingredients and cook briskly for a further 2 minutes. Serve piping hot.

Step 2 Rinse the split leek under running water, separating the leaves to wash out any grit or dirt.

Step 3 Cut the pieces of leek lengthwise into thin strips.

Cook's Notes

Time
Preparation takes 15 minutes, cooking takes approximately 10 minutes.

Cook's Tip
Sprout your own beans or lentils by putting them into a glass jar, rinse thoroughly and pour in fresh water each day, cover with muslin, and stand the jar on a sunny windowsill. After 3-4 days, the beans or lentils will have sprouted.

Serving Idea
Serve this dish with rice, and sprinkle it liberally with soy sauce.

SERVES 6

84 kilocalories per serving

RATATOUILLE

This delicious vegetable casserole from the south of France has become a great favorite the world over.

2 eggplants
Salt
4 zucchini
5 tbsps olive oil
2 Spanish onions
2 green or red peppers
2½ tsps chopped fresh basil
1 large clove garlic, minced
2 x 1lb 12 oz cans of peeled plum tomatoes
Salt and freshly ground black pepper
⅔ cup dry white wine

1. Cut the eggplants in half lengthwise and score each cut surface diagonally, using the point of a sharp knife.

2. Sprinkle the eggplants liberally with salt and allow to stand for 30 minutes to degorge. After this time, rinse them thoroughly and pat them dry.

3. Roughly chop the eggplants and slice the zucchini thickly. Set them to one side.

4. Peel the onions and half them. Cut them into thin slices with a sharp knife.

5. Cut the peppers in half lengthwise and remove and discard the seeds and white pith. Chop the flesh roughly.

6. Heat the oil in a large saucepan, and fry the onion slices for 5 minutes until they are soft and just beginning to brown.

7. Stir in the peppers and zucchini, and cook gently for 5 minutes until they begin to soften. Remove all the vegetables from the pan and set them aside.

8. Put the chopped eggplants into the saucepan with the

Step 5 Remove and discard the seeds and white pith from the halved peppers.

Step 8 Gently fry the chopped eggplant in the vegetable juices and oil, until they begin to brown.

vegetable juices. Cook gently until it begins to brown, then add all the other ingredients to the pan.

9. Add the cans of tomatoes, the garlic and the basil to the saucepan along with the sautéed vegetables, mixing well to blend in evenly. Bring to the boil, then reduce the heat and simmer for 15 minutes, or until the liquid in the pan has been reduced and is thick.

10. Add the wine to the pan and continue cooking for a further 15 minutes, before serving straight away, or chiling and serving cold.

Cook's Notes

Time
Preparation takes 20 minutes, plus 30 minutes standing time. Cooking takes approximately 35 minutes.

Preparation
Make sure that the degorged eggplant is rinsed thoroughly to remove any saltiness, otherwise this will spoil the flavor of the finished dish.

Cook's Tip
If the liquid in the pan is still thin and excessive after the full cooking time, remove the vegetables and boil the juices rapidly until they have reduced and thickened.

SERVES 4
239 kilocalories per serving

LIME ROASTED CHICKEN

This simply made, but unusual, main course is very low in calories and high in tangy flavor.

---

4 chicken breast portions, each weighing about 8oz
Salt and freshly ground black pepper
4 limes
2½ tsps white wine vinegar
6 tbsps olive oil
2½ tsps fresh chopped basil

---

1. Rub the chicken portions all over with salt and black pepper. Place in a shallow ovenproof dish, and set aside.

2. Carefully pare away thin strips of the rind only from 2 of the limes, using a lemon parrer. Cut these 2 limes in half and squeeze the juice.

3. Add the lime juice to the vinegar and 4 tbsps of the olive oil in a small dish, along with the strips of rind, and mix well.

4. Pour the oil and lime juice mixture over the chicken por-

tions in the dish. Cover and refrigerate for about 4 hours or overnight.

5. Remove the covering from the dish in which the chicken is marinating, and baste the chicken well with the marinade mixture. Place into a preheated oven 375°F and cook for 30-35 minutes, or until the chicken is well roasted and tender.

6. In the meantime, peel away the rind and white pith from the remaining 2 limes. Cut the limes into thin slices using a sharp knife.

7. Heat the remaining oil in a small frying pan and add the lime slices and basil. Cook quickly for 1 minute, or until the fragrance rises up from the basil and the limes just begin to soften.

8. Serve the chicken portions on a serving platter, garnished with the fried lime slices and a little extra fresh basil, if desired.

Step 5 After marinating for 4 hours, the chicken portions will look slightly cooked and the meat will have turned a pale opaque color.

Step 7 Fry the lime slices very quickly in the hot oil until they just begin to soften.

Cook's Notes

Time
Preparation takes 25 minutes, plus 4 hours marinating time. Cooking takes 40 minutes.

Preparation
The chicken can be prepared in advance and marinated overnight.

Variation
Use lemons instead of limes, and thyme instead of basil.

Watchpoint
Puncture the chicken with a skewer at its thickest point and when the resulting juices run clear, it is ready.

SERVES 4

230 kilocalories per serving

PAPRIKA SCHNITZEL

Thin slices of pork tenderloin are served with a rich tasting paprika sauce for a delicious low calorie meal.

8 thin slices pork tenderloin cut along the fillet
Salt and freshly ground black pepper
1 clove garlic, minced
3¾ tbsps vegetable oil
1 medium-sized onion
1 red pepper
1 green pepper
1¼ tbsps paprika
⅔ cup beef stock
½ cup red wine
3¾ tbsps tomato paste
⅔ cup natural low fat yogurt

Step 1 Flatten the pork slices out with a rolling pin until they are ¼-inch thick.

1. Trim the slices of pork to remove any fat, and flatten them out with a rolling pin until they are ¼-inch thick.

2. Rub both sides of the pork slices with salt, pepper, and garlic, then allow to stand in a refrigerator for 30 minutes.

3. Heat the oil in a large frying pan, and cook the pork slices in several batches if necessary, until they are well browned and cooked right through. This will take approximately 4 minutes on each side.

4. Remove the pork from the pan, set aside, and keep warm.

5. Peel the onion and thinly slice it into rings, steadying it with a fork as you cut. Cut the peppers in half and remove and discard the seeds and white pith. Slice the peppers lengthwise into thin strips.

6. Add the onion rings and the sliced peppers to the oil and meat juices in the frying pan, and cook quickly for about 3-4 minutes until they are soft but not browned.

7. Add the paprika, stock, wine and tomato paste to the frying pan with the vegetables, and bring the mixture to the boil.

8. Reduce the heat and simmer until the liquid has evapo-

Step 6 Fry the onions and peppers together for 3-4 minutes until they have softened but not browned.

rated and the sauce has thickened. Season with salt and pepper to taste.

9. Arrange the pork slices on a serving dish, and pour the paprika sauce over the top of them.

10. Beat the yogurt in a bowl until it is smooth.

11. Carefully drizzle the yogurt over the paprika sauce to make an attractive pattern. Swirl it gently into the sauce to blend, but take care not to incorporate it completely. Serve hot.

Cook's Notes

 Time
Preparation takes 30 minutes, cooking takes approximately 20 minutes.

 Freezing
This dish freezes well.

 Preparation
This dish may be made in advance, covered with foil, then reheated in a moderate oven when required.

 Cook's Tip
If the yogurt is too thick to drizzle properly, whisk in a little water or skim milk to thin it to the required consistency.

SERVES 4

198 kilocalories per serving

CHICKEN WITH BLACKCURRANT SAUCE

The sharp tang of blackcurrants makes an ideal partner for lightly cooked chicken.

4 chicken breasts, boned and skinned
4 tbsps sesame oil
1⅓ cups fresh blackcurrants
Juice of 1 orange
⅔ cup red wine
Artificial sweetener to taste
Orange slices and fresh blackcurrants to garnish

1. Season the chicken breasts with a little salt. Heat the oil in a shallow frying pan.

Step 2 Gently fry the chicken breasts in the hot oil until they are golden brown on all sides.

2. Gently fry the chicken breasts for 4-5 minutes on each side, until they are golden brown and tender.

3. Top and tail the blackcurrants and put them into a small pan, along with the orange juice and red wine. Bring to the boil, then cover and simmer gently until the blackcurrants are soft.

4. Using a liquidizer or food processor, blend the blackcurrants and the cooking juice for 30 seconds.

Step 5 Press the blackcurrant purée through a metal sieve with a wooden spoon, to remove all the pips and skins.

Step 6 Simmer the sieved fruit purée until it has thickened and the liquid has reduced.

5. Rub the blended purée through a nylon sieve with the back of a spoon, pressing the fruit through to reserve all the juice and pulp but leaving the pips in the sieve.

6. Put the sieved purée into a small saucepan and heat gently, stirring constantly until the liquid has reduced and the sauce is thick and smooth.

7. Arrange the chicken breasts on a serving dish, and spoon the blackcurrant sauce over. Garnish with orange slices and fresh blackcurrants.

Cook's Notes

Time
Preparation takes 15 minutes, cooking takes approximately 15 minutes.

Preparation
To test if the chicken breasts are cooked, insert a skewer into the thickest part, then press gently, if the juices run clear, the meat is cooked.

Variation
Use blackberries instead of blackcurrants in this recipe.

Serving Idea
Serve with a selection of fresh green vegetables.

SERVES 4
220 kilocalories per serving

KIDNEYS WITH MUSTARD SAUCE

Lambs' kidneys have a wonderful delicate flavor, and when served with a delicious mustard sauce, make a quick and very flavorful main course.

5 tbsps vegetable oil
1½lbs lambs' kidneys
1-2 shallots, peeled and finely chopped
1⅓ cups dry white wine
3¾ tbsps Dijon mustard
Salt, pepper and lemon juice to taste
2½ tbsps fresh chopped parsley

1. Cut the kidneys in half lengthwise, and carefully snip out the core and tough tubes.

2. Heat the oil in a large frying pan, and gently sauté the kidneys for about 10 minutes, stirring them frequently until they are light brown on all sides. Remove the kidneys from the pan and keep them warm.

3. Add the shallots to the sauté pan and cook for about 1 minute, stirring frequently until they soften, but do not brown.

4. Add the wine and bring to the boil, stirring constantly and scraping the pan to remove any brown juices.

5. Allow the wine to boil rapidly for 3-4 minutes, until it has reduced by about 2/3rds. Remove the pan from the heat.

6. Using an eggbeater or fork, mix the mustard into the reduced wine along with salt, pepper, lemon juice to taste, and half of the fresh chopped parsley.

7. Return the kidneys to the pan and cook over a low heat for 1-2 minutes, stirring all the time to heat the kidneys through evenly. Serve immediately, sprinkled with the remaining parsley.

Step 1 Trim any fat or tubes away from the core of each kidney, using a sharp knife or small pair of scissors.

Step 2 Sauté the kidneys in the hot oil, stirring them frequently to brown evenly on all sides.

Step 6 Using an eggbeater or fork, blend the mustard into the reduced wine, whisking well to keep the sauce smooth.

Cook's Notes

Time
Preparation takes about 25 minutes, cooking takes 15 minutes.

Variation
Use chicken livers in place of the lambs' kidney in this recipe.

Watchpoint
Take care not to cook the kidneys for too long as they will toughen if overcooked.

SERVES 4

254 kilocalories per serving

SOLE KEBABS

Fish is highly nutritious, economical to prepare, and makes an ideal contribution to a healthy diet.

8 fillets of sole
5 tbsps olive oil
1 clove garlic, minced
Juice ½ lemon
Finely grated rind ½ lemon
Salt and freshly ground black pepper
3 drops of Tabasco, or pepper sauce
3 medium-sized zucchini
1 medium-sized green pepper
Freshly chopped parsley for garnish

1. Using a sharp knife, carefully peel the skin from the backs of each sole fillet.

Step 1 Use a sharp knife to carefully cut between the meat of the fish and the skin. Lift the meat up and away as you cut, keeping the blade of the knife away from you.

Step 2 Cut the sole fillets in half lengthwise, and roll the slices up jelly roll fashion.

2. Cut each sole fillet in half lengthwise, and roll each slice up jelly roll fashion.

3. Mix together the oil, garlic, lemon juice, rind, and seasonings in a small bowl.

4. Put the rolls of fish into a shallow dish and pour over the lemon and oil marinade. Cover the dish and allow to stand in a cool place for at least 2 hours.

5. Cut the zucchini into ¼-inch slices.

6. Cut the peppers in half lengthwise and remove the white core and the seeds. Chop the pepper flesh into 1-inch squares.

7. Carefully thread the marinated sole fillets onto kebab skewers, alternating these with pieces of the prepared vegetables. Brush each kebab with a little of the oil and lemon marinade.

8. Arrange the kebabs on a broiler pan and cook under a moderately hot broiler for about 8 minutes, turning frequently to prevent them from burning, and brushing with the extra marinade to keep them moist.

9. Arrange the kebabs on a serving dish, and sprinkle with the chopped parsley for garnish.

Step 7 Thread the marinated rolls of fish onto kebab skewers, alternating these with vegetables for color.

Cook's Notes

Time
Preparation takes about 30 minutes, plus marinating time. Cooking takes approximately 8 minutes.

Preparation
After 2 hours marinating, the sole will look opaque and have a partially cooked appearance.

Cook's Tip
These kebabs are ideal for cooking out of doors on a barbeque.

SERVES 6
275 kilocalories per serving

CASSEROLE OF VEAL AND MUSHROOMS

Veal is a low fat meat and is delicious when served in this tomato and mushroom sauce.

3lbs lean pie veal
Salt and freshly ground black pepper
5 tbsps olive oil
2 shallots, finely chopped
½ clove garlic, minced
½ cup dry white wine
1⅓ cups strong brown stock
1 cup canned tomatoes, drained and chopped
1 bouquet garni
2 strips lemon peel
1 cup small button mushrooms
2½ tbsps fresh chopped parsley

1. Dice the meat into bite-sized pieces, using a sharp knife.

2. Sprinkle the pieces of meat with salt and pepper, then allow to stand for about 30 minutes.

3. Heat half of the oil in a large frying pan, and cook the pieces of meat for 5-10 minutes, stirring them frequently until they are browned on all sides. Remove the meat from the pan and set it aside.

4. Add the shallots and garlic to the oil and meat juices in the pan, lower the heat and cook until softened, but not colored. Return the veal to the pan and mix well.

5. Add the wine, stock, tomatoes, bouquet garni and lemon peel to the meat mixture, and bring to the boil.

6. Transfer the veal to an ovenproof casserole. Cover with a tight-fitting lid and bake in a pre-heated oven 325°F for

Step 3 Gently brown the veal in the hot oil, stirring it frequently until it has browned on all sides.

Step 4 Cook the garlic and shallots in the hot oil and meat juices gently, taking care to soften, but not brown them.

about 1¼ hours, or until the meat is tender.

7. Heat the remaining oil in a clean frying pan, and gently stir in the mushrooms, cooking them for 2-3 minutes until they begin to soften, but are not properly cooked.

8. After the casserole cooking time has finished, stir in the partially cooked mushrooms and continue cooking in the oven for a further 15 minutes.

9. Sprinkle with the chopped parsley before serving.

Cook's Notes

Time
Preparation takes about 30 minutes, cooking takes approximately 1½ hours.

Variation
Use lamb, or beef, instead of the veal in this recipe.

Serving Idea
Serve with new potatoes, pasta, or rice.

Watchpoint
Do not allow the garlic and onions to brown, or it will impair the flavor of the veal.

SERVES 4
157 kilocalories per serving
EGGPLANT AND CHICKEN CHILI

This unusual dish is both delicious and filling.

2 medium-sized eggplants
5 tbsps sesame oil
2 cloves garlic, minced
4 green onions
1 green chili, finely chopped
¾lb boned and skinned chicken breast
5 tbsps light soy sauce
2½ tbsps stock, or water
1¼ tbsps tomato paste
1 tsp cornstarch
Liquid sweetener to taste

Step 6 Cut the green onions diagonally into small pieces, approximately ½ inch long.

1. Cut the eggplant into quarters lengthwise, using a sharp knife. Slice the eggplant quarters into pieces approximately ½-inch thick.

2. Put the eggplant slices into a bowl and sprinkle liberally with salt. Stir well to coat evenly. Cover with plastic wrap and leave to stand for 30 minutes.

3. Rinse the eggplant slices very thoroughly under running water, then pat dry with a clean tea cloth.

4. Heat half of the oil in a wok, or large frying pan, and gently cook the garlic until it is soft, but not colored.

5. Add the eggplant slices to the wok and cook, stirring frequently, for 3-4 minutes.

6. Using a sharp knife, slice the green onions into thin diagonal strips. Stir the green onions together with the chili into the cooked eggplant, and cook for a further 1 minute. Remove the eggplant and onion from the pan, and set aside, keeping warm.

7. Cut the chicken breast into thin slices with a sharp knife.

8. Heat the remaining oil in the wok, and fry the chicken pieces for approximately 2 minutes or until they have turned white and are cooked thoroughly.

9. Return the eggplant and onions to the pan and cook, stirring continuously, for 2 minutes or until heated through completely.

10. Mix together the remaining ingredients and pour these over the chicken and eggplants in the wok, stirring constantly until the sauce has thickened and cleared. Serve immediately.

Cook's Notes

Time
Preparation takes about 10 minutes, cooking takes approximately 15 minutes.

Cook's Tip
The vegetables can be prepared well in advance, but the eggplants should be removed from the salt after 30 minutes, or they will become too dehydrated.

Variation
Use turkey instead of chicken in this recipe, and zucchini in place of the eggplants.

Serving Idea
Serve this recipe as part of a more extensive Chinese style meal.

SERVES 4

170 kilocalories per serving

FRUIT PLATE

This medley of fruit can be varied to suit your taste and is served without a syrupy liquid, so is low in calories.

1 green fig
2 kiwi fruit
2 fresh dates
1 guava
1 paw paw
¾ cup lychees
½ small pineapple
1 fresh mango
¾ cup seedless grapes
½ small melon
½lb watermelon
2½ tbsps orange juice
2½ tbsps lemon juice
½ cup chopped walnuts, or pine kernels (optional)

1. Select a large, shallow serving platter on which to arrange the fruit.

2. Cut the figs into quarters lengthwise and arrange on a plate.

3. Peel the kiwi fruits, and remove any hard core from the stem end. Slice the fruit thinly and arrange alongside the figs, reserving a few slices for the watermelon.

4. Cut the dates in half lengthwise and remove the stones. Place the dates on the serving plate.

5. Cut the guavas in half and slice these into wedges with a sharp knife. Peel the paw paw and slice this into thin crescents. Arrange the guava slices and paw paw alternately onto the plate along with the other prepared fruit.

6. Peel the lychees and remove the stones from the stalk end, using the rounded tip of a swivel potato peeler. Discard the stones, and place the fruit on the serving platter.

7. Peel the pineapple and cut away any brown eyes which may remain in the flesh. Cut the pineapple into slices and remove the core, using a sharp knife or apple corer. Cut the pineapple slices into small wedges and arrange on the plate.

8. Peel the mango and cut the flesh into slices, discarding the stone.

9. Halve the seedless grapes. Place the mango and grapes in an alternate pattern, alongside the rest of the fruit on the serving plate.

10. Peel the melon, cut into half, and remove the seeds. Slice the melon flesh into small wedges.

11. Leave the peel and pips in the watermelon, and cut this into small wedges, approximately the same size as the previous melon. Arrange the melon wedges on either side of the plate and decorate with the remaining kiwi fruit if used.

12. Mix together the lemon, juice, orange juice and chopped nuts, and sprinkle this dressing evenly over the fruit on the plate. Cover with plastic wrap and chill well before serving.

Step 6 Remove the stones from the lychees by scooping them out from the stalk end with the rounded end of a potato peeler.

Cook's Notes

Time
Preparation takes about 30 minutes, plus chiling time.

Preparation
Canned lychees could be used in place of the fresh fruit in this recipe, as could canned pineapples, kiwis and mangoes, but make sure they are packed in natural juice which should be drained before serving.

Variation
Use any selection of your favorite fruits in this recipe.

Low Calorie Notes

Low Calorie
Notes

PASTA
COOKING

Introduction

Pasta has become increasingly popular over the last few years. Pasta is literally a paste made with flour and eggs. Commercial pasta is usually made from hard durum wheat, but fresh pasta can be made with almost any kind of flour. It can also be made in a variety of different colors with the addition of ingredients such as spinach and tomato paste.

You can make pasta at home, but it is often more convenient to buy the fresh varieties now available in supermarkets. A wide range of dried, packaged pastas are also on offer, but these do not match the taste of the real thing! Pasta comes in a bewildering array of names and shapes. Because the Italian names often vary depending on which region the pasta originates from, it is often easier to look for the shape of the particular pasta you require.

Pasta is the perfect complement to a wide range of other ingredients. It can simply be mixed with olive oil and garlic or fresh herbs, or it can be enhanced with everything from tomatoes and cheese to ham and olives. Tomatoes, cheese and herbs are the most common ingredients in pasta sauces and fillings, but even within these categories there are numerous flavors and uses. Parmesan is treasured for its wonderful flavor, while ricotta is perfect for stuffing pasta as it adds body and holds its shape well. One of the joys of cooking pasta is that it combines so well with numerous ingredients, so experiment with your favorites to find flavors that you enjoy.

One of the bonuses of pasta is that it is simple and quick to cook, but a few guidelines should be followed. Never overcook pasta as it will quickly become sticky. Remember that fresh pasta cooks more quickly than the dried variety. Whole wheat pasta takes longer to cook and cooking times will also vary according to the thickness of the pasta. Most important, pasta should be cooked in a large, uncovered saucepan of boiling, salted water. A little olive oil can be added to prevent the pasta sticking, and the water boiling over.

The ease of cooking and variety of shapes and flavors ensures that pasta is here to stay, so start experimenting with some of the recipes in this book, and you will find that producing the perfect pasta dish is simplicity itself.

Contents

MEATBALL SOUP

*A filling soup which makes a meal
in itself when served with bread.*

SERVES 4

1 lb beef bones (see Cook's Tip)
1 carrot
1 onion, chopped
1 celery stalk, chopped
1 egg, beaten
½ lb ground beef
½ cup bread crumbs
Salt and pepper
1 tbsp oil
14 oz can crushed plum tomatoes
¾ cup small pasta
1 tbsp chopped fresh parsley

1. Place bones, carrot, onion and celery in a large saucepan and cover with cold water. Bring to a boil, cover and simmer for at least one hour.

2. Meanwhile, mix lightly beaten egg with ground beef, bread crumbs and plenty of seasoning.

3. Take a teaspoon of the mixture and roll into small balls. Heat oil in a roasting pan and put in the balls. Bake in a preheated oven at 350°F for 45 minutes, turning occasionally.

4. Strain stock into a saucepan.

5. Add tomatoes to stock. Bring to a boil, and simmer for 15 minutes. Add pasta and cook for 10 minutes, stirring frequently.

6. Add meatballs, adjust seasoning, and stir in chopped parsley. Serve hot.

TIME: Preparation takes 10 minutes, cooking takes 1 hour 40 minutes.

COOK'S TIP: Use a beef stock cube instead of the beef bones. Dissolve the stock cube in a little boiling water, add to the saucepan with the vegetables and cover with cold water.

MINESTRA

*Some of Italy's finest ingredients
make up this warming soup.*

SERVES 4

1 onion
1 carrot
1 celery stalk
2 tbsps olive oil
6 cups water
Salt and pepper
½ lb fresh spinach
2 tomatoes
4 oz elbow macaroni
2 cloves garlic, crushed
2 tbsps chopped fresh parsley
1 tsp fresh rosemary or ½ tsp dried
¼ cup Parmesan cheese, grated

1. Cut onion, carrot and celery into thick, julienne.

2. Heat oil in a large, heavy pan and fry vegetable strips until just brown, stirring occasionally. Pour on water, season with salt and pepper, and simmer for 20 minutes.

3. Meanwhile, wash and cut spinach leaves into shreds, add to soup and simmer for 10 minutes.

4. Blanch and peel tomatoes and chop coarsely, removing seeds.

5. Add tomatoes, macaroni, garlic, parsley and rosemary to the soup, and simmer another 10 minutes. Adjust seasoning. Serve with grated Parmesan cheese if desired.

TIME: Preparation takes 15 minutes, cooking takes 45 minutes.

MACARONI WITH OLIVE SAUCE

Macaroni is served here with butter, garlic and finely chopped olives.
A very tasty dish that makes an ideal appetizer.

SERVES 4

11 oz macaroni
¼ cup butter
1 clove garlic, finely chopped
10 pitted olives, green and/or black, finely
   chopped
Salt and pepper

1. Cook the macaroni to your liking in salted, boiling water. Rinse in hot water and set aside to drain.

2. Melt the butter in a saucepan and add the garlic and olives. Cook for 1 minute and then stir in the macaroni.

3. Check the seasoning, adding salt and pepper as necessary. Serve hot.

TIME: Preparation takes about 10 minutes, cooking takes approximately 20 minutes.

VARIATION: Add a few chopped capers to the olives, but reduce the amount of salt.

COOK'S TIP: Rinse the macaroni really well under hot water to prevent it from sticking together.

VERMICELLI PESCATORE

*This impressive dish is simple to prepare
and perfect for special guests.*

SERVES 4

12 mussels
12 clams
½ lb cod fillets
¼ lb squid, cleaned
4 large shrimp, cooked
4 fresh oysters, cooked
3 cups tomato sauce
¼ cup olive oil
1 cup dry white wine
Half a green pepper, diced
Salt and pepper
9 oz package vermicelli

1. Prepare seafood. If using fresh mussels, clean closed mussels, removing beard, and cook in boiling water for 3 minutes until they open. (Discard any that remain closed).

2. Cool and remove from shells, keeping a few in shells for garnish if desired. Cut cod into ½ inch pieces.

3. Cut squid into rings.

4. Heat 2 tbsps oil in a pan and add the squid. Fry gently until golden brown, then add wine, tomato sauce, green pepper, and salt and pepper to taste. Simmer for 20 minutes and then add cod. Simmer for another 10 minutes, stirring occasionally.

5. Add clams and mussels and bring mixture back to a boil; adjust seasoning. Meanwhile, cook vermicelli in plenty of boiling, salted water for 10 minutes, or until tender but still firm. Drain well. Add seafood mixture and toss. Garnish with shrimps and oysters.

TIME: Preparation takes 15 minutes, cooking takes 40 minutes.

CABBAGE AND PASTA SOUP

Chicken stock flavored with bacon, cabbage, pasta and garlic is the base for this light and tasty appetizer.

SERVES 4

6 leaves white cabbage
1 tbsp olive oil
5 oz small pasta shells
2 slices bacon
1 clove garlic, chopped
3 cups chicken stock
Salt and pepper

1. Cut the cabbage into thin strips. To do this, roll the leaves into cigar shapes and cut with a very sharp knife.

2. Heat the olive oil. Trim excess fat from bacon, dice meat and fry the bacon, garlic and cabbage together for 2 minutes.

3. Pour over the stock, season with salt and pepper and cook on a moderate heat for 15 minutes.

4. Add the pasta to the soup and cook for another 15 minutes.

5. Check the seasoning and serve.

TIME: Preparation takes about 5 minutes, cooking takes approximately 35 minutes.

SERVING IDEA: Sprinkle over a little grated Parmesan cheese just before serving the soup.

VARIATION: Leave the piece of bacon whole and remove before serving the soup.

CHICK PEA SOUP

This unusual sounding soup is a wonderful mixture
of chick peas and classic Italian ingredients.

SERVES 4

1 cup dried chick peas
3 tbsps olive oil
2 cloves garlic
1½ cups plum tomatoes, chopped
3 cups water
1 tsp fresh basil or ½ tsp dried
1 chicken bouillon cube
Salt and pepper
1 cup small pasta or elbow macaroni
2 tbsps Parmesan cheese, grated

1. Soak chick peas overnight in enough water to cover by 1 inch. Drain and discard water. Place the chick peas in a large, heavy pan, and cover with 1 inch of water. Bring to a boil and simmer, covered, for about 1 hour until chick peas are tender. Make sure they do not boil dry.

2. Heat olive oil in a heavy pan and sauté garlic cloves. When browned, remove and discard garlic cloves. Add tomatoes and their juice, water and basil, and simmer for 20 minutes.

3. Add drained chick peas, crumbled bouillon cube, and salt and pepper to taste. Stir well and simmer another 10 minutes. Bring back to a boil. Add pasta and cook, stirring frequently, for 10 minutes.

4. Mix in half of the Parmesan cheese. Adjust seasoning and serve immediately, with remaining Parmesan cheese sprinkled on top.

TIME: Preparation takes overnight soaking for the chick peas plus 5 minutes, cooking takes 1 hour 20 minutes.

COOK'S TIP: Soup may be puréed before pasta is added, if desired.

BEAN SOUP

*Kidney beans and pasta combine to produce
a filling soup suitable for all the family.*

SERVES 4-6

15 oz can kidney beans
2 slices bacon, chopped
1 celery stalk, chopped
1 small onion, chopped
1 clove garlic, crushed
½ cup plum tomatoes, chopped
   and seeds removed
1 tbsp chopped fresh parsley
1 tsp fresh basil or ½ tsp dried
4 cups water
1 chicken bouillon cube
Salt and pepper
1 cup whole wheat pasta

1. Place kidney beans, bacon, celery, onion, garlic, parsley, basil, tomatoes and water in a large saucepan. Bring to a boil and add bouillon cube and salt and pepper to taste. Cover and cook on a low heat for about 1½ hours.

2. Raise heat and add pasta, stirring well. Stir frequently until pasta is cooked but still firm – about 10 minutes. Serve immediately.

TIME: Preparation takes 15 minutes, cooking takes 1 hour 45 minutes.

161

Mariner's Salad

*Seafood mixes very well with pasta and the
ingredients can be adapted according to availability.*

SERVES 6

1 lb pasta shells, plain and spinach
4 large scallops, cleaned
1 cup mussels
½ cup lemon juice and water mixed
¾ cup cooked, peeled and de-veined
   shrimp
½ cup clams, cooked
4 oz cooked crab meat, diced
4 green onions, chopped
1 tbsp chopped fresh parsley

Dressing
Grated rind and juice of half a lemon
1 cup mayonnaise
2 tsps paprika
⅓ cup sour cream or plain yogurt
Salt and pepper

1. Cook the pasta for 10 minutes in a large pan of boiling, salted water with 1 tbsp oil. Drain and rinse under hot water. Leave in cold water until ready to use.

2. Cook the scallops and mussels in the lemon juice and water mixture for about 5 minutes, or until fairly firm.

3. Cut the scallops into 2 or 3 pieces, depending upon size.

4. Prepare the dressing and drain the pasta thoroughly.

5. Mix all ingredients together and coat completely with dressing. Stir carefully so that the shellfish do not break-up. Chill for up to 1 hour before serving.

TIME: Preparation takes 25 minutes, cooking takes 15 minutes.

CURRIED SHRIMP SALAD

*An unusual salad which is perfect
for a summer lunch.*

SERVES 4

2 tbsps olive oil
1 clove garlic, crushed
1 small onion, chopped
1½ tsps curry powder
1 tsp paprika
1 tsp tomato paste
½ cup water
2 slices lemon
Salt and pepper
1 tsp apricot preserve
1 cup mayonnaise
1½ cups small pasta or elbow macaroni
½ lb cooked shrimp, peeled and de-veined
Juice of ½ a lemon

1. Heat oil, and fry garlic and onion gently until soft but not colored. Add curry powder and paprika, and cook for 2 minutes.

2. Stir in tomato paste and water. Add lemon slices, and salt and pepper to taste. Cook slowly for 10 minutes.

3. Stir in the preserve, and bring to a boil, simmering for 2 minutes. Strain and leave to cool. Add mayonnaise.

4. Meanwhile, cook pasta in plenty of boiling salted water for 10 minutes, or until tender, but still firm. Rinse under cold water and drain well.

5. Toss in lemon juice, and put in serving dish. Arrange shrimp on top, and pour over curry sauce. Toss well. Sprinkle with paprika.

TIME: Preparation takes 10 minutes, cooking takes 20 minutes.

PASTA AND VEGETABLES IN PARMESAN DRESSING

Fresh vegetables and pasta in a delicious dressing.

SERVES 6

1 lb pasta spirals or other shapes
½ lb assorted vegetables such as:
Zucchini, cut in rounds or julienne
Broccoli, trimmed into very small florets
Snow peas, ends trimmed
Carrots, cut in rounds or julienne
Celery, cut in julienne
Cucumber, cut in julienne
Green onion, thinly shredded or sliced
Asparagus tips
Green beans, sliced
Red or yellow peppers, thinly sliced

Dressing
½ cup olive oil
3 tbsps lemon juice
1 tbsp sherry
1 tbsp fresh parsley, chopped
1 tbsp fresh basil, chopped, or ½ tbsp dried
¼ cup freshly grated Parmesan cheese
2 tbsps mild mustard
Salt and pepper
Pinch sugar

1. Cook pasta in a large saucepan of boiling, salted water with 1 tbsp oil for 10-12 minutes or until just tender. Rinse under hot water to remove starch. Leave in cold water.

2. Place all the vegetables except the cucumber into boiling salted water for 3 minutes until just tender. Rinse in cold water and leave to drain.

3. Mix the dressing ingredients together very well. Drain the pasta thoroughly and toss with the dressing. Add the vegetables and toss to coat. Refrigerate for up to 1 hour before serving.

TIME: Preparation takes 25 minutes, cooking takes 13-15 minutes.

ITALIAN PASTA SALAD

*Buy your favorite Italian cold cuts
for this delicious salad.*

SERVES 4-6

1 lb pasta shapes
½ cup frozen peas
8 oz assorted Italian cold cuts, cut in strips:
    salami, mortadella, prosciutto
4 oz provolone or mozzarella cheese, cut
    in strips
15 black olives, halved and pitted
4 tbsps capers
1 small red onion or 2 shallots, chopped
2 cups oyster mushrooms, stems trimmed
    and sliced

Dressing
3 tbsps white wine vinegar
½ cup olive oil
½ clove garlic, crushed
1 tsp fennel seed, crushed
1 tbsp fresh parsley, chopped
1 tbsp fresh basil, chopped, or ½ tsp dried
1 tbsp prepared mustard
Salt and pepper

1. Put the pasta in a large saucepan of boiling water with a pinch of salt and 1 tbsp oil. Cook for about 10 minutes or until just tender.

2. Add the frozen peas during the last 3 minutes of cooking. Drain the pasta and peas and rinse under hot water. Leave in cold water until ready to use.

3. Mix the dressing ingredients together well.

4. Drain the pasta and peas thoroughly. Mix the pasta and peas with the cold cuts and cheese, olives, capers, chopped onion or shallot and sliced mushrooms.

5. Pour the dressing over the salad and toss all the ingredients together to coat. Do not over-mix.

6. Leave the salad to chill for up to 1 hour before serving.

TIME: Preparation takes 25 minutes, cooking takes 10 minutes.

NIÇOISE SALAD

*A classic French salad using
Italy's favorite ingredients!*

SERVES 4

1½ cups penne
7 oz can tuna, drained and flaked
3 tomatoes, quartered
1 cucumber, cut into julienne
1 cup green beans, cooked
12 black olives, halved, with stones
    removed
6-8 anchovy fillets, drained, and soaked in
    milk if desired (see Cook's Tip)
½ cup oil and vinegar dressing

1. Cook penne in plenty of boiling, salted water until tender, but still firm.

2. Rinse in cold water, drain, and leave to dry.

3. Put flaked tuna in the bottom of a salad dish. Toss pasta with tomatoes, cucumber, green beans, olives, and anchovies, and then pour on dressing. Mix together well.

TIME: Preparation takes 15 minutes, cooking takes 15 minutes.

COOK'S TIP: Soaking the anchovy fillets in milk removes any excess salt
from the fish. Drain well before using.

TUNA AND TOMATO SALAD

*An economical salad which uses few
ingredients – perfect for unexpected guests.*

SERVES 4

1 tbsp chopped fresh basil or marjoram,
 or 1 tsp dried basil or oregano
6 tbsps vinaigrette dressing (see Cook's Tip)
3 cups pasta shells
7 oz can tuna, flaked
6 tomatoes

1. Mix herbs with vinaigrette dressing.

2. Cook pasta shells in a large saucepan of boiling salted water until tender – about 10 minutes. Rinse with cold water and drain, shaking off excess water. Toss with 3 tablespoons of vinaigrette dressing. Leave to cool.

3. Meanwhile, slice enough of the tomatoes to arrange around the outside of the serving dish.

4. Chop the rest, pour the remaining vinaigrette dressing over them, and place in the center of the dish.

5. Add tuna to the pasta shells, and toss gently. Serve in the center of the dish over the chopped tomatoes.

TIME: Preparation takes 10 minutes, cooking takes 15 minutes.

COOK'S TIP: To make your own vinaigrette dressing, mix 4½ tbsps olive oil with 1½ tbsps white wine vinegar, a pinch of salt and pepper and about ⅛-¼ tsp of prepared mustard.

MEXICAN CHICKEN SALAD

A simple salad which is both quick and tasty.

SERVES 4

1¼ cups pasta shells
2 cups cooked chicken, shredded
7 oz can corn, drained
1 celery stalk, sliced
1 red pepper, diced
1 green pepper, diced

Dressing
1 tbsp mayonnaise
2 tbsps vinegar
Salt and pepper

1. Cook pasta in plenty of boiling salted water until just tender. Drain well and leave to cool.

2. Meanwhile, combine mayonnaise with vinegar and salt and pepper to taste.

3. When the pasta has cooled, add chicken, corn, celery and peppers.

4. Toss together well and serve with the dressing.

TIME: Preparation takes 10 minutes, cooking takes 15 minutes.

GIANFOTTERE SALAD

Eggplant, zucchini and peppers are
combined with pasta in this simple salad.

SERVES 4

1 eggplant
2 tomatoes
1 zucchini
1 red pepper
1 green pepper
1 onion
4 tbsps olive oil
1 clove garlic
Salt and pepper
1 lb whole wheat pasta spirals or bows

1. Cut eggplant into ½ inch slices. Sprinkle with salt and set aside for 30 minutes.

2. Peel the tomatoes – put them into boiling water for 20 seconds, rinse in cold water, and peel the skins off. Chop coarsely.

3. Cut zucchini into ½ inch slices. Chop the peppers coarsely.

4. Chop the onion and garlic.

5. Heat 3 tbsps olive oil in pan and fry onion gently until transparent.

6. Meanwhile, rinse salt from eggplant, and pat dry with paper towels. Chop coarsely.

7. Add eggplant, zucchini, peppers, tomatoes and garlic to onion, and fry gently for 20 minutes. Season with salt and pepper. Allow to cool.

8. Meanwhile, cook pasta spirals in plenty of boiling, salted water for 10 minutes, or until tender but still firm. Rinse in cold water and drain well. Toss in the remaining 1 tbsp olive oil.

9. Toss vegetables together with pasta spirals.

TIME: Preparation takes 40 minutes, cooking takes 30 minutes.

Tuna and Pasta with Red Kidney Beans

The perfect summer salad for lunch or a light dinner.

SERVES 4-6

1½ cups small pasta shells
8 oz can red kidney beans, drained
   and rinsed
1 cup small mushrooms, quartered
14 oz can tuna, drained and flaked
4 green onions, sliced
2 tbsps mixed fresh herbs chopped, or
   1 tbsp dried

Dressing
½ cup olive oil
3 tbsps white wine vinegar
Squeeze of lemon juice
1 tbsp Dijon mustard
Salt and pepper

1. Cook the pasta shells in boiling, salted water with 1 tbsp oil for 10 minutes or until just tender. Rinse under hot water and then place in cold water until ready to use.

2. Mix the dressing ingredients together thoroughly.

3. Drain the pasta shells. Mix the pasta with the beans, mushrooms, tuna, green onions and herbs.

4. Pour over the dressing and toss to coat. Chill up to 1 hour in the refrigerator before serving.

TIME: Preparation takes 20 minutes, cooking takes 10 minutes.

SPAGHETTI AMATRICIANA

This is another quickly cooked sauce with a rich spicy taste.
Reduce the amount of chili pepper for a less fiery flavor.

SERVES 4

1 onion
6 slices Canadian bacon
1 lb ripe tomatoes
1 red chili pepper, diced
1½ tbsps oil
12 oz spaghetti
Parmesan cheese (optional)

1. Slice the onion thinly. Cut the bacon into thin strips.

2. Drop the tomatoes into boiling water for 6-8 seconds. Remove with a draining spoon, place in cold water, and leave to cool completely. This will make the skin easier to remove.

3. Peel the tomatoes, cut them in half and remove the seeds and pulp with a teaspoon. Rub the seeds and pulp through a strainer and retain juice to use in the sauce if desired. Chop the tomato flesh roughly and set it aside.

4. Heat the oil in a sauté pan and add the onion and bacon. Stir over medium heat for about 5 minutes, until the onion is transparent. Drain off excess fat, add the tomatoes and pepper, and mix well. Simmer the sauce gently, uncovered, for about 5 minutes, stirring occasionally.

5. Meanwhile, cook the spaghetti in boiling, salted water with 1 tbsp oil for about 10-12 minutes. Drain and rinse in hot water and toss in a colander to dry. To serve, spoon the sauce on top of the spaghetti and sprinkle with freshly grated Parmesan cheese, if desired.

TIME: Preparation takes about 20-25 minutes, cooking takes about 10-12 minutes for the spaghetti and about 8 minutes for the sauce.

181

PASTA SPIRALS WITH CREAMY PARSLEY SAUCE

Serve this quick and easy dish with French bread for the perfect mid-week dinner.

SERVES 3-4

2 tbsps butter or margarine
1 tbsp flour
1 cup milk
9 oz pasta spirals
1 tbsp chopped fresh parsley
1 tbsp lemon juice or 1 tsp vinegar

1. Heat butter in pan; when melted, stir in flour. Heat gently for 1 minute. Remove from heat, and gradually stir in milk. Return to heat, and stir continuously until boiling. Cook for 2 minutes.

2. Meanwhile, cook pasta spirals in plenty of boiling, salted water for 10 minutes, or until tender, but still firm. Rinse in hot water, and drain well.

3. Just before serving, add parsley and lemon juice to sauce, and pour over pasta. Serve immediately.

TIME: Preparation takes 5 minutes, cooking takes 15 minutes.

183

TORTIGLIONI ALLA PUTTANESCA

*Anchovy fillets add a special flavor
to this classic Italian dish.*

SERVES 4

7 oz can plum tomatoes, drained
6-8 anchovy fillets
10 oz tortiglioni (pasta spirals)
2 tbsps olive oil
2 cloves garlic, crushed
½ tsp fresh or pinch dried basil
Pinch chili powder
½ cup black olives, pitted and chopped
2 tbsps chopped fresh parsley
Salt and pepper

1. Chop tomatoes and anchovies.

2. Cook pasta in plenty of boiling salted water for 10 minutes, or until tender but still firm. Rinse in hot water and drain. Pour into a warmed bowl.

3. Meanwhile, heat oil in pan, add garlic, basil and chili powder, and cook for 1 minute.

4. Add tomatoes, olives, parsley and anchovies, and cook for a few minutes.

5. Season with salt and pepper. Pour sauce over pasta and mix together thoroughly. Serve immediately.

TIME: Preparation takes 10 minutes, cooking takes 15 minutes.

185

PASTA SHELLS WITH MUSHROOM SAUCE

This adaptable dish can be served for lunch or dinner.

SERVES 3-4

½ lb mushrooms
2 tbsps butter or margarine
1 tbsp flour
1 cup milk
Salt and pepper
10 oz pasta shells

1. Rinse the mushrooms and chop them coarsely.

2. Melt butter in a saucepan and add mushrooms. Fry for 5 minutes, stirring occasionally. Stir in the flour and cook for 1 minute.

3. Reduce the heat, and add milk gradually, stirring continuously. Bring to a boil and cook for 3 minutes. Season with salt and pepper.

4. Meanwhile, cook the pasta shells in plenty of boiling salted water for 10 minutes, or until tender, but still firm.

5. Rinse in hot water and drain well. Place in a warmed serving dish, and pour over mushroom sauce. Serve immediately.

TIME: Preparation takes 5 minutes, cooking takes 15 minutes.

187

TAGLIATELLE WITH CREAMY LIVER SAUCE

Chicken livers are lovely mixed with cream and mushrooms;
add pasta to the mixture and you have the perfect mid-week treat.

SERVES 3-4

3 tbsps olive oil
2 medium onions, sliced
1 clove garlic, crushed
¾ cup mushrooms, sliced
1 lb chicken livers, cleaned and sliced
⅓ cup heavy cream
2 eggs, beaten
Salt and pepper
10 oz tagliatelle
1 tbsp chopped fresh parsley

1. Melt 2 tbsps of the oil in a large frying pan and cook onions and garlic gently until softened.

2. Add mushrooms and cook for 3 minutes. Add chicken livers, and cook until lightly browned. Remove from heat and stir in cream. Return to low heat and cook, uncovered, for another 2 minutes.

3. Remove from heat and stir in lightly beaten eggs. Season with salt and pepper to taste.

4. Meanwhile, cook the tagliatelle in plenty of boiling, salted water for 10 minutes, or until tender but still firm, stirring occasionally.

5. Drain tagliatelle, toss in remaining oil, and black pepper. Serve sauce over tagliatelle and sprinkle with parsley.

TIME: Preparation takes 10 minutes, cooking takes 15 minutes.

SPAGHETTI WITH TOMATO, SALAMI AND GREEN OLIVES

*Vary the quantities of salami and green olives
in this recipe according to your taste.*

SERVES 2-3

14 oz can plum tomatoes
⅓ lb salami, sliced and shredded
1 cup green olives, stoned and chopped
½ tbsp dried oregano
Salt and pepper
10 oz spaghetti
2 tbsps olive oil
1 clove garlic, crushed
¼ cup pecorino cheese, grated

1. Purée tomatoes in a blender or food processor and put into a saucepan. Add oregano, olives and salami and heat gently. Add salt and pepper to taste.

2. Meanwhile, cook spaghetti in plenty of boiling, salted water for 10 minutes, or until tender but still firm. Drain well.

3. Heat olive oil in the pan used to cook the spaghetti, and add garlic and freshly-ground black pepper.

4. Add spaghetti and pour the sauce over. Toss well. Serve immediately with pecorino cheese.

TIME: Preparation takes 15 minutes, cooking takes 15 minutes.

MACARONI CHEESE WITH HOT DOGS

Kids and adults alike will love this delicious, filling meal.

SERVES 4

8 hot dogs
1 lb macaroni
¼ cup butter or margarine
¾ cup all-purpose flour
2 cups milk
1½ cups cheddar cheese, grated
1 tsp dry mustard
Salt and pepper

Garnish
½ red pepper, cut into thin strips

1. Poach the hot dogs for 5-8 minutes. Remove skins and, when cold, cut into diagonal slices.

2. Cook macaroni in plenty of boiling salted water for about 10 minutes, or until tender but still firm. Rinse in hot water and drain well.

3. Meanwhile, melt the butter in a pan. Stir in the flour and cook gently for 1 minute. Reduce heat and gradually add milk, stirring all the time. Bring to a boil, stirring continuously, reduce heat and cook gently for 3 minutes.

4. Add hot dogs, grated cheese, mustard, and salt and pepper to taste. Stir well.

5. Add macaroni and mix in well. Pour mixture into an oven-proof dish and sprinkle the remaining cheese over the top.

6. Make a lattice of pepper, and cook under a preheated broiler until golden brown. Serve immediately.

TIME: Preparation takes 10 minutes, cooking takes 20 minutes.

SPIRALI WITH SPINACH AND BACON

Pasta doesn't have to have a sauce that cooks for hours. This whole dish takes about 15 minutes. True Italian "fast food!"

SERVES 4

12 oz pasta spirals
8 oz fresh spinach
3 oz bacon
1 small red or green chili pepper
1 small red pepper
1 small onion
1 clove garlic, crushed
3 tbsps olive oil
Salt and pepper

1. Cook the pasta in boiling, salted water for about 10-12 minutes or until just tender. Drain the pasta in a colander and rinse it under hot water. Keep the pasta in a bowl of water until ready to use.

2. Tear the stalks off the spinach and wash the leaves well in the water several times. Set aside to drain.

3. Dice the bacon finely. Slice the chili and the red pepper finely. Slice the onion thinly.

4. Roll up several of the spinach leaves into a cigar shape and then shred them finely. Repeat until all the spinach is shredded.

5. Heat the oil in a sauté pan and add garlic, onion, peppers and bacon. Fry for 2 minutes, add the spinach and fry for another 2 minutes, stirring continuously. Season with salt and pepper.

6. Drain the pasta spirals and toss them in a colander to remove excess water. Mix with the spinach sauce and serve immediately.

TIME: Preparation takes 20 minutes, cooking takes about 15 minutes.

Penne with Ham and Asparagus

*The Italian word penne means quills, due to the
diagonal cut on both ends.*

SERVES 4

8 oz penne
12 oz fresh asparagus
4 oz cooked ham
2 tbsps butter or margarine
1 cup heavy cream
Parmesan cheese (optional)

1. Trim asparagus spears about 1 inch from the bottom.

2. Cut the ham into strips about ½-inch thick.

3. Steam the asparagus spears for about 2 minutes. Drain and allow to cool.

4. Cut the asparagus into 1 inch lengths, leaving the tips whole.

5. Melt the butter in the sauté pan and add the asparagus and ham. Cook briefly to evaporate the liquid and then add the cream. Bring to a boil and cook for about 5 minutes to thicken the cream.

6. Meanwhile, cook the pasta in boiling salted water with 1 tbsp oil for about 10-12 minutes.

7. Drain the pasta and rinse under hot water. Toss in a colander to drain and mix with the sauce. Serve with grated Parmesan cheese, if desired.

TIME: Preparation takes about 20 minutes, cooking takes 10-12 minutes for the pasta and 8 minutes for the sauce.

197

HOMEMADE TAGLIATELLE WITH SUMMER SAUCE

Pasta making is not as difficult as you might think. It is well worth it, too, because homemade pasta is in a class by itself.

SERVES 4

Pasta Dough
1 cup all-purpose flour
1 cup bread flour
2 large eggs
2 tsps olive oil
Pinch salt

Sauce
1 lb unpeeled tomatoes, seeded and diced
1 large green pepper, diced
1 onion, diced
1 tbsp fresh basil, chopped, or ½ tsp dried
1 tbsp fresh parsley, chopped
2 cloves garlic, crushed
½ cup olive oil and vegetable oil, mixed

1. Combine all the sauce ingredients, mixing well. Cover and refrigerate overnight.

2. Place the flours in a mound on a work surface and make a well in the center. Place the eggs, oil and salt in the center of the well.

3. Using a fork, beat the ingredients in the center to blend them and gradually incorporate the flour from the outside edge. The dough may also be mixed in a food processor.

4. When half the flour is incorporated, start kneading using the palms of the hands until all the flour is incorporated. This may also be done in a food processor. Cover the dough and leave it to rest for 15 minutes.

5. Divide the dough in quarters and roll out thinly with a rolling pin on a floured surface, dusting dough lightly with flour before rolling. If using a pasta machine, following the manufacturer's directions. Allow the sheets of pasta to dry for about 10 minutes on a floured surface or tea towels. Cut the sheets into strips about ¼ inch wide by hand or machine, dusting lightly with flour while cutting. Leave the cut pasta to dry for 5-10 minutes.

6. Cook the pasta for 5-6 minutes in boiling, salted water with a spoonful of oil. Drain the pasta and rinse under very hot water. Toss in a colander to drain excess water. Place the hot pasta in serving dish. Pour the cold sauce over and toss well.

TIME: Preparation takes about 30 minutes, cooking takes about 5-6 minutes.

199

LASAGNE WITH FOUR CHEESES

Adapt this dish by using your own
favorite Italian cheeses.

SERVES 2-3

1 tbsp olive oil
½ lb green lasagne
¼ cup butter
3 tbsps all-purpose flour
3¼ cups milk
6 tbsps grated Parmesan cheese
¼ cup grated gruyére cheese
¼ cup mozzarella, diced
¼ cup pecorino, diced
Salt, pepper and nutmeg

1. Fill a large pan with salted water. Add the olive oil. Cook the lasagne 4 or 5 sheets at a time for 7-10 minutes. Lift each batch out carefully and plunge into cold water. When all the pasta has been cooked, drain well on absorbent paper.

2. Melt the butter over gentle heat. When melted, add the flour and mix well. Heat the mixture gently until it turns a pale straw color. Stir in the milk gradually, stirring constantly until thick. Add the cheeses to the sauce, reserving 2 tbsps Parmesan. Season with salt, pepper and nutmeg.

3. Stir until the cheeses have melted.

4. Butter a deep baking dish generously. Add alternate layers of lasagne and sauce – there should be at least four layers. Finish with a layer of sauce, and sprinkle with the reserved grated Parmesan. Cook at 350°F for 45 minutes until bubbling and golden brown.

TIME: Preparation takes 15-20 minutes, cooking takes 45 minutes.

MEAT RAVIOLI WITH RED PEPPER SAUCE

*Pepper-flavored pasta dough is rolled thinly, cut into squares, filled with a
delicious meat stuffing and served with a creamy red pepper sauce.*

SERVES 4

2 red peppers, seeded
1¾ cups all-purpose flour, sifted
2 eggs
1 cup ground beef
1 tbsp fresh parsley, finely chopped
½ onion, chopped
½ cup light cream
½ cup butter
Salt and pepper

1. Place the red peppers in a food processor and blend until liquid. Place in a small bowl and set aside, giving time for the pulp to rise to the surface. This takes approximately 30 minutes.

2. To make the dough, place the sifted flour in a bowl with a pinch of salt. Add 1 egg and 3 tbsps of the pepper pulp (not the juice).

3. Mix together really well and form into a ball. Set the dough aside for 30 minutes.

4. Mix together the meat, parsley and onion, and season with salt and pepper.

5. Roll the dough out very thinly, using a pasta machine if available, and cut into small squares. Place a little stuffing on half of the cut squares. Beat the remaining egg and brush the edges of the squares with the egg. Cover with another square of dough and seal the edges by pinching together with your fingers.

6. Bring a large saucepan of salted water to a boil and cook the ravioli for approximately 3 minutes – longer if you prefer your pasta well cooked.

7. While the ravioli are cooking, prepare the sauce by heating the cream with ½ cup of the red pepper pulp. Bring to a boil and then whisk in the butter.

8. Drain the ravioli and then pat them dry with a tea towel. Serve with the hot cream sauce.

TIME: Preparation takes about 50 minutes, resting time is 30 minutes and cooking time approximately 15 minutes.

VARIATION: Add a little wine vinegar (1 tsp) and a few drops of Tabasco to the sauce to give it a slightly peppery taste.

WATCHPOINT: When rolling out the dough, flour it well so that it does not stick to the rolling pin or pasta machine rollers.

SPAGHETTI WITH CRAB AND BACON

This recipe includes a wonderful preparation of home-made parsley pasta.
It is tossed and served with a seafood sauce, crab and bacon.

SERVES 4-6

1 bunch parsley (approximately 6 tbsps)
4¼ cups all-purpose flour
4 eggs
8 oz bacon
1 tbsp olive oil
¾ lb crab meat, chopped
1½ cups heavy cream
3 tbps butter
Fresh chervil, optional
Salt and pepper

1. Trim the leaves off the parsley, discard the stalks. Cook for 10 minutes in boiling water. Pass through a fine sieve and reserve the cooking liquid.

2. Purée the parsley with 3 tbsps of the cooking liquid in a blender.

3. In a bowl, mix together the flour, salt, eggs and 1½ tbsps parsley purée. Form into a ball.

4. Quarter the dough and form these pieces into balls. Press each ball flat and run it through a pasta machine, or roll out with a rolling pin.

5. Thin the dough progressively by passing it through the machine several times. Flour the dough frequently throughout the operation.

6. Run the flattened strips of dough through the spaghetti cutter or cut with a knife.

7. Cut the bacon first into strips and then into small rectangles.

8. Add the olive oil to boiling, salted water and cook the spaghetti for 5 minutes. Strain and rinse.

9. Break up the crab meat into small pieces with your fingers.

10. Heat the cream gently with the crab and bacon pieces.

11. Meanwhile, heat the butter in a pan and when it bubbles, add the spaghetti (first reheated by plunging for 30 seconds in boiling water). Mix well and season with salt and pepper.

12. Place the buttered spaghetti around the edges of the dinner plates and arrange the crab/bacon mixture in the center. Garnish with the fresh chervil.

TIME: Preparation takes 1 hour, cooking takes 20 minutes.

Cook's Tip: If you do not wish to prepare the spaghetti yourself you can buy fresh spaghetti, either parsley or plain verde, at a delicatessen or supermarket.

TAGLIATELLE WITH BLUE CHEESE

Fruit and cheese marries well to give a sweet and savory dish.

SERVES 6

4¼ cups all-purpose flour
5 eggs
1 tbsp olive oil
4 oz blue cheese (roquefort or stilton)
1 cup dried apricots
1¼ cups heavy cream
¼ cup milk
¼ cup pine nuts
½ bunch chives
Salt and pepper

1. In a bowl, work together the flour, a pinch of salt and eggs to form a soft ball of dough.

2. Quarter the dough and flatten each piece. Coat each piece with plenty of flour. Flour the rollers of a pasta machine and pass the dough through the machine, or roll it out with a rolling pin.

3. Continue rolling the pasta until thin. Flour frequently during the process.

4. Thread the dough strips through the tagliatelle cutter or cut into strips with a knife. Dredge the noodles with flour and allow to dry for 2 hours.

5. Bring to a boil a saucepan of salted water with 1 tbsp oil. Cook the pasta for 2 to 4 minutes, stirring with a fork.

6. Drain the tagliatelle and rinse in plenty of cold water to prevent sticking. Set aside.

7. Break up the cheese and force through a sieve with the back of a spoon.

8. Cut the apricots into strips, then dice.

9. Slowly heat the cream in a saucepan. Stir in the cheese and milk. Blend until smooth with a hand-held electric blender.

10. While the sauce is hot, stir in the tagliatelle and apricots, and season as necessary. Heat through quickly so the cream does not curdle or the noodles overcook.

11. Mix the pasta with two forks. Remove from the heat and mix in the pine nuts.

12. Chop the chives finely and sprinkle them over the tagliatelle; serve immediately.

TIME: Preparation takes 1 hour, cooking takes 16 minutes.
Drying the pasta takes 2 hours.

207

Pasta with Leeks and Mussels

*An easy pasta dish to prepare, ideal
for unexpected guests.*

SERVES 6

1 lb mussels
½ cup white wine
1 shallot, chopped
2 medium-sized leeks
¾ cup heavy cream
1 lb spiral-shaped pasta
1 tbsp oil
2 slices ham
1½ tbsps butter
Fresh chives to garnish
Salt and pepper

1. Scrub the mussels; remove the beards and wash in several changes of water to remove any sand.

2. In a large, covered saucepan, cook the mussels in the white wine with the chopped shallot for approximately 5 minutes, over a high heat.

3. Cool and remove the opened mussels from their shells. Reserve the cooking liquid.

4. Quarter each leek lengthwise, wash thoroughly and slice finely.

5. In a covered saucepan, cook the leeks in the cream, with salt and pepper to taste, for 10 minutes over a low heat.

6. In a large saucepan of boiling water, cook the pasta with 1 tbsp oil. Stir the pasta as it cooks, to prevent sticking.

7. Drain after 5 or 6 minutes. Rinse in cold water to prevent sticking.

8. Slice the ham into small pieces.

9. Strain the mussel cooking liquid through a sieve lined with cheesecloth. Measure out approximately ½ cup.

10. Add the shelled mussels and the mussel liquid to the cream mixture, and cook for 4 minutes, stirring constantly.

11. Melt the butter in a deep frying pan and reheat the pasta gently with the ham. Season to taste.

12. When the pasta is heated through, add the cream and leek sauce, and serve garnished with the chopped chives.

TIME: Preparation takes 30 minutes, cooking takes 25 minutes.

FISH RAVIOLI

This recipe has quite a few ingredients but it is not too difficult to prepare and the end result tastes wonderful.

SERVES 4

Dough
1¼ cups bread flour
Pinch of salt
3 eggs

Filling
½ lb sole or flounder fillets
1 slice of onion
1 slice of lemon
6 peppercorns
1 bay leaf
1 tbsp lemon juice
1 cup water
2 eggs, beaten
2 tbsps bread crumbs
1 green onion, finely chopped

Lemon sauce
2 tbsps butter or margarine
2 tbsps flour
1 cup strained cooking liquid from fish
2 tbsps heavy cream
2 tbsps lemon juice
Salt and pepper

Filling

1. Preheat oven to 350°F.

2. Wash and dry fish. Place in oven-proof dish with slice of onion, slice of lemon, peppercorns, bay leaf, lemon juice and water. Cover and cook for 20 minutes.

3. Remove fish from liquid and allow to drain. Strain liquid and set aside. When fish is cool, beat with the back of a spoon to a pulp.

4. Add eggs, bread crumbs and green onion, and salt and pepper to taste. Mix well.

Dough

1. Sift flour and salt into a bowl. Make a well in the center, and add the eggs. Work the flour and eggs together with a spoon, and then knead by hand until a smooth dough is formed. Leave to rest for 15 minutes.

2. Lightly flour a pastry board and roll out dough thinly into a rectangle. Cut dough in half.

3. Shape the filling into small balls and set them about 1½ inches apart on one half of the dough. Place the other half of the dough on top and cut with a ravioli cutter or small pastry cutter. Seal the edges.

4. Cook in batches in a large pan with plenty of boiling, salted water until tender – about 8 minutes. Remove carefully with a slotted spoon. Meanwhile, make sauce.

Sauce

1. Melt butter in a pan. Stir in flour and cook gently for 30 seconds. Reduce the heat and gradually stir in liquid from cooked fish. Return to heat and bring to a boil. Simmer for 4 minutes, stirring continuously.

2. Add cream and mix well. Season to taste. Remove from heat and gradually stir in lemon juice and seasoning. Do not reboil. Pour sauce over ravioli and serve immediately.

TIME: Preparation takes 30 minutes, cooking takes 30 minutes.

PASTITSIO

*This is like an Italian version of Shepherd's Pie
with macaroni instead of potato.*

SERVES 4

8 oz macaroni
4 tbsps butter or margarine
¼ cup Parmesan cheese, grated
Pinch of grated nutmeg
2 eggs, beaten
1 medium onion, chopped
1 clove garlic, crushed
1 lb ground beef
2 tbsps tomato paste
¼ cup red wine
½ cup beef stock
2 tbsps chopped fresh parsley
2 tbsps all-purpose flour
½ cup milk
Salt
Pepper

1. Preheat oven to 375°F.

2. Cook macaroni in plenty of boiling, salted water for 10 minutes, or until tender but still firm. Rinse under hot water. Drain.

3. Put one-third of the butter in the pan and return macaroni to it. Add half the cheese, nutmeg, and salt and pepper to taste. Leave to cool. Mix in half the beaten egg and put aside.

4. Melt half of the remaining butter in a pan and fry the onion and garlic gently until onion is soft. Increase temperature, add meat, and fry until browned.

5. Add tomato paste, stock, parsley and wine, and season with salt and pepper. Simmer for 20 minutes.

6. In a small pan, melt the rest of the butter. Stir in the flour and cook for 30 seconds. Remove from heat and stir in milk. Bring to a boil, stirring continuously, until the sauce thickens.

7. Beat in the remaining egg and season to taste. Spoon half the macaroni into a serving dish and cover with the meat sauce.

8. Put on another layer of macaroni and smooth over. Pour over white sauce, sprinkle with remaining cheese, and bake in the oven for 30 minutes until golden brown. Serve immediately.

TIME: Preparation takes 10 minutes, cooking takes 1 hour.

TORTELLINI

*Vary the amount of Parmesan cheese in
this recipe to suit your own taste.*

SERVES 4

Dough
1¼ cups bread flour
Pinch of salt
1 tbsp water
1 tbsp oil
3 eggs

Filling
2 tbsps cream cheese
1 cooked chicken breast, finely diced
2 tbsps ham, finely diced
2 spinach leaves, stalks removed, cooked
 and chopped finely
1 tbsp grated Parmesan cheese
1 egg, beaten
Salt and pepper

Sauce
1 cup heavy cream
¼ lb mushrooms, cleaned and sliced
¼ cup Parmesan cheese, grated
1 tbsp chopped fresh parsley
Salt and pepper

Filling

1. Beat the cream cheese until soft and
smooth. Add chicken, ham, spinach and
Parmesan cheese, and mix well. Add egg
gradually, and salt and pepper to taste. Set
aside.

Dough

1. Sift flour and salt onto a board. Make a
well in the center. Mix water, oil and lightly
beaten eggs together, and gradually pour into
well, working in the flour with the other hand,
a little at a time. Continue until the mixture
comes together in a firm ball of dough.

2. Knead on a lightly-floured board for 5
minutes, or until smooth and elastic. Put
into a bowl, cover with a cloth, and leave
to stand for 15 minutes.

3. Roll dough out on a lightly-floured
board as thinly as possible. Using a 2 inch
cutter, cut out circles. Put ½ teaspoon of
filling into the center of each circle. Fold
in half, pressing edges together firmly.
Wrap around forefinger, and press ends
together. Cook in batches in a large pan, in
plenty of boiling salted water for about 10
minutes until tender, stirring occasionally.

Sauce

1. Meanwhile, gently heat cream in a pan.
Add mushrooms, Parmesan cheese,
parsley, and salt and pepper to taste.
Gently cook for 3 minutes.

To serve, toss sauce together with
tortellini and sprinkle with parsley.

TIME: Preparation takes 30 minutes, cooking takes 15 minutes.

215

MEAT RAVIOLI

Preparing your own pasta dough is very satisfying as it almost always tastes better than packaged varieties.

SERVES 4

Dough
1¼ cups bread flour
Pinch of salt
3 eggs

Filling
4 tbsps butter or margarine
1 clove garlic, crushed
1 onion, grated
½ lb ground beef
½ cup red wine
Salt and pepper
2 tbsps bread crumbs
½ cup cooked spinach, chopped
2 eggs, beaten

Sauce
14 oz can plum tomatoes
1 small onion, grated
1 small carrot, diced finely
1 bay leaf
3 parsley stalks
Salt and pepper
½ cup Parmesan cheese, grated

Filling

1. Heat butter in a frying pan. Add garlic and onion, and fry gently for 1 minute. Add ground beef and fry until browned. Add red wine, and salt and pepper to taste, and cook, uncovered, for 15 minutes.

2. Strain juices and reserve them for the sauce. Allow to cool.

3. Add bread crumbs, chopped spinach, and beaten eggs to bind.

4. Adjust salt and pepper to taste.

Dough

1. Sift flour in a bowl with salt. Make a well in the center and add the eggs. Work flour and eggs together with a spoon, then knead by hand, until a smooth dough is formed. Leave dough to rest for 15 minutes.

2. Lightly flour board, and roll out dough thinly into a rectangle. Cut dough in half.

3. Shape the filling into small balls, and set them about 1½ inches apart on one half of the dough.

4. Place the other half of dough on top and cut with a ravioli cutter or small pastry cutter. Seal the edges by pinching together or pressing with a fork.

5. Cook in batches in a large, wide pan with plenty of boiling, salted water until tender – about 8 minutes. Remove carefully with a slotted spoon. Meanwhile, make the sauce.

Sauce

1. Put all the sauce ingredients in a saucepan. Add juice from cooked meat and bring to a boil. Simmer for 10 minutes. Push through a sieve, and return smooth sauce to pan. Adjust seasoning.

To serve, put ravioli in a warm dish and cover with tomato sauce. Serve immediately, sprinkled with grated Parmesan cheese.

TIME: Preparation takes 30 minutes, cooking takes 5 minutes.

FETTUCINE ESCARGOTS WITH LEEKS AND SUN-DRIED TOMATOES

*These dried tomatoes keep for a long time and allow you to add a
sunny taste to dishes whatever the time of year.*

SERVES 4-6

6 sun-dried tomatoes
14 oz can escargots (snails), drained
12 oz fresh or dried whole wheat fettucine
3 tbsps olive oil
2 cloves garlic, crushed
1 large or 2 small leeks, trimmed, split,
  well washed and finely sliced
6 oyster, shittake or other large mushrooms
4 tbsps chicken or vegetable stock
3 tbsps dry white wine
6 tbsps heavy cream
2 tsps fresh basil, chopped
2 tsps fresh parsley, chopped
Salt and pepper

1. Drain the escargots well and dry with
paper towels.

2. Place the fettucine in boiling salted
water and cook for about 10-12 minutes,
or until al dente. Drain, rinse under hot
water and leave in a colander to drain dry.

3. Meanwhile, heat the olive oil in a frying
pan and add the garlic and leeks. Cook
slowly to soften slightly. Add the
mushrooms and cook until the leeks are
tender crisp. Remove to a plate. Add the
drained escargots to the pan and cook
over high heat for about 2 minutes,
stirring constantly.

4. Pour on the stock and wine and bring
to a boil. Boil to reduce by about a
quarter and add the cream and tomatoes.
Bring to a boil then cook slowly for about
3 minutes. Add the herbs, and salt and
pepper to taste.

5. Add the leeks, mushrooms and
fettucine to the pan and heat through.
Serve immediately.

TIME: Preparation takes about 15-20 minutes.

LASAGNE NAPOLETANA

This is a lasagne as it is cooked and eaten in Naples.
With its layer of red, green and white it looks as delicious
as it tastes and is very easy to prepare.

SERVES 6

9 sheets spinach lasagne pasta
1 tbsp olive oil

Tomato Sauce
2 tbsps olive oil
2 cloves garlic, crushed
2 lbs fresh tomatoes, peeled, or canned
   tomatoes, drained
2 tbsps fresh basil, chopped, or 1 tbsp
   dried
Salt and pepper
Pinch sugar
6 whole basil leaves to garnish

Cheese filling
1 lb ricotta cheese
4 tbsps unsalted butter
2 cups Mozzarella cheese, grated
Salt and pepper
Pinch nutmeg

1. Cook the pasta for 8 minutes in boiling salted water with 1 tbsp oil. Drain and rinse under hot water and place in a single layer on a damp cloth. Cover with another damp cloth and set aside.

2. To prepare the sauce, cook the garlic in oil for about 1 minute in a large saucepan. When pale brown, add the tomatoes, basil, salt, pepper and sugar. (If using fresh tomatoes, drop into boiling water for 6-8 seconds. Transfer to cold water and leave to cool completely. This will make the skin easier to remove.)

3. Lower the heat and simmer the sauce for 35 minutes. Add more seasoning or sugar to taste.

4. Beat the ricotta cheese and butter together until creamy and stir into the remaining filling ingredients.

5. To assemble the lasagne, oil a rectangular baking dish and place 3 sheets of lasagne on the base. Cover with one third of the sauce and carefully spread on a layer of cheese. Place another 3 layers of pasta over the cheese and cover with another third of the sauce. Add the remaining cheese filling and cover with the remaining pasta. Spoon the remaining sauce on top.

6. Cover with foil and bake for 20 minutes at 375°F. Uncover and cook for 10 minutes longer. Garnish with the fresh basil leaves (if available) and leave to stand for 10-15 minutes before serving.

TIME: Preparation takes about 25 minutes, cooking takes about 1-1¼ hours.

ITALIAN CASSEROLE

*Serve this hearty main course with a
green salad or broccoli, and fresh bread.*

SERVES 4

1 cup small macaroni
2 tbsps butter or margarine
1 clove garlic, crushed
1 onion, chopped
2 16 oz cans plum tomatoes
1 tbsp tomato paste
1 red pepper, chopped coarsely
1 green pepper, chopped coarsely
½ lb salami, cut into chunks
10 pitted black olives, halved
½ lb mozzarella cheese, sliced thinly
Salt and pepper

1. Cook the macaroni in plenty of boiling salted water for 10 minutes, or until tender but still firm. Rinse under hot water and drain well. Place in a shallow, oven-proof dish.

2. Meanwhile, heat butter in pan, and fry onion and garlic gently until soft.

3. Add undrained tomatoes, tomato paste, red and green peppers, salami and olives, and stir well. Simmer uncovered for 5 minutes. Season with salt and pepper.

4. Pour over the macaroni, stir, and cover with the sliced cheese. Bake, uncovered, in a moderate oven at 350°F for 20 minutes, until cheese has melted. Serve immediately.

TIME: Preparation takes 15 minutes, cooking takes 40 minutes.

223

SPINACH LASAGNE

*Everyone will be asking for seconds when
they taste this delicious lasagne.*

SERVES 4

8 sheets green lasagne pasta

Spinach sauce
4 tbsps butter or margarine
3 tbsps flour
½ cup milk
1½ cups frozen spinach, thawed and
   chopped finely
Pinch of ground nutmeg
Salt
Pepper

Mornay sauce
2 tbsps butter or margarine
2 tbsps flour
1 cup milk
⅓ cup Parmesan cheese, grated
1 tsp Dijon mustard
Salt

1. To make spinach sauce, heat butter in
pan, stir in flour and cook gently for 30
seconds.

2. Remove from heat and stir in milk
gradually. Return to heat and bring to a
boil, stirring continuously. Cook for 3
minutes.

3. Add spinach, nutmeg, and salt and
pepper to taste. Set aside.

4. Cook spinach lasagne in lots of boiling
salted water for 10 minutes, or until
tender. Rinse in cold water, and drain
carefully. Dry on a clean cloth.

5. To make mornay sauce, heat butter in a
saucepan and stir in flour, cooking for 30
seconds.

6. Remove from heat and stir in milk.
Return to heat, stirring continuously, until
boiling. Continue stirring and simmer for 3
minutes.

7. Remove from heat and add mustard
and two-thirds of cheese, and salt to taste.

8. Preheat oven to 400°F. Grease an ovenproof baking dish. Line the bottom with a
layer of lasagne, followed by some of the
spinach mixture and a layer of the cheese
sauce. Repeat the process, finishing with a
layer of lasagne and a covering of cheese
sauce.

9. Sprinkle with the remaining cheese.
Bake in a hot oven until golden on top.
Serve immediately.

TIME: Preparation takes 10 minutes, cooking takes 30 minutes.

VANILLA CREAM MELBA

Elbow macaroni is enhanced with a delicious raspberry sauce and peaches in this easy-to-prepare dessert.

SERVES 4

⅔ cup small pasta or elbow macaroni
1½ cups milk
2½ tsps brown sugar
Few drops vanilla extract
½ cup heavy cream, lightly whipped
16 oz can peach halves
1 tsp cinnamon

Melba sauce
1 cup raspberries
2 tbsps confectioners sugar

1. Cook pasta in milk and sugar until soft. Stir regularly, being careful not to allow it to boil over. Remove from heat and stir in vanilla extract.

2. Pour pasta into a bowl to cool. When cool, fold in cream. Chill.

3. Meanwhile, make melba sauce. Push raspberries through a sieve, or purée in a blender or food processor. Mix in confectioners sugar to desired thickness and taste.

4. Serve pasta with peach halves and melba sauce. Dust with cinnamon if desired.

TIME: Preparation takes 15 minutes, cooking takes 10 minutes.

BLACK CHERRY RAVIOLI WITH SOUR CREAM SAUCE

*A simple dough is mixed with cherries and
cream to make the perfect ending to a meal.*

SERVES 4

Dough

1¾ cups bread flour
1 tbsp sugar
3 eggs, lightly beaten

Large can pitted black cherries
¼ cup sugar
1 tsp cornstarch
½ cup sour cream
½ cup heavy cream

1. Put cherries in a sieve. Strain off the juice and reserve.

2. Make the dough by sifting flour and sugar in a bowl. Make a well in the center and add lightly-beaten eggs. Work flour and eggs together with a spoon, and then by hand, until a smooth dough is formed. Knead gently.

3. Lightly flour board, and roll dough out thinly into a rectangle. Cut dough in half. Put well-drained cherries about 1½ inches apart on the dough.

4. Place the other half on top and cut with a small glass or pastry cutter. Seal well around edges with back of a fork.

5. Boil plenty of water in a large saucepan, and drop in cherry pasta. Cook for about 10 minutes, or until they rise to the surface. Remove with a slotted spoon and keep warm. Keep 2 tablespoons cherry juice aside.

6. Mix 1 tablespoon cherry juice with cornstarch; mix remaining juice with sugar, put in small saucepan and set over heat. Add cornstarch mixture, and heat until it thickens.

7. Meanwhile mix sour cream and heavy cream together, and marble 1 tablespoon of cherry juice through it.

8. Pour hot, thickened cherry juice over cherry ravioli. Serve hot with cream sauce.

TIME: Preparation takes 30 minutes, cooking takes 15 minutes.

CHOCOLATE CREAM HELÈNE

*Pears, cream and pasta combine perfectly
in this simply delicious dessert.*

SERVES 4

⅔ cup small pasta or elbow macaroni
1½ cups milk
2½ tbsps sugar
1 tsp cocoa
½ cup heavy cream, lightly whipped
1 tbsp hot water
16 oz can pear halves

Garnish
Chocolate, grated

1. Cook pasta in milk and sugar until soft. Stir regularly, being careful not to allow it to boil over. Remove from heat.

2. Meanwhile, dissolve cocoa in hot water, and stir into pasta.

3. Pour pasta into a bowl to cool. When cool, fold in lightly-whipped cream. Chill. Serve with pear halves and a sprinkling of grated chocolate.

TIME: Preparation takes 15 minutes, cooking takes 10 minutes.

Pasta Notes

Pasta
Notes

SUGAR FREE

Introduction

In today's health-conscious atmosphere we are all becoming more aware of the disadvantages of a high sugar intake – increasing levels of obesity and tooth decay are the most obvious results of just such a diet. We now eat as much sugar in two weeks as people of two centuries ago did in one year, yet as we live less active lives, we actually require less energy than our forefathers.

There are many misconceptions about the properties of sugar. Contrary to what many people believe, sugar does not contain any nutrients and all types of sugar, whether white or brown, or in the form of honey or maple syrup, have the same calorific value. Sugar, or sucrose to give it its technical name, is a complex carbohydrate made up of two simple sugars. The first, fructose, is the sweetest and is found naturally in fruits. The second, glucose, is formed by the body during the digestion of plants and vegetables. Sugars are all digested in the same way: the sugar is broken down into glucose, which then travels around in the blood as energy; if this energy isn't used, it is stored as fat reserves.

By eating naturally sweet foods we can educate our palates to prefer these to over-sweet, sugared foods. The extra chewing needed will also produce more saliva to clean away the sugary film from the teeth and help prevent decay. As naturally sweet foods also take longer to digest, our bodies will not experience the short-lived artificial "highs" that refined sugars produce.

Unfortunately, it is not always possible to leave sugar out of recipes as it can be vital for a dish's preservation or structure. However, cutting down our sugar intake gradually and avoiding those processed foods which contain sugar is a big step towards a more healthful diet. In addition, eating more naturally sweet foods containing fructose, such as strawberries, not only reduces calorie intake but also provides some nutritional benefits from the food, including vitamins and fiber.

Switching to a healthful diet does not mean sacrificing taste but rather replacing refined sugars with more natural sugars and sweet fruits. The recipes in this book do just that, providing a varied selection of wholesome dishes that are delicious too!

SERVES 6-8

GOLDEN RAISIN SODA BREAD

*Golden raisins add a natural sweetness which makes this bread ideal for
serving as a tea-time treat.*

1lb all-purpose white flour
1¼ tsps salt
1¼ tsps baking soda
1¼ tsps cream of tartar
1⅓ cups sour milk
⅔ cup golden raisins

1. Sift together the flour, salt, baking soda and cream of tartar in a mixing bowl.

2. Add the golden raisins and mix into the flour quickly, making a slight well in the center of the flour as you do so.

3. Pour the milk into the well in the flour, and mix with a round bladed knife to form a firm, but not too stiff dough.

4. Turn the dough onto a lightly floured board, and knead quickly to bring all the ingredients together well.

5. Shape the dough into a round, and flatten it slightly with the palm of your hand.

6. Place the dough round on a lightly greased and floured cookie sheet. Cut a deep cross into the top of the dough with a sharp knife.

7. Bake the dough in a preheated oven 400°F for 25 minutes.

8. After this time, turn the loaf upside down on the cookie sheet and return to the oven for a further 10 minutes to dry out completely.

9. Wrap the baked loaf in a damp cloth, and place on a wire rack to cool completely.

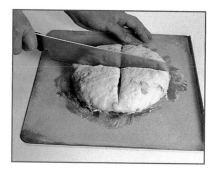

Step 6 Cut a deep cross into the top of the bread dough using a sharp knife.

Step 8 Turn the loaf upside down on the cookie sheet before returning to the oven for a further 10 minutes.

Cook's Notes

Time
Preparation takes 15 minutes, cooking takes 35 minutes.

Variation
Use whole-wheat flour instead of the white flour in this recipe.

Preparation
To test that the loaf is completely cooked, tap the base with your fingers and if it sounds hollow it is ready.

Cook's Tip
If you do not have sour milk, use fresh milk with 1 tbsp of natural yogurt added.

Freezing
This bread freezes well.

MAKES 10-12

RICH FRUIT BISCUITS

Fruit biscuits are always a firm favorite and do not need any added sugar when made with plenty of fruit.

½lb all-purpose flour
1¼ tsps cream of tartar
¾ tsp baking soda
⅓ tsp salt
3 tbsps butter
½ cup golden raisins
¾ tbsp sunflower seeds
½oz fresh stem ginger
2 eggs
Extra milk for blending
Beaten egg, for glaze

Step 2 Rub the butter into the sieved flour until the mixture resembles fine breadcrumbs.

1. Mix the flour, cream of tartar, baking soda and salt together, and sieve it twice through a metal sieve to aerate completely.

2. Put the sieved flour into a large bowl, and rub in the butter until the mixture resembles fine breadcrumbs.

3. Stir the golden raisins and the sunflower seeds into the flour and butter mixture.

Step 9 Roll out the dough to no less than ½-inch thick.

4. Peel the ginger, and cut or grate it into very small pieces.

5. Using a pestle and mortar or the handle of a large knife, crush the ginger until it becomes a paste.

6. Put the ginger into a small bowl along with the eggs, and beat together with a fork until they are evenly blended.

7. Add the beaten eggs and ginger to the flour and raisin mixture, mixing well to form a soft dough, and adding a little extra milk if the dough is too stiff.

8. Lightly flour a work surface. Turn out the dough and knead it lightly until it becomes smooth.

9. Roll the dough out to approximately ½-inch thick.

10. Cut the dough into 2-inch rounds using a biscuit cutter.

11. Place the biscuits on a greased cookie sheet, and brush each one with the extra beaten egg. Bake in a preheated oven 400°F for 10-15 minutes, or until golden brown and well risen.

Cook's Notes

Time
Preparation takes approximately 15 minutes, cooking takes 10-15 minutes.

Preparation
Do not roll the dough out too thinly, otherwise the biscuits will not rise properly.

Variation
Use other combinations of dried fruit and nuts, or seeds, in place of the golden raisins and sunflower seeds in this recipe.

SERVES 6-8

SUGAR-FREE FRUIT CAKE

There is no need for sugar in a recipe rich in the natural sweetness of dried fruits.

¼lbs all-purpose flour
¾ tsp baking soda
1¼ tsps mixed spice
1¼ tsps ground nutmeg
1 cup butter
2 cups raisins
1⅓ cups currants
2 cups golden raisins
⅔ cup mixed peel
1¼ cups Guinness, or stout
3 eggs

Step 9 The cake batter should drop easily into the prepared pan, but not be too runny, or it will seep around the lining paper.

1. Sift the flour, baking soda, mixed spice and nutmeg into a large bowl, using a metal sieve.

2. Cut the butter into small dice, and rub into the flour using the fingertips, until the mixture resembles fine breadcrumbs.

3. Add all the fruit to the flour and mix well to distribute evenly.

4. Push the flour and fruit mixture away from the center of the bowl to form a slight well.

5. Put the Guinness and the eggs into a large jug and whisk together thoroughly, until frothy.

6. Pour the Guinness and eggs into the well in the center of the flour mixture.

7. Mix the Guinness and eggs together to form a soft batter, using a round bladed knife.

8. Grease and line a 9-inch round cake pan with wax paper.

9. Pour the cake batter into the pan and bake in the center of a preheated oven 325°F for 2 hours. Reduce the temperature to 275°F after the first hour if the cake appears to be cooking too quickly.

10. Test the cake with a skewer to see when it is done. If it is cooked, the skewer will come out clean. Turn the cake onto a wire rack, remove the lining paper and cool it completely before storing in an airtight tin for 2-3 days, before serving.

Cook's Notes

 Time
Preparation takes approximately 30 minutes, cooking takes 2 hours.

 Variation
Use whole-wheat flour in place of the white flour in this recipe, cider instead of Guinness, and grated apple instead of mixed peel.

 Preparation
If the cake is cooking too quickly, the sides will become brown and the center of the cake will rise up into a point. If this should happen, reduce the temperature and cook at a much slower heat. Cover the top of the cake with aluminium foil to prevent it from browning further.

 Cook's Tip
The flavor of this cake really does improve if it can be kept in an airtight container for a few days before using.

 Freezing
This cake freezes very well for up to 3 months.

SERVES 4-6

GRIDDLE SCONES

The whole fun of these cakes is that they can be eaten directly from the pan in which they are cooked. So gather family and friends around you for a traditional tea-time treat.

1 cup self-rising flour
Pinch salt
3 tbsps butter or margarine
⅔ cup currants
¾ tsp ground nutmeg
1 egg
⅓ cup milk

Step 4 Using a wooden spoon, mix the egg and flour mixture into the flour, stirring from the center of the bowl and drawing the flour in from the sides to form a smooth, thick batter.

Step 1 Rub the butter into the flour with your fingertips, until the mixture resembles fine breadcrumbs.

Step 6 Fry tablespoons of the batter in a hot pan until the undersides have browned lightly and the tops are just set.

1. Mix the flour and salt together, and rub in the butter until the mixture resembles fine breadcrumbs.

2. Stir in the currants and the nutmeg, then push the mixture gently to the sides of the bowl to form a well in the center.

3. Beat together the egg and the milk, and pour the into the well in the center of the flour.

4. Using a wooden spoon, mix the egg and milk mixture into the flour, stirring from the center of the bowl and drawing the flour in from the sides to form a smooth, thick batter.

5. Heat a heavy-based frying pan on top of a moderate heat, and grease with a little butter or oil.

6. Drop tablespoons of the batter into the hot pan, and cook for 2-3 minutes, or until the bases are set and have turned golden brown.

7. Turn the scones over and cook on the other side in the same way.

8. Serve from the pan with sugar-free preserves.

Cook's Notes

 Time
Preparation takes 15 minutes, cooking takes about 4 minutes per scone.

 Preparation
If the batter is too thick, add a little extra milk until it becomes a soft dropping consistency.

Freezing
These scones freeze well, and can be re-heated by wrapping in a clean dish towel and standing in a warm oven until they are heated through.

SERVES 6-8

FRUIT LOAF

There is no need to add sugar to this recipe as the easy-blend yeast will work on the natural sugars provided by the fruit.

1lb all-purpose flour
¾ tsp cinnamon
¾ tsp nutmeg
¾ tsp salt
1⅓ cups golden raisins
1⅓ cups currants
⅓ cup cut mixed peel
1 package of easy blend yeast
2½ tbsps vegetable oil
1¼ cups lukewarm milk
1 large egg

1. Put the flour, spices and salt into a large mixing bowl.

2. Stir in the golden raisins, currants and mixed peel, mixing well to distribute the fruit evenly.

3. Sprinkle over the yeast, and mix this directly into the dry ingredients.

4. Put the oil, milk and egg into a large jug, and beat together with a fork until the egg is broken up evenly. Add the mixture to the flour, and mix together, stirring until the batter becomes stiff and elastic.

5. Turn the batter onto a lightly floured board, and knead until smooth – approximately 10 minutes.

6. Return the batter to the bowl and cover with a damp cloth or a piece of plastic wrap. Leave the batter in a warm place for about 1 hour to allow the dough to rise.

7. After this time, the dough should be approximately double its original size.

8. Punch the dough down to remove the air, and turn it out once again onto the lightly floured surface.

9. Continue kneading the dough for approximately 5 minutes, then cut in two.

Step 4 Mix the milk mixture into the flour and yeast mixture, stirring until a soft, but elastic, dough is formed.

Step 10 Shape the pieces of dough to fit into 2 lightly greased, or non-stick loaf pans.

10. Shape each piece of dough to fit 2 x 7-inch non-stick loaf pans. Cover each pan lightly with plastic wrap or a damp cloth, and leave once again in a warm place until the loaves have risen to double their size.

11. Bake the loaves for 30-40 minutes in the center of a preheated oven 400°F, removing the loaves from the oven after 20 minutes, and brushing the surfaces with a little milk.

12. To test if the loaves are cooked, turn out of the pans and tap the bases with your knuckles, if it sounds hollow, the loaves are ready.

13. Serve warm, or allow to cool and serve sliced, with butter.

Cook's Notes

Time
Preparation takes approximately 2 hours, cooking takes 40 minutes.

Variation
Use any combination of your favorite dried fruits in this recipe.

Freezing
This recipe freezes well for up to 2 months.

MAKES 10

FRUIT TRUFFLES

These delicious little cakes get all the sweetness they require from fresh bananas.

2 bananas
Juice ½ orange
Finely grated rind 1 orange
1¼ cups ground almonds
¼ cup blanched almonds
1¼ tbsps plain cocoa

1. Chop the bananas into a large bowl and using a potato masher, mash them until they are smooth.

2. Mix in the orange juice and rind.

3. Stir in the ground almonds, mixing well to blend evenly. Place the mixture in a refrigerator and chill for approximately 30 minutes.

4. Using a sharp knife, finely chop the blanched almonds into small pieces.

5. Mix the chopped almonds into the cocoa powder, and place on a flat plate.

Step 1 Mash the bananas to a smooth pulp using a potato masher.

Step 7 Roll the banana mixture into 10 even-sized balls, using lightly floured hands.

Step 8 Cover each banana truffle with an even coating of chopped nuts and cocoa, pressing this gently onto the surface to ensure it stays in place.

6. Remove the banana mixture from the refrigerator, and divide into 10 portions.

7. Roll each portion into a small ball, using lightly floured hands.

8. Roll each ball into the cocoa and almond mixture, rolling each one evenly to give a good coating. Press gently before placing into a small paper cases, and chilling once again.

Cook's Notes

Time
Preparation takes approximately 25 minutes, plus chilling time.

Cook's Tip
Do not keep these delicious sweets for long after they have been made, or the banana will go brown and wet.

Variation
Use walnuts in place of almonds in this recipe.

MAKES 2lbs

COCONUT RELISH

This unusual relish is a welcome change from the more common fruit relishes.

2 fresh coconuts
½-inch piece fresh root ginger
2 green chilies
1¼ tsps cumin seed
5 tbsps finely chopped fresh coriander leaves
3¾ tbsps lemon juice
¾ tsp salt

1. Crack the coconuts in half, and carefully pour out and reserve the milk.

2. Remove the coconut flesh from inside the shells, and peel off the brown outer skin.

3. Chop the peeled coconut into small pieces.

4. Peel the root ginger and finely chop or grate the flesh.

5. Cut the green chilies in half, remove and discard the seeds, and finely chop the outer flesh.

6. Put the coconut, ginger, chilies, cumin seeds, coriander, lemon and salt into a liquidizer or food processor, and blend with enough coconut milk to produce a thick creamy relish.

7. Pour the mixture into pots and seal well.

8. Keep in a refrigerator and use within 2-3 weeks.

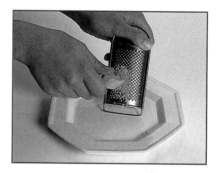

Step 4 Finely chop or grate the peeled root ginger.

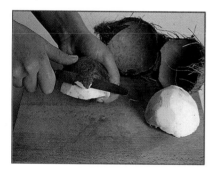

Step 2 Peel away the brown skin from the flesh of the coconut using a sharp knife.

Step 6 Blend the relish ingredients with coconut milk in a liquidizer or food processor until it is thick and creamy.

Cook's Notes

Time
Preparation takes approximately 20 minutes.

Freezing
This recipe freezes well.

Preparation
If you do not have a liquidizer or a food processor, the coconut and other ingredients can be grated, but this will not produce such a smooth textured relish.

Serving Idea
This relish is delicious served with cold meats, curries, or in sandwiches.

MAKES APPROXIMATELY 5lbs

FRUIT CHUTNEY

The use of canned fruit means that this delicious chutney can be prepared at any time of the year.

15oz can pears in natural juice
15oz can peach slices in natural juice
12oz can pineapple chunks in natural juice
8oz can prunes in natural juice
1lb plums
4 cooking apples
½ cup fresh dates, pitted
½ cup ready-to-use dried apricots
1-inch piece fresh root ginger, peeled and thinly sliced
1 cup blanched almonds
1 cup cashew nuts
5 tbsps malt vinegar
¾ tsp ground cloves
1¼ tsps chili powder
2-inch piece cinnamon stick
2 bananas, peeled and sliced

1. Remove the stones from the plums and chop the flesh into fairly large pieces.

2. Drain the fruit juices from the cans of fruit, and set aside. Chop the fruit into large pieces.

3. Cut the apples into four and remove the cores, but do not peel.

4. Finely slice the apple and mix this with the chopped fruit in a large saucepan.

5. Chop the dates and the dried apricots into small pieces. Add the apricots and dates to the saucepan of fruit, along with all the remaining ingredients, except for the reserved juice.

6. Pour over enough of the reserved juice to just cover the fruit.

7. Cover the pan, and bring the chutney to the boil. Reduce the heat and simmer for 15-20 minutes.

8. Remove the lid of the pan and stir the chutney well. Add a little extra juice if required, and continue cooking for a further 10 minutes, uncovered, stirring occasionally to prevent the mixture from burning.

9. When the chutney is thick and most of the liquid has evaporated, divide it between clean warm glass jars. Cover with waxed paper and a tight fitting lid, then store for up to 3 months in a refrigerator.

Step 1 Cut the plums in half and carefully remove the stones. Chop the flesh into fairly large pieces.

Step 9 When cooked, the chutney should be thick and most of the liquid should have evaporated.

Cook's Notes

Time
Preparation takes approximately 15 minutes, cooking takes 30 minutes.

Serving Idea
Serve with cold meats, cheeses, or in sandwiches.

Cook's Tip
Check that the chutney does not stick to the base of the pan, by stirring occasionally whilst it is cooking.

Variation
If you cannot get fresh plums, try using mangoes or apricots.

Freezing
This recipe will freeze well.

MAKES APPROXIMATELY 2lbs

SUGAR-FREE MINCEMEAT

Not only is this recipe free from refined sugar, it is also completely fat free, making it extremely healthful.

3 large red eating apples
1⅓ cups raisins
1⅓ cups currants
1⅓ cups golden raisins
⅔ cup fresh dates
½ cup blanched almonds
⅔ cup brandy or sherry

Step 3 Blend the pitted dates with the nuts and brandy, or sherry, until they are fairly coarsely chopped.

Step 1 Quarter the apples, remove the cores and chop the flesh roughly.

Step 4 Mix the date mixture with the apple and fruit mixture, stirring well to blend evenly.

1. Quarter the apples, remove the cores and chop the apple flesh.

2. Put the apples into a liquidizer or food processor, along with the raisins, currants and golden raisins. Chop the fruit finely, then transfer to a large mixing bowl.

3. Carefully remove the stones from the dates and put the fruit into a food processor or liquidizer, along with the nuts

and the brandy or sherry. Process until the dates and nuts are roughly chopped.

4. Mix the date mixture into the apple and dried fruit mixture, stirring well to blend all ingredients thoroughly.

5. Divide the mixture between 2-3 clean glass jars, then cover and allow to stand for up to 3 weeks before using.

Cook's Notes

Time
Preparation takes approximately 20 minutes.

Serving Idea
Use in minced pies or apple pie as a natural sweetener.

Freezing
This recipe will freeze, but should be stirred well when thawed to distribute the alcohol evenly.

MAKES 2 cups

CHOCOLATE BUTTER SAUCE

The sugar-free (diabetic) chocolate used in this recipe is readily available in most health food shops.

1 cup water
2 cups sugar-free chocolate, chopped
½ cup butter, cut into small pieces
1¼ tbsps brandy

Step 1 Melt the chocolate in the water over a low heat, stirring until the mixture is smooth.

1. Put the water and the chocolate into a saucepan, and heat over a low heat, stirring until the chocolate has melted.

2. Remove the melted chocolate and water from the heat and slowly stir in the butter, piece by piece, until the mixture becomes thick and glossy.

3. Whisk the brandy into the butter sauce and spoon into an attractive serving dish. This sauce can be served hot or cold.

Step 2 Drop the butter into the melted chocolate, piece by piece, stirring well until it has melted.

Step 3 Beat the brandy into the sauce, whisking until it is thick and glossy.

Cook's Notes

Time
Preparation takes approximately 5 minutes, cooking takes 10 minutes.

Preparation
After melting the chocolate and water together, the mixture should be smooth, with no lumps in it.

Serving Idea
Serve with fresh fruit or pancakes.

Watchpoint
Do not heat the chocolate and water too rapidly or the mixture will curdle.

MAKES 1 cup

MOCHA SAUCE

This unusual coffee chocolate sauce gets its sweetness from the delightfully tangy apricot purée.

1 cup sugar-free chocolate
3¾ tbsps very strong black coffee
½ cup heavy cream
½ cup thick apricot purée (see separate recipe)

Step 3 Stir the heavy cream into the chocolate and coffee mixture, mixing well to blend evenly.

Step 2 Melt the chocolate and coffee together in a bowl which is standing over a saucepan of hot water.

1. Grate the chocolate, or chop it into small pieces with a sharp knife.

2. Put the chocolate and the coffee into a large bowl, and stand the bowl over a saucepan half filled with simmering water. Remove the saucepan and the bowl from the heat, and stir the chocolate gently until it has melted.

3. Add the heavy cream to the melted chocolate, mixing well to blend evenly.

4. Stir in the apricot purée, transfer the chocolate sauce to a serving dish and chill thoroughly.

Cook's Notes

Time
Preparation takes approximately 5 minutes, cooking takes 15 minutes.

Serving Idea
Serve this delicious sauce with fruit or pancakes.

Watchpoint
Take great care not to cook the chocolate and the coffee together too quickly, or the chocolate will separate and curdle.

MAKES APPROXIMATELY 1½ cups

APRICOT PURÉE

This delicious tangy sauce is made with canned apricots in natural juice,
thus making use of the natural sweetness of fruit sugars.

15oz can apricot halves in natural juice
Juice and rind 1 lime
2½ tbsps apricot brandy (optional)

1. Purée the apricots in their juice, using a liquidizer or food processor.

2. Put the apricot purée into a small saucepan.

3. Stir the lime juice and rind into the apricot mixture, and heat over a low temperature until it begins to boil.

4. Continue simmering over a low temperature until the sauce is thick and liquid has reduced.

Step 1 Purée the apricots in a liquidizer or food processor until they are smooth.

Step 3 Stir the lime juice and rind into the fruit purée, mixing well to blend evenly.

Step 4 Cook the apricot mixture over a low heat until the sauce has thickened and the liquid has evaporated.

5. Cool the purée in a refrigerator until required, and serve after stirring in the apricot brandy.

Cook's Notes

Time
Preparation takes 2 minutes, cooking takes 5 minutes.

Variation
Use canned pears or prunes in place of the apricots in this recipe.

Serving Idea
Serve with pancakes, or fresh fruit.

SERVES 10-12

APPLE SAUCE

This sauce is extremely versatile and can be used as an accompaniment to meats or fish, as well as being included in ingredients for desserts.

2lbs cooking apples
1¼ cups apple juice
⅓ tsp ground cloves
Finely pared rind ½ orange

1. Wash the apples and cut away any bruised or discolored pieces. Cut the fruit into large pieces.

2. Put the chopped fruit into a large pan, along with the apple juice, ground cloves and the orange rind. Bring to the boil and simmer until most of the liquid has evaporated and the fruit has softened.

3. Cool the cooked apples.

4. Put the cooled apples into a nylon sieve over a large bowl, and press through using the back of a wooden spoon, to remove all skin, pips and cores.

5. Put the apple purée into cartons or jars, and store or freeze until required.

6. Serve in a bowl and decorate with a sprig of mint.

Step 1 Wash the apples and cut away any bruising or discolored pieces.

Step 2 Cook the apples in the fruit juice until the liquid has reduced, and the fruit is soft and pulpy.

Step 4 Press the cooled fruit through a nylon sieve into a bowl, using the back of a wooden spoon to push the fruit purée through and to remove the cores, skin and pips.

Cook's Notes

Time
Preparation takes approximately 30 minutes, cooking takes about 20 minutes.

Preparation
If preferred, the cooked apples can be puréed in a liquidizer or food processor before pressing through the sieve to remove the skins and cores.

Variation
Use cinnamon instead of the cloves in this recipe.

Freezing
This sauce can be frozen for up to 4 months.

MAKES 10-12 PANCAKES
CREPES

These tasty pancakes are delicious with both sweet and tangy sauces.

1 cup all-purpose flour
Pinch salt
1 egg
1¼ cups milk
1¼ tsps vegetable oil
Juice and rind of a lemon and orange

1. Sieve the flour and the salt into a large bowl. Push the flour gently towards the sides of the bowl to make a well in the center.

2. Put the egg and the milk into a jug and beat well.

3. Gradually add the egg and milk mixture to the flour, pouring it into the center of the bowl, and mixing gently by stirring and drawing the flour in from the sides.

4. Continue adding the egg mixture gradually and beat until all the flour has been incorporated.

5. Heat a little oil in a small frying pan, and pour in enough batter to make a thin pancake.

6. Quickly tilt and rotate the frying pan so that the batter coats the bottom of it evenly.

7. Cook the pancake over a moderate heat until the underside has turned brown and the top has set.

8. Carefully turn the pancake over and brown the other side in the same way.

9. Turn each pancake out onto wax paper and keep them warm until required.

10. Serve the pancakes hot with freshly squeezed orange and lemon juice and decorate with the pared citrus rind.

Step 1 Gently push the flour towards the sides of the bowl to make a well in the center.

Step 3 Gradually add the egg and milk to the flour, mixing from the center of the bowl and drawing the flour into the liquid.

Step 6 Quickly tilt and rotate the frying pan so that the batter coats the bottom thinly.

Cook's Notes

Time
Preparation takes approximately 10 minutes, cooking takes about 20 minutes for all the pancakes.

Watchpoint
Do not overheat your frying pan or the base of the pancake will burn before the top has set. Also, do not attempt to turn the pancakes until the underside is properly cooked.

Freezing
Pancakes can be made in greater quantities than this recipe, and frozen until required.

MAKES 2 x 2 PINT PUDDINGS

PLUM PUDDING

Plum puddings are always thought of as being sweet and heavy. Try this sugar-free recipe for a fresh tasting change.

1lb mixed dried fruit
1 cup seedless raisins
1 cup pitted dates
1 cup pitted, ready to use prunes
½ cup blanched shredded almonds
3 cups fresh white breadcrumbs
⅔ cup shredded suet
1½ cups all-purpose flour
½ tsp ground nutmeg
¾ tsp ground cinnamon
¼ tsp salt
1 carrot, grated
1 cooking apple, grated
Grated rind and juice 1 orange
⅔ cup brandy, or stout
1 egg

1. Put all the fruit into a mincer or food processor and chop finely.

2. Put the chopped fruits into a large mixing bowl, add all the remaining ingredients, and mix well.

3. Grease 2 x 2 pint pudding bowls, and divide the mixture evenly between both bowls.

4. Cover the top of the puddings with a buttered circle of wax paper.

5. Make a foil pudding lid by cutting a large piece of aluminum foil, and pleating it down the center. Tie this lid securely onto the bowls.

6. Stand the puddings on an up-turned saucer or trivet, in a large saucepan.

7. Add enough boiling water to the saucepans to come two thirds of the way up the side of the pudding bowls.

8. Cover the saucepans and boil the puddings for 4-5 hours, keeping the water topped up as it evaporates.

9. Remove the bowls from the water and remove the covering paper.

10. Up-turn a serving plate over the puddings, and turn the whole pudding over, shaking it gently to help it drop out of the bowl onto the serving plate.

11. Serve ignited with brandy, if desired.

Step 2 Mix the minced fruit together in a large bowl with all the remaining ingredients, stirring well to blend thoroughly.

Step 5 Cover the pudding with a pleated foil pudding lid, tying this down securely before boiling.

Cook's Notes

Time
Preparation takes approximately 30 minutes, cooking takes about 5 hours.

Serving Idea
Serve with brandy butter or fresh cream.

Preparation
To be at its best this pudding should be prepared at least 3 months in advance.

Cook's Tip
This pudding can be stored for up to a year. To re-heat before use, pop into a pan of simmering water and cook for 3 hours.

SERVES 4-6

COCONUT SORBET

Naturally sweet coconut milk and dark rum blend lusciously to produce a sorbet rich with the flavors of the Caribbean.

14oz can coconut milk
⅓ cup mineral water
⅓ cup dark rum
2 egg whites
Liquid sweetener to taste (optional)
2 bananas, thinly sliced and brushed with lemon juice and flaked coconut, to decorate

1. Mix the coconut milk with the mineral water, rum and liquid sweetener to taste, if required. Pour into a large freezer container and put into the freezer for 1 hour, or until the sides are beginning to freeze.

2. Using a fork, break the frozen coconut mixture up into a thin slush, making sure that there are no large ice crystals left in the mixture. Return to the freezer and continue freezing for a further hour.

3. Remove the coconut mixture from the freezer, and break up as before with a fork to make a thicker slush. Return the mixture to the freezer whilst you whisk the egg whites.

4. Whisk the egg whites until they form soft peaks.

5. Remove the partially frozen coconut mixture from the freezer and make sure that it can be easily stirred.

6. Carefully fold the egg whites into the coconut mixture, mixing lightly but thoroughly to blend evenly.

Step 2 Break the crystals away from the edge of the freezer dish using a fork, and mixing well to make a thin slush.

Step 6 Fold the softly whipped egg whites into the partially frozen slush, mixing lightly but thoroughly, to blend evenly.

7. Return the sorbet to the freezer and freeze until completely set.

8. To serve, remove the sorbet from the freezer 10 minutes before it is required and break it up with a fork into large ice crystals. Pile the crystals into serving dishes and decorate with the banana and the flakes of coconut.

Cook's Notes

Time
Preparation takes approximately 20 minutes, freezing takes 2-3 hours.

Variation
Use pineapple juice in place of the rum, and serve with pineapple pieces and coconut flakes.

Preparation
Make sure that the ice crystals are not too wet when you fold in the egg whites, otherwise the mixture will separate during freezing.

Cook's Tip
Make double quantities of this sorbet, as it freezes well for up to 3 months and is ideal as a stand-by dessert.

SERVES 4-6

EXOTIC FRUIT SALAD

Mangoes are exceptionally sweet when ripe, and give this lovely fruit salad a natural tangy sweetness.

3 ripe peaches
3 kiwi fruits
1 large star fruit
⅔ cup fresh strawberries
2 well-ripened mangoes, each weighing about 12oz
Juice of half a lime
1 cup redcurrants
Few strawberry leaves for decoration

Step 9 Press the mango purée through a wire sieve, using a wooden spoon to remove the pips and skins from the redcurrants.

Step 5 Cut away any brown pieces from the skin of the star fruit using a sharp knife.

1. Plunge the peaches into boiling water for a few seconds, then carefully peel away the skin using a sharp knife.

2. Carefully cut the peaches in half and remove the stone.

3. Cut the peach halves into thin slices and arrange on a serving plate.

4. Cut away the peel from the kiwi fruits and slice them crosswise to show their attractive color.

5. Trim away any dark pieces from the skin of the star fruit, cut the flesh into thin slices, and remove any small pips you may find.

6. Leave the green stems on the strawberries and cut them in half lengthways. Arrange all the prepared fruit on the serving platter with the peaches.

7. Peel the mango and chop away the flesh from the large inner stone.

8. Put the chopped mango flesh into a liquidizer or food processor, along with the lime juice and half of the redcurrants.

9. Purée the mixture until smooth, then press the purée through a nylon sieve to remove the redcurrant skins and pips.

10. Sprinkle the remaining redcurrants over the fruit on the serving platter, removing any hard stems or leaves as you do so.

11. Pour the fruit purée evenly over the fruit salad, and chill for at least 1 hour before serving, decorated with the strawberry leaves.

Cook's Notes

Time
Preparation takes approximately 25 minutes, plus 1 hour chilling time.

Variation
Use any combination of your favorite fruits in the fruit salad, but do not change the mango purée.

Preparation
If you do not have a liquidizer or food processor, a really ripe mango will rub easily through a wire sieve and will not need to be reduced to a purée first.

Cook's Tip
Add 3 tbsps rum to the mango purée to give extra flavor for a special occasion.

SERVES 6
RASPBERRY SOUFFLÉ
This light dessert is the perfect finale for a dinner party.

1lb raspberries
Liquid sweetener to taste
2 tbsps gelatin
⅔ cup hot water
4 eggs, separated
1¼ cups heavy cream

1. Prepare a 6-inch souffle dish by tightly tying a lightly oiled sheet of wax paper carefully around the outside edge of the souffle dish, allowing it to stand approximately 4 inches above the rim of the dish.

2. Reserve a few of the raspberries for decoration, and purée the remainder using a liquidizer or food processor.

3. Rub the puréed raspberries through a nylon sieve to remove the hard pips.

4. Sweeten the smooth raspberry purée with the liquid sweetener and set aside.

5. Dissolve the gelatin in the hot water, stirring gently until it is completely dissolved and the liquid is clear.

6. Allow the gelatin to cool slightly and then beat it into the raspberry purée along with the egg yolks, mixing until all ingredients are well blended. Chill in the refrigerator until partially set.

7. Whisk the egg whites until they form soft peaks.

8. Lightly whip half of the heavy cream until it is softly stiff.

9. Remove the partially set raspberry mixture from the refrigerator, and carefully fold in the cream and the egg

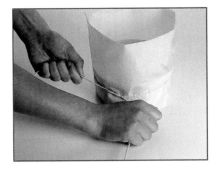

Step 1 Tie a sheet of wax paper around the souffle dish, to form a collar rising above the rim of the dish.

Step 3 Press the raspberry purée through a metal sieve, to remove the pips.

whites, blending lightly but thoroughly until the mixture is smooth.

10. Turn the prepared souffle mixture into the dish, allowing it to rise about 1 inch above the rim of the dish inside the paper collar. Allow to set in the refrigerator.

11. When completely set, remove the collar carefully and decorate the souffle with the remaining whipped cream and the reserved raspberries.

Cook's Notes

Time
Preparation takes approximately 40 minutes, plus chilling time.

Watchpoint
Do not add the gelatin to boiling water, or this will impair its setting qualities.

Preparation
Take great care not to overmix the souffle mixture when adding the egg whites, or there will not be enough to rise up over the rim of the dish inside the collar.

Variation
Use strawberries, or any other favorite fresh fruit in place of the raspberries in this recipe.

Freezing
Cold souffles freeze very well for up to 6 weeks, but should be decorated after they have thawed.

SERVES 4

PASSION FRUIT ICE CREAM

Fruit ice creams are actually more refreshing without added sugar, but if you must have added sweetness use liquid sweetener.

6 passion fruits
1¼ cups natural yogurt
2 egg yolks
Liquid sweetener to taste (optional)
1-2 passion fruits, halved and scooped for decoration

Step 1 Cut the 6 passion fruits in half and scoop all the center pulp into a bowl using a small spoon.

Step 2 Beat together the yogurt, egg yolks and passion fruit pulp until they are well blended.

Step 4 Break up the partially frozen passion fruit ice cream using a fork, and mixing until a smooth slush is formed.

1. Halve the 6 passion fruits, and scoop out all the center pulp into a bowl.

2. Add the yogurt and egg yolks to the passion fruit pulp, and mix together well, adding liquid sweetener to taste, if desired.

3. Pour the passion fruit mixture into a shallow container, and freeze until partially set – approximately 1 hour.

4. Break the ice crystals in the partially set passion fruit mixture using a fork, and mixing well until they form a smooth slush.

5. Return the ice cream to the freezer and freeze until completely firm.

6. To serve, remove the ice cream from the freezer for 10 minutes, then pile scoops of ice cream into stemmed glasses, and serve with passion fruit pulp poured over each portion.

Cook's Notes

Time
Preparation takes approximately 20 minutes, plus freezing time.

Variation
Add 2 tbsps rum or brandy to the ice cream mixture before freezing.

Watchpoint
This ice cream goes extremely hard when frozen, so it is important to remember to remove it from the freezer 10 minutes before serving.

SERVES 4

STUFFED FIGS

Fresh figs are now easily available from most major supermarkets and good greengrocers. When ripe, they go a luscious purple black and are soft to the touch.

4 large ripe figs
5 tbsps ground almonds
2½ tbsps orange juice
2½ tbsps finely chopped dried apricots
5 tbsps natural yogurt
Finely grated rind ½ orange
Wedges of figs and mint, or strawberry leaves for
   decoration

Step 2 Ease the four sections of each fig outwards to form a flower shape.

Step 1 Carefully cut a cross into each fig, making sure that you do not cut right through the base.

Step 4 Divide the almond mixture evenly between the four figs, and press it into the center of each one.

1. Cut each fig into four quarters using a sharp knife, and taking care not to cut right down through the base.

2. Ease the four sections of each fig outward to form a flower shape.

3. Put the ground almonds, orange juice and chopped apricots into a small bowl and mix together thoroughly.

4. Divide this mixture into four, and press it into the center

of each fig.

5. For the sauce, mix the yogurt with the orange rind, and thin it down with just a little water, or orange juice.

6. Spoon a small pool of orange yogurt onto each of four plates, and sit a stuffed fig into the center of each pool. Decorate with the additional wedges of fig, and the mint or strawberry leaves.

Cook's Notes

Time
Preparation takes
approximately 25 minutes.

Variation
Use peach halves instead of
the figs in this recipe.

Watchpoint
Do not add too much water or
orange juice to the sauce, or it
will become too thin.

SERVES 6

CHERRIES IN SYRUP

Black cherries and apple juice combine perfectly in this tasty dessert.

1½lbs fresh black cherries
2 cups apple or grape juice
1¾ tsps finely grated lemon rind
3 tbsps cornstarch or arrowroot
3¾ tbsps brandy (optional)

1. Remove the stones from the cherries, using a cherry pitter or the rounded end of a potato peeler.

2. Put the pitted cherries into a saucepan, along with the apple or grape juice and the lemon rind. Bring to the boil over a moderate heat, then simmer for 10 minutes, or until the cherries are gently poached.

3. Remove the cherries from the juice with a slotted spoon, leaving the juice in the saucepan. Arrange the cherries in a serving bowl.

4. Blend the cornstarch with 5 tbsps of the cherry juice.

5. Add the blended cornstarch or arrowroot to the cherry juice in the pan, and bring to the boil stirring constantly until the sauce has thickened. Stir in the brandy if used.

6. Pour the thickened cherry sauce over the cherries in the bowl, and chill well before serving.

Step 1 Remove the stones from the cherries using a cherry pitter or the rounded end of a potato peeler.

Step 4 Blend cornstarch or arrowroot with 5 tbsps of the cherry juice.

Step 5 Bring the cherry juice and blended cornstarch or arrowroot, slowly to the boil, stirring all the time until the sauce thickens and clears.

Cook's Notes

Time
Preparation takes 15-20 minutes, cooking takes about 5 minutes plus chilling time.

Cook's Tip
Arrowroot will produce a clearer sauce than cornstarch.

Variation
Use apricots instead of cherries in this recipe.

Freezing
This recipe freezes well.

SERVES 4-6

ORANGE AND APRICOT MOUSSE

This delicious light mousse makes an ideal end to any meal.

2 oranges
3 x 14oz cans of apricots in natural juice, drained
Artificial sweetener to taste (optional)
2 tbsps powdered gelatin
⅔ cup natural yogurt
2 egg whites
Extra orange rind to decorate

1. Finely grate the rind from half of one orange using a fine grater.

2. Cut all the oranges in half and squeeze out the juice.

3. Put the drained apricots, all but 3 tbsps of the orange juice, and the orange rind into a liquidizer or food processor, and purée until smooth. Pour into a large bowl and set aside.

4. Put the 3 tbsps of orange juice into a small pan and heat gently, but do not boil.

5. Sprinkle the gelatin over the warm orange juice, and allow to stand until dissolved and clear.

6. Stir the gelatin mixture into the apricot purée, along with the natural yogurt, mixing well to blend evenly. Put in a refrigerator for about 30 minutes until almost set.

7. Whisk the egg whites until they form soft peaks.

8. Fold the whisked egg whites lightly, but thoroughly, into the partially set apricot mixture.

9. Divide the fruit mousse evenly into serving glasses and chill until completely set.

Step 3 Purée the orange juice, rind and apricots together in a liquidizer or food processor until smooth.

Step 6 Allow the fruit purée and gelatin to chill in a refrigerator until it is just beginning to set.

Step 8 Fold the egg whites carefully, but thoroughly, into the thickening fruit mixture, taking care not to over mix and lose the air in the egg whites.

Cook's Notes

Time
Preparation takes 30-35 minutes, plus chilling time.

Variation
Use strawberries or peaches in place of the apricots.

Serving Idea
Serve decorated with twisted strips of orange peel and a crisp biscuit if liked.

SERVES 6

BAKED APPLES IN PASTRY

Pastry sweetened with cinnamon and spices combines with a rich fruit filling to make this warming winter dessert.

3 cups all-purpose flour
¼ tsp salt
⅓ tsp cinnamon
⅓ tsp ground nutmeg
¾ cup butter
6-8 tbsps iced water
6 medium-sized dessert apples
6 prunes, pitted
6 dried apricots
2½ tbsps raisins
1 egg, beaten to glaze
Fresh cream to serve
Fresh mint to serve

1. Sift the flour, salt and spices into a large bowl.

2. Cut the butter into dice and rub into the flour until the mixture resembles fine breadcrumbs.

3. Mix in enough water to produce a smooth pliable dough.

4. Divide the dough into six pieces and roll out into a square approximately 8 inches.

5. Peel the apples with a sharp knife and carefully remove the center cores with an apple corer.

6. Chop the prunes and the apricots and mix these with the raisins.

Step 8 Draw the sides of the pastry square up and over each apple, sealing the edges well with a little water.

7. Place one prepared apple into the center of each pastry square, and fill the cavities with equal amounts of the dried fruit mixture.

8. Brush the edges of each square with a little water, and draw them up and around the sides of the apples, sealing them well with a little water and trimming off any excess pastry to give a neat finish.

9. Roll out the pastry trimmings, cut into decorative leaves and stick the leaves onto each apple for decoration.

10. Glaze each pastry apple with the beaten egg and place on a lightly greased cookie sheet.

11. Bake the apples in a preheated oven 350°F for 20-25 minutes, or until golden brown.

12. Serve hot with the fresh cream and sprigs of fresh mint.

Cook's Notes

Time
Preparation takes approximately 30 minutes, cooking time takes 20-25 minutes.

Cook's Tip
For an extra rich pastry, use 1 egg yolk and half the amount of water in this recipe.

Variation
Use pears instead of apples in this recipe.

Freezing
These apples freeze well after baking and should be thawed, then re-heated, before eating.

SERVES 6

ALMOND-YOGURT SHAKE

This healthy, sugar-free yogurt shake has a slightly salty, but refreshing flavor.

1¾ cups water
2 cups natural yogurt
2½ tsps lemon juice
2½ tbsps ground almonds
¼ tsp saffron strands
2½ tsps rose water
¼ tsp salt

1. Lightly moisten the rims of six tumblers with a little water or lightly whipped egg white. Spread a thin layer of salt onto a saucer and dip the moistened rims into it to coat lightly.

2. Put half of the water into a liquidizer and add the yogurt, lemon juice, almonds, saffron and rose water. Blend until smooth.

3. Mix in the remaining water and the salt.

4. Measure 1 pint of ice cubes into a measuring jug.

5. Pour the yogurt mixture from the liquidizer into another large jug.

6. Put half of the ice into the liquidizer and pour over half of the yogurt and saffron mixture. Blend to a thick slush, then repeat with the remaining ice and yogurt mixture. Serve in the prepared tumblers.

Step 2 Blend the water, yogurt, lemon juice, almonds, saffron and rose water in a liquidizer or food processor, until smooth.

Step 1 Lightly moisten the rims of six tumblers with a little water or lightly whipped egg white. Spread a thin layer of salt onto a saucer and dip the moistened rims into it to coat lightly.

Step 6 Blend half of the ice with half of the liquid in the liquidizer until it forms a smooth slush.

Cook's Notes

Time
Preparation takes 10 minutes.

Cook's Tip
If you haven't got a liquidizer or food processor, use a rolling pin to crush the ice.

Variation
Use the juice of ½ an orange in place of the lemon juice in this recipe.

SERVES 6

KIWI AND PINEAPPLE SHAKE

Sugar-free lemonade is easily available in supermarkets, and adds a tangy fizz to this delicious fruity drink.

1 cup pineapple juice
3 kiwi fruits
1¼ cups natural yogurt
1 lemon
Liquid sweetener to taste
2 cups ice cubes
1¼ cups sugar-free lemonade
1 kiwi fruit for decoration

Step 1 Purée the pineapple juice and kiwi fruits together in a liquidizer or food processor, until smooth.

1. Carefully peel the 3 kiwi fruits and roughly chop the flesh. Put the kiwi flesh into a food processor or liquidizer, along with the pineapple juice, and blend until smooth.

2. Finely grate the rind from half of the lemon and squeeze the juice. Mix the juice into the yogurt in a large jug, along with the fruit purée and liquid sweetener.

3. Put the ice cubes into the food processor or liquidizer, and pour over the pineapple and yogurt mixture. Blend for

15-30 seconds until it becomes a smooth slush.

4. Divide this mixture between six glasses and top up with lemonade, stirring well with a long handled spoon to blend in the glass.

5. Cut the unpeeled kiwi fruit into thin slices and slit each slice halfway through. Stand each slice of kiwi onto the sides of each glass for decoration.

Step 2 Blend the yogurt, lemon rind and juice, liquid sweetener, and the pineapple and kiwi fruit mixture together in a large jug.

Step 3 Blend together the ice and the pineapple yogurt mixture until it becomes a smooth slush.

Cook's Notes

Time
Preparation takes 5-10 minutes.

Cook's Tip
Do not use set yogurt in this drink as it will not blend smoothly.

Variation
Use orange juice in place of the pineapple juice in this recipe.

SERVES 4

TROPICAL FRUIT HEALTH DRINK

This healthful fruit drink is an ideal breakfast time treat.

3 kiwi fruits
2 ripe nectarines or peaches
2 slices fresh pineapple
1 lime
1¼ cups unsweetened pineapple juice
1 kiwi fruit or lime, for decoration

Step 2 Carefully peel away the skin from the blanched nectarines or peaches, using a sharp knife.

Step 3 Cut the peaches in half and twist them carefully apart to remove the stones.

Step 5 Blend the fruit and the juices in a liquidizer or food processor, until smooth.

1. Carefully remove the peel from the kiwi fruit and roughly chop the flesh.

2. Plunge the nectarines or peaches into boiling water for 30 seconds and carefully peel off the blanched skins.

3. Halve the peaches or nectarines, and remove the stones. Chop the flesh and put this into a liquidizer or food processor, along with the kiwi fruit.

4. Remove the peel from the pineapple slices and cut into quarters. Cut away the tough core from the pineapple and add the remaining flesh to the kiwi and peaches in the liquidizer or food processor.

5. Squeeze the juice from the lime and add this, with the pineapple juice, to the fruit in the food processor. Blend until smooth, and pour into individual serving glasses.

6. Decorate the edge of the glasses with thin slices of un-peeled kiwi fruit or lime.

Cook's Notes

Time
Preparation takes approximately 10 minutes.

Variation
Add 1¼ cups sugar-free lemonade to this recipe for a lighter more refreshing fruit drink.

Serving Idea
Serve spooned over muesli for a refreshing breakfast.

Sugar Free
Notes

Sugar Free
Notes

THE CHICKEN
COOKBOOK

Introduction

Chicken is one of the most popular meats eaten today. This is due, to a certain extent, to the large numbers of people who are eating less red meat in an attempt to reduce their fat and cholesterol intakes. In addition to being perfect for both healthy and low-calorie diets, chicken has the added advantage of being quick and easy to cook, as well as lending itself to a whole variety of cooking methods and complementary ingredients.

When choosing a fresh chicken, look at the skin. It should be pale and moist-looking, and the breast meat should be plump. Make sure that the packaging is intact, so that the chicken hasn't been exposed to the air – this goes for frozen chicken as well. Fresh chicken should be removed from its packaging and kept covered, for no more than three days in the refrigerator. Frozen chicken should be thoroughly defrosted before using, and then cooked immediately. All chicken should be cooked from room temperature, but that does not mean that it should be left standing in the warm for a long time. When stuffing a chicken, do not pack the cavity tightly. Hot air must be allowed to circulate round to ensure that it cooks thoroughly. Chicken should never be cooked from frozen or partially thawed and never be eaten pink or bloody.

As chicken is so popular, it can be bought in many forms; whole, quartered, or in portions – with or without bones. Although buying portions is convenient for the cook, it is expensive. It is much cheaper to buy a whole chicken and joint it yourself. Whole birds can also be bought as free-range or corn-fed (with a yellow-tinted skin), and these have a very good flavor. Young chickens, known as Cornish game hens, are also readily available. Depending on their size, they will each feed one or two people and make a very neat and attractive dish. Whole birds can also be boned and stuffed for special occasions, or "spatchcocked", by splitting them in half lengthwise up the underside and then flattening them out on skewers. Boneless breast fillets are one of the most popular portions, simply because they are so convenient for slicing, grinding, and cutting into bite-sized pieces.

With such a choice of cuts and cooking methods it is little wonder so many recipes for chicken exist. This book contains a variety of delicious recipes suitable for all occasions, and includes recipes from around the world, as well as more familiar appetizers and entrées. So, whether you want a dish for a cold winter's day, a dinner party, a lunch, or a Chinese meal, you need look no further than the recipes in this book.

Contents

CHICKEN-STUFFED PEPPERS

This is a lighter stuffing than the usual meat-and-rice mixture.

SERVES 6

3 large green or red bell peppers
¼ butter or margarine
1 small onion, minced
1 stick celery, finely chopped
1 clove garlic, crushed
3 chicken breasts, skinned, boned, and
　　diced
2 tsps chopped parsley
Salt and pepper
½ loaf of stale white bread, made into
　　crumbs
1-2 eggs, beaten
6 tsps dry breadcrumbs

1. Cut the peppers in half lengthwise and remove the cores and seeds. Leave the stems attached, if wished.

2. Melt the butter in a skillet and add the onion, celery, garlic, and chicken. Cook over moderate heat until the vegetables are softened and the chicken is cooked. Add the parsley. Season with salt and pepper.

3. Stir in the stale breadcrumbs and add enough beaten egg to make the mixture hold together.

4. Spoon the filling into each pepper half, mounding the top slightly. Place the peppers in a baking dish that holds them closely together.

5. Pour enough water around the peppers to come about ½ inch up their sides. Cover, and bake in a pre-heated 350°F oven for about 45 minutes, or until the peppers are just tender.

6. Sprinkle each with the dried breadcrumbs and place under a preheated broiler. Broil until golden-brown.

TIME: Preparation takes about 30 minutes and cooking takes about 45-50 minutes.

VARIATIONS: Use green onions in place of the small onion. Add chopped nuts or black olives to the filling, if wished.

SERVING IDEAS: Serve as a first course, either hot or cold, or as a light lunch or supper with a salad.

Paotzu Steamed Buns with Chicken, Cabbage, and Mushrooms

The steamed dumplings could be eaten as part of a Chinese Dim Sum meal.

MAKES about 16

3 cups self-rising flour
2 tsps salt
1 tsp fresh yeast or 1 envelope dried yeast
1 cup warm water
½ cup shredded cabbage
6 dried black Chinese mushrooms (shiitake or cloud ear) pre-soaked and sliced
2 tsps sesame oil
1 cup ground chicken
1 tbsp chopped fresh root ginger
1 tbsp soy sauce
1 tbsp oyster sauce
Black pepper

1. Place the flour and salt in a large bowl. Sprinkle the yeast over the warm water, stir and leave for 10 minutes or until foaming.

2. Make a well in the center of the flour, add the liquid and stir in well, gradually incorporating the flour. Cover with a damp cloth or plastic wrap and leave in a warm place for 2 hours or until doubled in volume.

3. Combine the shredded cabbage and mushrooms. Heat the oil in a wok and add the cabbage, mushrooms, and chicken. Stir-fry rapidly for a few minutes. Add the remaining ingredients, stir together and remove from the wok. Leave to cool.

4. Knead the dough for 2-3 minutes, then cut into about 16 pieces. Roll each piece out to a 4-inch circle and place about 2 tsps of filling in the center of each circle.

5. Draw up the edges of the dough over the filling and pinch together. Place pieces of oiled nonstick baking parchment over the pinched ends and turn the buns over so they stand on the paper.

6. Leave the buns to stand, covered with the damp cloth, for 15-20 minutes, then place in a steamer and steam rapidly for 10-15 minutes or until firm, springy, and well risen. Serve immediately.

TIME: Preparation takes about 40 minutes, plus 2 hours 20 minutes for rising. Cooking takes 10-15 minutes.

WATCHPOINT: When steaming the buns, leave enough space between them for expansion. If necessary, cook in batches.

PREPARATION: Soak the mushrooms for 20 minutes in boiling water. Discard tough stalks before using.

TACOS

Packaged taco shells make this famous Mexican snack easy to prepare, so spend the extra time on imaginative fillings.

MAKES 12

12 taco shells

Chicken Filling

3 tbsps butter or margarine

1 medium onion, chopped

1 small red bell pepper, chopped

2 tbsps flaked almonds

12 ounces chicken breasts, skinned and
   finely chopped

Salt and pepper

1 piece fresh ginger, peeled and chopped

6 tbsps milk

2 tsps cornstarch

⅔ cup sour cream

Toppings

Shredded lettuce

Grated cheese

Tomatoes, seeded and chopped

Chopped green onions

Avocado slices

Sour cream

Jalapeño peppers

Taco sauce

1. Melt 2 tbsps of the butter or margarine in a medium saucepan and add the onion. Cook slowly until softened.

2. Add the red bell pepper and almonds, and cook slowly until the almonds are lightly browned. Stir often during cooking. Remove to a plate and set aside.

3. Melt the remaining butter in the same saucepan and cook the chicken for about 5 minutes, turning frequently. Season and return the onion mixture to the pan, along with the chopped ginger.

4. Blend the milk and cornstarch and stir into the chicken mixture. Bring to the boil and stir until very thick. Mix in the sour cream and cook gently to heat through. Do not boil.

5. Heat the taco shells on a cookie sheet in a preheated 350°F oven for 2-3 minutes. Place on the sheet with the open ends downward.

6. To fill, hold the shell in one hand and spoon in about 1 tbsp of chicken filling.

7. Next, add a layer of shredded lettuce, followed by a layer of grated cheese. Add your choice of other toppings and finally spoon some taco sauce over the mixture.

TIME: Preparation takes about 30 minutes. Cooking takes about 15 minutes for the chicken filling and 2-3 minutes to heat the taco shells.

COOK'S TIP: Placing the taco shells on their open ends when reheating keeps them from closing up and makes filling easier.

SERVING IDEAS: For a buffet, place all the ingredients out separately for guests to help themselves and create their own combinations.

SZECHUAN BANG-BANG CHICKEN

Serve this dish as an appetizer. The diners should toss and mix the ingredients together themselves.

SERVES 4

---

2 chicken breasts
1 medium cucumber

Sauce
4 tbsps smooth peanut butter
2 tsps sesame oil
½ tsp sugar
¼ tsp salt
2 tsps broth
½ tsp chili sauce

1. Simmer the chicken in a pan of water for 30 minutes or until tender. Remove the chicken breasts and cut them into ½-inch-thick strips.

2. Thinly slice the cucumber. Spread the cucumber on a large serving platter and pile the shredded chicken on top.

3. Mix the peanut butter with the sesame oil, sugar, salt, and broth. Pour the sauce evenly over the chicken. Sprinkle the chili sauce evenly over the top.

TIME: Preparation takes about 15 minutes and cooking takes 30 minutes.

VARIATIONS: Use crunchy peanut butter or tahini in place of smooth peanut butter.

PREPARATION: The chicken is cooked if the juices run clear when a sharp knife or skewer is inserted into the thickest part of the meat.

SALADE BRESSE

As well as being famous for its cheese, Bresse, in Burgundy, is renowned for its special breed of chickens, reputed to be the best in France.

SERVES 4-6

1 head radicchio, leaves separated and washed
1 head romaine lettuce, washed
1 bunch lamb's lettuce or watercress, washed
4 chicken breasts, cooked, skinned, and thinly sliced
½ cup Bresse Bleu or other blue cheese, cut in small pieces
16 cornichons (small pickles), thinly sliced
8-10 cherry tomatoes, halved and cored
2 tbsps walnut halves

Dressing

2 tbsps vegetable and walnut oil mixed
2 tsps white wine vinegar
¾ cup crème frâiche
2 tsps chopped fresh tarragon
Salt and pepper

1. Tear the radicchio and romaine lettuce into bite-size pieces. Leave the lamb's lettuce in whole leaves. If using watercress, wash thoroughly, remove the thick stems and any yellow leaves.

2. Toss the leaves together and pile onto a salad plate.

3. Place the chicken, cheese, cornichons, tomatoes, and walnuts on top of the lettuce.

4. Mix the oils and vinegar together and whisk well to emulsify.

5. Fold in the crème frâiche and add the tarragon, salt, and pepper.

6. Sprinkle some of the dressing over the salad to serve and hand the rest of the dressing separately.

TIME: Preparation takes about 20 minutes.

VARIATIONS: Use goat's cheese instead of Bresse Bleu, and yogurt or sour cream in place of the crème frâiche.

PREPARATION: The dressing can be made in advance and kept refrigerated.

Peking Egg Chicken with Beansprouts, in Onion and Garlic Sauce

This exciting mixture results in a simply delicious dish.

SERVES 3

3 chicken breasts
Salt and pepper
2 eggs
2 cloves garlic
2 green onions
4 tbsps oil
⅔ cup fresh beansprouts
4 tbsps broth
Wine vinegar to taste

1. Cut each chicken breast crosswise into 1-inch slices. Rub with salt and pepper.

2. Beat eggs lightly, and add the chicken slices to the eggs.

3. Crush the garlic and cut the green onions into 2.5cm/1-inch pieces.

4. Heat the oil in the wok. Add the chicken pieces one by one, and reduce heat to low. Leave to sauté for 2-3 minutes.

5. Once the egg has set, sprinkle the chicken with garlic, green onion, and beansprouts.

6. Finally, add the broth and vinegar to taste. Simmer gently for 4 minutes.

7. Remove the chicken, cut each piece into small regular pieces, and serve on a heated platter. Pour the remaining sauce from the wok over the chicken.

TIME: Preparation takes 10 minutes, cooking takes about 10 minutes.

COOK'S TIP: Buy the beansprouts on the day you intend to use them as they deteriorate rapidly.

SERVING IDEAS: Serve with a chili dipping sauce and rice.

305

CHICKEN WITH WALNUTS AND CELERY

Oyster sauce lends a subtle, slightly salty taste to this Cantonese dish.

SERVES 4

8 ounces chicken meat, cut into 1-inch
  pieces
2 tsps soy sauce
2 tsps brandy
1 tsp cornstarch
Salt and pepper
2 tbsps oil
1 clove garlic
½ cup walnut halves
3 sticks celery, cut in diagonal slices
⅔ cup chicken broth
2 tsps oyster sauce

1. Combine the chicken with the soy sauce, brandy, cornstarch, salt and pepper.

2. Heat a wok and add the oil and garlic. Cook for about 1 minute to flavor the oil.

3. Remove the garlic and add the chicken in two batches. Stir-fry quickly to cook the chicken but without allowing it to brown. Remove the chicken and add the walnuts to the wok. Cook for about 2 minutes until the walnuts are slightly brown and crisp.

4. Add the celery to the wok and cook for about 1 minute. Add the broth and oyster sauce and bring to the boil. When boiling, return the chicken to the pan and stir to coat all the ingredients well. Serve immediately.

TIME: Preparation takes about 20 minutes, cooking takes about 8 minutes.

WATCHPOINT: Nuts can burn very easily. Stir them constantly for even browning.

VARIATIONS: Almonds or cashew nuts may be used instead of the walnuts. If the cashew nuts are already roasted, add them along with the celery.

FLAUTAS

Traditionally, these are long, thin rolls of tortillas with savory fillings, topped with sour cream.

SERVES 6

8 ounces chicken, skinned, boned and ground or finely chopped

1 tbsp oil

1 small onion, minced

½ green bell pepper, finely chopped

½-1 chili, seeded and finely chopped

½ cup fresh or frozen sweetcorn

6 black olives, pitted and chopped

½ cup heavy cream

Salt

12 corn or flour tortillas

Sour cream, guacamole, and taco sauce for toppings

1. Use a food processor or meat grinder to prepare the chicken, or chop by hand.

2. Heat the oil in a medium skillet and add the chicken, onion, and green bell pepper. Cook over a moderate heat, stirring frequently to break up the pieces of chicken.

3. When the chicken is cooked and the vegetables are softened, add the chili, corn, olives, cream, and salt. Bring to the boil over a high heat and boil rapidly, stirring continuously, to reduce and thicken the cream.

4. Place 2 tortillas on a clean work surface, overlapping them by about 2 inches. Spoon some of the chicken mixture onto the tortillas, roll up and secure with cocktail sticks.

5. Fry the flautas in about ½ inch oil in a large skillet. Do not allow the tortillas to get very brown. Drain on kitchen paper.

6. Arrange flautas on serving plates and top with sour cream, guacamole, and taco sauce.

TIME: Preparation takes about 15 minutes and cooking takes about 15 minutes.

VARIATIONS: Use guacamole instead of heavy cream.

SERVING IDEAS: Flautas are often served with rice, refried beans, and a salad.

CHICKEN WITH CLOUD EARS

Cloud ears is the delightful name for an edible tree fungus which is mushroom-like in taste and texture.

SERVES 6

12 cloud ears, wood ears, or other dried Chinese mushrooms, soaked in boiling water for 5 minutes
1 pound chicken breasts, boned and thinly sliced crosswise
1 egg white
2 tsps cornstarch
2 tsps white wine
2 tsps sesame oil
1¼ cups oil
1-inch piece fresh root ginger
1 clove garlic
1¼ cups chicken broth
1 tbsp cornstarch
3 tbsps light soy sauce
Pinch salt and pepper

1. Soak the mushrooms until they soften and swell. Remove all the skin and bone from the chicken and cut it into thin slices. Mix the chicken with the egg white, cornstarch, wine, and sesame oil.

2. Heat the wok for a few minutes and add the oil. Add the whole piece of ginger and whole garlic clove to the oil and cook about 1 minute. Remove them and reduce the heat.

3. Add about a quarter of the chicken at a time and stir-fry for about 1 minute. Remove, and continue cooking until all the chicken is fried. Remove all but about 2 tbsps of the oil from the wok.

4. Drain the mushrooms and squeeze them to extract all the liquid. If using mushrooms with stems, remove the stems before slicing the caps thinly. Cut cloud ears or wood ears into smaller pieces. Add to the wok and cook for about 1 minute.

5. Add the broth and allow it to come almost to the boil. Mix together the cornstarch and soy sauce and add a tablespoon of the hot broth. Add the mixture to the wok, stirring constantly, and bring to the boil. Allow to boil for 1-2 minutes or until thickened. The sauce will clear when the cornstarch has cooked sufficiently.

6. Return the chicken to the wok and add salt and pepper. Stir thoroughly for about 1 minute and serve immediately.

TIME: Preparation takes about 25 minutes, cooking takes about 5 minutes.

VARIATIONS: Flat, cup, or button mushrooms may be used instead of the dried mushrooms. Eliminate the soaking and slice them thickly. Cook as for the dried variety. Two tsps bottled oyster sauce may be added with the broth.

SERVING SUGGESTION: Cloud ears or wood ears are both available from oriental supermarkets and some delicatessens. Shiitake mushrooms are more readily available fresh or dried. Both keep a long time in their dried state.

CHICKEN, HAM, AND LEEK PIE

The addition of cream and egg yolks at the end of the cooking time makes this pie extra special.

SERVES 6-8

1 × 3-pound chicken
1 onion
1 bayleaf
Parsley stalks
Salt and black pepper
1 pound leeks
2 tbsps butter
½ cup chopped cooked ham
1 tbsp parsley
1¼ cups chicken broth
12-14 ounces puff dough
⅔ cup heavy cream
1 egg, lightly beaten for glazing

1. Put the cleaned chicken in a large saucepan together with the onion, bayleaf, parsley stalks, and salt and pepper. Cover with cold water and bring gently to the boil. Allow to simmer for about 45 minutes until the chicken is tender. Leave it to cool in the pan.

2. Meanwhile, wash and trim the leeks, and cut into 1½-inch pieces. Melt the butter in a small pan and gently sauté the leeks for about 5 minutes. Remove from the heat.

3. Take the cooled chicken out of the pan, remove the skin, and strip off the flesh. Cut it into good-sized pieces.

4. Put the chicken, ham, leeks, and parsley into a large pie dish with plenty of seasoning. Add 1¼ cups of the cooking liquid from the chicken.

5. Roll out the dough slightly larger than the size of the pie dish. Use the trimmings to line the rim of the dish. Dampen them and put on the dough lid. Trim and seal the edges together firmly. Any surplus dough can be used to make decorative leaves. Cut a few slits in the dough to allow the steam to escape. Brush the dough well with beaten egg.

6. Bake in the center of a preheated 450°F oven for 15 minutes. Remove and glaze again with beaten egg. Reduce the temperature of the oven to 400°F. Return the pie to the oven for another 20 minutes.

7. When the pie crust is well risen and golden-brown, remove it from the oven. Carefully lift off a segment of pastry and pour in the cream which has been gently warmed together with the remaining beaten egg.

TIME: Preparation takes about 45 minutes for the chicken, plus extra cooling time and 20 minutes to prepare the pie. Cooking takes about 35 minutes.

SERVING IDEAS: Serve with creamed potatoes and a green vegetable.

CRUMB-FRIED CHICKEN

A southern speciality, this dish has a slightly misleading name since most of the "frying" takes place in the oven!

SERVES 4-6

---

1 ✗ 3-pound chicken
1 cup dry breadcrumbs
½ cup Parmesan cheese
¼ tsp ground ginger
2 eggs, mixed with a pinch of salt
3 tbsps oil
¼ cup butter or margarine
Lemons and parsley for garnish

---

1. Preheat the oven to 400°F. To joint the chicken, first cut off the legs, bending them outward to break the ball-and-socket joint. Cut in between the ball-and-socket joint to completely remove the legs.

2. Cut down the breastbone with sharp poultry shears to separate the two halves. Use the poultry shears to cut through the rib cage. Use the notch in the shears to separate the wing joints from the back.

3. Use a sharp knife to separate the drumstick from the thigh. Cut the breasts in half with poultry shears.

4. Mix the breadcrumbs, Parmesan cheese, and ground ginger together. First dip the chicken into the egg and then coat with the crumbs.

5. Heat the oil in a large skillet and add the butter. When hot, place in the chicken, skin side down first. Cook both sides until golden-brown.

6. Transfer with a slotted spoon to a cookie sheet and place in the oven for 20-30 minutes, or until the juices run clear when the chicken is tested with a knife or a fork. Serve garnished with small bunches of parsley and lemon wedges or slices.

TIME: Preparation takes about 30 minutes. If using chicken portions, allow about 15-20 minutes for preparation. Chicken will take about 10-15 minutes to brown and 20-30 minutes to finish cooking in the oven.

PREPARATION: Mix the crumbs, cheese, and ginger on a sheet of wax or parchment paper. Place the chicken on the crumbs and shake the paper from side to side to coat easily and completely.

VARIATIONS: If wished, omit the Parmesan cheese and ginger, and add extra breadcrumbs, paprika, salt, pepper, and a pinch of thyme.

315

INDIAN CHICKEN

Marinating chicken with spices allows their full flavors to penetrate the meat.

SERVES 4-6

1 × 3-pound chicken, cut into 8 pieces
2½ cups plain yogurt
2 tsps ground coriander
2 tsps paprika
1 tsp ground turmeric
Juice of 1 lime
1 tbsp honey
½ clove garlic, crushed
1 small piece ginger, peeled and grated

1. Pierce the chicken all over with a fork or skewer.

2. Combine all the remaining ingredients and spread half the mixture over the chicken, rubbing in well.

3. Place the chicken in a shallow dish or a plastic bag and cover or tie it. Leave for at least 4 hours or overnight in the refrigerator.

4. Arrange the chicken, skin side down, under a moderate pre-heated broiler and cook until lightly browned. Turn over and cook the second side until lightly browned. This should take about 30 minutes in all. Baste frequently with remaining marinade.

5. Reduce the broiler heat and cook for 15 minutes, turning and basting frequently, until the chicken is brown and the skin is crisp.

6. Alternatively, bake the chicken in a covered pan in the oven at 325°F for 45 minutes - 1 hour and broil it for the last 15 minutes for flavor and color.

7. Serve any remaining yogurt mixture separately as a sauce.

TIME: Preparation takes about 15 minutes and marinating at least 4 hours, cooking takes about 45 minutes.

COOK'S TIP: The chicken can also be barbecued. Make sure the shelf is on the level furthest from the coals so that the chicken has time to cook without burning.

VARIATIONS: Use chicken breasts only for this dish.

CHICKEN AND VEGETABLE STEW

A combination of chicken, lima beans, peppers, and onions made into an aromatic stew.

SERVES 4-6

1 × 3-pound chicken, cut in 8 pieces
⅓ cup butter or margarine
3 tbsps flour
1 large red bell pepper, diced
1 large green bell pepper, diced
6 green onions, chopped
2 cups chicken broth
⅔ cup canned or fresh lima beans
1 tsp chopped thyme
Salt, pepper, and a pinch of nutmeg

1. To cut the chicken in 8 pieces, remove the legs first. Cut between the legs and the body of the chicken.

2. Bend the legs outward to break the joint and cut away from the body.

3. Cut the drumstick and thigh joints in half.

4. Cut down the breastbone with a sharp knife, and then use poultry shears to cut through the bone and ribcage to remove the breast joints from the back.

5. Cut both breast joints in half, leaving some white meat attached to the wing joint.

6. Heat the butter in a large skillet and when foaming add the chicken, skin side down. Brown on one side, turn over and brown the other side. Remove the chicken and add the flour to the pan. Cook to a pale straw color. Add the peppers and onions and cook briefly.

7. Gradually stir in the chicken broth and bring to the boil. Stir constantly until thickened. Add the chicken, lima beans, thyme, seasoning, and nutmeg. Cover the pan and cook about 25 minutes, or until the chicken is tender.

TIME: Preparation takes about 35 minutes and cooking takes about 40 minutes.

PREPARATION: For crisper vegetables, add them after the chicken and sauce have cooked for about 15 minutes.

SERVING SUGGESTION: Buying a whole chicken and jointing it yourself is cheaper than buying chicken joints.

CHICKEN WITH SAFFRON RICE AND PEAS

Saffron is frequently used in Spanish recipes. While it is expensive, it gives rice and sauces a lovely golden color and delicate flavor.

SERVES 4

2 tbsps oil

1 × 2-3 pound chicken, cut into 8 pieces, skinned if wished

Salt and pepper

1 small onion, minced

2 tsps paprika

1 clove garlic, crushed

8 tomatoes, skinned, seeded, and chopped

1¼ cups rice

3 cups boiling water

Large pinch saffron or ¼ tsp ground saffron

¾ cup frozen peas

2 tbsps chopped parsley

1. Heat the oil in a large skillet. Season the chicken with salt and pepper and place it in the hot oil, skin side down first. Cook over moderate heat, turning the chicken frequently to brown it lightly. Set the chicken aside.

2. Add the onions to the oil and cook slowly until softened but not colored.

3. Add the paprika and cook for about 2 minutes, stirring frequently until the paprika loses some of its red color. Add the garlic and the tomatoes.

4. Cook the mixture over high heat for about 5 minutes to evaporate the liquid from the tomatoes. The mixture should be of dropping consistency when done. Add the rice, water, and saffron and stir together.

5. Return the chicken to the casserole and bring to the boil over high heat. Reduce to simmering, cover tightly, and cook for about 20 minutes. Remove chicken and add the peas and parsley. Cook a further 5-10 minutes, or until rice is tender. Combine with the chicken to serve.

TIME: Preparation takes about 20-25 minutes and cooking takes about 25-35 minutes.

VARIATIONS: Use fresh peas, podded, in which case allow about 3 cups of peas in their pods. Cook fresh peas with the rice and chicken.

SERVING IDEAS: This is a very casual, peasant-type dish which is traditionally served in the casserole in which it was cooked.

CHICKEN COBBLER

This dish is warming winter fare with its creamy sauce and tender, light topping.

SERVES 6

4 chicken joints (2 breasts and 2 legs)
1½ quarts water
1 bayleaf
4 whole peppercorns
2 carrots, peeled and diced
24 pearl onions, peeled
6 tbsps frozen sweetcorn
⅔ cup heavy cream
Salt

Cobbler Topping

3½ cups all-purpose flour
1½ tbsps double-action baking powder
Pinch salt
5 tbsps butter or margarine
1½ cups milk
1 egg, beaten with a pinch of salt

1. Place the chicken in a deep saucepan with the water, bayleaf, and peppercorns. Cover and bring to the boil. Reduce the heat and allow to simmer for 20-30 minutes, or until the chicken is tender. Remove the chicken from the pan and allow to cool. Skim and discard the fat from the surface of the cooking liquid.

2. Continue to simmer the broth until reduced by about half. Meanwhile, skin the chicken and remove the meat from the bones. Strain the broth and add the carrots and onions. Cook until tender and add the corn. Stir in the cream, season and add the chicken. Pour into a warmed casserole or into individual baking dishes and keep hot.

3. To prepare the topping, sift the dry ingredients into a bowl or place them in a food processor and process once or twice to sift.

4. Rub in the butter or margarine until the mixture resembles breadcrumbs. Stir in enough of the milk to allow the mixture to stick together. If using a food processor, trickle the milk in down the food tube and process in short bursts to avoid overmixing.

5. Turn out onto a floured surface and knead lightly. Roll out with a floured rolling pin until the dough is about ½-inch thick.

6. Cut the dough into rounds using a 2-inch cookie cutter to form the cobbles. Place the rounds on top of the chicken mixture. Brush the surface of the cobbler with the egg and salt mixture and bake for 10-15 minutes in a pre-heated oven at 375°F. Serve immediately.

TIME: Preparation takes about 20-30 minutes for the chicken, about 20 minutes to prepare the sauce, and the cobbler takes about 10 minutes to prepare. Final cooking takes about 10-15 minutes.

PREPARATION: Once the topping has been prepared, it must be baked immediately or the baking powder will stop working and the cobbler topping will not rise.

LEMON CHICKEN

*Chicken, lemon, and basil is an ideal flavor combination and one that is used
often in Greek cookery.*

SERVES 4-6

2 tbsps olive oil
2 tbsps butter or margarine
1 × 3-pound chicken, jointed
1 small onion, cut in thin strips
2 sticks celery, shredded
2 carrots, cut in julienne strips
1 tbsp chopped fresh basil
1 bayleaf
Grated rind and juice of 2 small lemons
⅔ cup water
Salt and pepper
Pinch sugar (optional)
Lemon slices for garnishing

1. Heat the oil in a large skillet. Add the butter or margarine and, when foaming, add the chicken, skin side down, in one layer. Brown and turn over. Brown the other side. Cook the chicken in two batches if necessary. Remove the chicken to a plate and set aside.

2. Add the vegetables and cook for 2-3 minutes over a moderate heat. Add the basil, bayleaf, lemon rind, and juice, water, salt, and pepper and replace the chicken. Bring the mixture to the boil.

3. Cover the pan and reduce the heat. Allow to simmer about 35-45 minutes or until the chicken is tender and the juices run clear when the thighs are pierced with a fork.

4. Remove the chicken and vegetables to a serving dish and discard the bayleaf. The sauce should be thick, so boil to reduce if necessary. If the sauce is too tart, add a pinch of sugar. Spoon the sauce over the chicken to serve and garnish with the lemon slices.

TIME: Preparation takes about 30 minutes, cooking takes about 45-55 minutes total, including browning of chicken.

VARIATIONS: Use limes instead of lemons and oregano instead of basil.

SERVING IDEAS: In Greece, this dish is often served with pasta. Rice is also a good accompaniment, along with a green salad.

TOMATO AND BACON FRIED CHICKEN

This unusual version of fried chicken is cooked in a tomato sauce flavored with garlic, herbs, and wine.

SERVES 6

Flour for dredging
Salt and pepper
1 × 3-pound chicken, cut into portions
6 tbsps oil
5 tbsps butter or margarine
1 clove garlic, crushed
1 small onion, finely chopped
½ cup diced bacon
6 tomatoes, skinned and chopped
2 tsps fresh thyme or 1 tsp dried thyme
Salt and pepper
⅔ cup white wine
2 tbsps chopped parsley

1. Mix the flour with salt and pepper and dredge the chicken lightly, shaking the pieces to remove any excess. Heat the oil in a large skillet and, when hot, add the butter.

2. Add the chicken drumstick and thigh pieces, skin side down, and allow to brown. Turn the pieces over and brown on the other side. Brown over moderately low heat so that the chicken cooks as well as browns. Push the chicken to one side of the pan, add the breast meat, and brown in the same way.

3. Add the garlic, onion, and bacon to the pan and reduce the heat. Cook slowly for about 10 minutes, or until the bacon browns slightly. Add the tomatoes and thyme, and reduce the heat. Cook until the chicken is just tender and the tomatoes are softened.

4. Using a slotted spoon, transfer the chicken and other ingredients to a serving dish and keep warm. Remove all but about 4 tbsps of the fat from the pan and deglaze with the wine, scraping up the browned bits from the bottom. Bring to the boil and allow to reduce slightly. Pour this gravy over the chicken to serve, and sprinkle with chopped parsley.

TIME: Preparation takes about 25 minutes and cooking takes about 30-40 minutes.

PREPARATION: Brown the chicken slowly so that it cooks at the same time as it browns. This will cut down on the length of cooking time needed once all the ingredients are added.

Spicy Spanish Chicken

Chili, coriander, and bright red tomatoes add a warm Spanish flavor to broiled chicken.

SERVES 6

6 boned chicken breasts

Grated rind and juice of 1 lime

2 tbsps olive oil

Coarsely ground black pepper

6 tbsps whole-grain mustard

2 tsps paprika

4 ripe tomatoes, skinned, de-seeded, and quartered

2 shallots, chopped

1 clove garlic, crushed

½ jalapeño pepper or other chili, seeded and chopped

1 tsp wine vinegar

Pinch salt

2 tbsps chopped fresh coriander

Whole coriander leaves to garnish

1. Place the chicken breasts in a shallow dish with the lime rind and juice, oil, pepper, mustard, and paprika. Marinate for about 1 hour, turning occasionally.

2. To skin the tomatoes easily, drop them into boiling water for about 5 seconds or less, depending on ripeness. Place immediately in cold water. Skins should come off easily.

3. Place the tomatoes, shallots, garlic, chili, vinegar, and salt in a food processor or blender, and process until coarsely chopped. Stir in the coriander by hand.

4. Place the chicken on a broiler pan and reserve the marinade. Cook the chicken, skin side uppermost, for about 7-10 minutes, depending on how close it is to the heat source. Baste frequently with the remaining marinade. Broil the other side in the same way. Sprinkle with salt after broiling.

5. Place the chicken on serving dishes and garnish the top with coriander leaves or sprigs. Serve with a spoonful of the tomato relish on one side.

TIME: Preparation takes about 1 hour including marinating, and cooking takes 14-20 minutes.

PREPARATION: The tomato relish can be prepared in advance and kept in the refrigerator.

WATCHPOINT: When preparing chilies, wear rubber gloves or at least be sure to wash hands thoroughly after handling them. Do not touch eyes or face before washing hands.

CHICKEN POLISH STYLE

Choose small, young chickens for a truly Polish-style dish. A dry white roll was originally used for stuffing, but breadcrumbs are easier.

SERVES 4

2 × 2-pound chickens
1 tbsp butter or margarine
2 chicken livers
6 slices crustless bread, made into crumbs
2 tsps minced parsley
1 tsp chopped dill
1 egg
Salt and pepper
⅔ cup chicken broth

1. Remove the fat from just inside the cavities of the chickens and discard it. Melt the butter in a small skillet. Pick over the chicken livers and cut away any discolored parts. Add chicken livers to the butter and cook until just brown. Chop and set aside.

2. Combine the breadcrumbs, herbs, egg, salt, and pepper and mix well. Mix in the chopped chicken livers.

3. Stuff the cavities of the chickens and sew up the openings. Tie the legs together.

4. Place the chickens in a roasting pan and spread the breasts and legs lightly with more butter. Pour the broth around the chickens and roast in a preheated 375°F oven for about 40-45 minutes. Baste frequently with the pan juices during roasting.

5. To check if the chickens are done, pierce the thickest part of the thigh with a skewer or small, sharp knife. If the juices run clear the chickens are ready. If the juices are pink, return to the oven for another 5-10 minutes.

6. When the chickens are done, remove them from the roasting pan, remove the string, and keep them warm. Skim any fat from the surface of the pan juices. If a lot of liquid has accumulated, pour into a small saucepan and reduce over high heat. Pour the juices over the chicken to serve.

TIME: Preparation takes about 20 minutes and cooking takes about 45 minutes.

SERVING IDEAS: Serve with a cucumber salad or a Polish style lettuce salad and new potatoes tossed with butter and dill.

VARIATIONS: Chopped mushrooms or onions may be added to the stuffing, if wished.

CHICKEN, SAUSAGE, AND OKRA STEW

There is an exotic flavor to this economical chicken stew. The garlic sausage adds flavor instantly.

SERVES 4-6

½ cup oil
1 × 3-pound chicken, cut into 6-8 pieces
1 cup flour
1 large onion, minced
1 large green bell pepper, roughly chopped
3 sticks celery, finely chopped
2 cloves garlic, crushed
8 ounces garlic sausage, diced
5 cups chicken broth
1 bayleaf
Dash Tabasco
Salt and pepper
1 cup fresh okra
Cooked rice to serve

1. Heat the oil in a large skillet and brown the chicken all over, 3-4 pieces at a time. Transfer the chicken to a plate and set it aside.

2. Reduce the heat under the pan and add the flour. Cook over a very low heat for about 30 minutes, stirring constantly until the flour turns a rich, dark brown. Take the pan off the heat occasionally, so that the flour does not burn.

3. Add the onion, green bell pepper, celery, garlic, and sausage to the pan and cook for about 5 minutes over very low heat, stirring continuously.

4. Slowly add the broth, stirring constantly, and bring to the boil. Add the bayleaf, a dash of Tabasco and seasoning. Return the chicken to the pan, cover and cook for about 30 minutes or until the chicken is tender.

5. Top and tail the okra and cut each into 2-3 pieces. If the okra are small, leave whole. Add to the chicken and cook for a further 10-15 minutes. Remove the bayleaf and serve over rice.

TIME: Preparation takes about 30 minutes and cooking takes about 1 hour 25 minutes.

COOK'S TIP: The oil-and-flour paste may be made ahead of time and kept in the refrigerator to use whenever needed. If the paste is cold, heat the liquid before adding.

FRIED CHICKEN

Fried Chicken is easy to make at home and it's much tastier than a takeout!

SERVES 4

2 eggs
3 pounds chicken portions
2 cups flour
1 tsp each salt, paprika, and sage
½ tsp black pepper
Pinch cayenne pepper (optional)
Oil for frying
Parsley or watercress to garnish

1. Beat the eggs in a large bowl and add the chicken one piece at a time, turning to coat.

2. Mix flour and seasonings in a large plastic bag.

3. Place the chicken in the bag one piece at a time, close bag tightly, and shake to coat. Alternatively, dip each chicken piece in a bowl of seasoned flour, shaking off the excess.

4. Heat about ½ inch of oil in a large skillet.

5. When the oil is hot, add the chicken, skin side downward first. Fry for about 12 minutes and then turn over. Fry a further 12 minutes or until the juices run clear.

6. Drain the chicken on kitchen paper and serve immediately. Garnish with parsley or watercress.

TIME: Preparation takes about 20 minutes and cooking takes about 24 minutes.

PREPARATION: The chicken should not be crowded in the skillet. If the pan is small, fry the chicken in several batches.

COOK'S TIP: When coating food for frying, be sure to coat it just before cooking. If left to stand, the coating can become soggy.

TANGERINE PEEL CHICKEN

An exotic mixture of flavors blends perfectly in this delicious chicken dish.

SERVES 2

1 pound boned chicken breast, cut into
  1-inch pieces

Seasoning

½ tsp salt

1½ tsps sugar

½ tsp monosodium glutamate (optional)

1 tsp dark soy sauce

2 tsps light soy sauce

1 tsp rice wine or dry sherry

2 tsps vinegar

1 tsp sesame oil

2 tsps cornstarch

Oil for deep frying

1-2 red or green chilies, chopped

½-inch fresh root ginger, peeled and finely
  chopped

2 inches dried tangerine peel, coarsely
  ground or crumbled

2 green onions, finely chopped

Sauce

½ tsp cornstarch

1-2 tbsps water or broth

1. Mix the chicken pieces with the seasoning ingredients and stir well. Leave to marinate for 10-15 minutes. Remove the chicken pieces and reserve the marinade.

2. Heat a wok and add the oil for deep frying. Heat to 350°F, add the chicken pieces, and fry for 4-5 minutes until golden. Drain chicken on kitchen paper and keep hot.

3. Allow the oil to cool then pour off, leaving 1 tbsp oil in the wok. Stir-fry the chilies, ginger, tangerine peel, and green onions for 2-3 minutes. When they begin to turn color add the chicken and stir-fry for 1 minute.

4. Mix the reserved marinade with the sauce ingredients and pour this over the chicken. Stir and cook for 2-3 minutes until the sauce thickens and the chicken is tender. Serve immediately.

TIME: Preparation takes 20 minutes including marinating time, cooking takes 15-20 minutes.

PREPARATION: Cook the chicken in batches.

COOK'S TIP: Have all the ingredients ready prepared before starting to cook.

CHICKEN WITH BEANSPROUTS

Marinated chicken, is stir-fried with beansprouts and served with a sauce based on the marinade.

SERVES 4

4 boneless chicken breasts, skinned
1 tbsp Chinese rice wine
2 tsps cornstarch
½ cup beansprouts
2 tbsps oil
2 green onions, finely sliced
1 tsp sugar
1¼ cups chicken broth
Salt and pepper

1. Cut the chicken into thin slices or strips.

2. Place the chicken on a plate and pour the Chinese rice wine over it.

3. Sprinkle with the cornstarch and stir together well. Leave to marinate for 30 minutes.

4. Blanch the beansprouts in boiling, lightly-salted water for 1 minute. Rinse under cold running water and set aside to drain.

5. Remove the chicken from the marinade with a slotted spoon. Heat the oil in a wok and stir-fry the green onions and the chicken for 2-3 minutes.

6. Add the drained beansprouts and the sugar. Add the marinade and the broth. Allow to heat through. Check the seasoning, adding salt and pepper to taste. Serve immediately.

TIME: Preparation takes about 20 minutes, marinating takes 30 minutes and cooking takes approximately 8-10 minutes.

VARIATIONS: Use half a small ordinary onion if green onions are not available.

WATCHPOINT: As soon as you add the marinade to the wok, the mixture will thicken so have the stock ready to pour in immediately and stir continuously until all the ingredients have been fully incorporated.

CHICKEN AND SAUSAGE RISOTTO

This is a one-pot meal you can cook on the stove top.

SERVES 4-6

3 pounds chicken portions, skinned, boned, and cut into cubes
3 tbsps butter or margarine
1 large onion, coarsely chopped
3 sticks celery, coarsely chopped
1 large green bell pepper, coarsely chopped
1 clove garlic, crushed
Salt and pepper
1 cup uncooked rice
1 × 14-ounce can tomatoes
6 ounces smoked sausage, cut into ½-inch dice
4 cups chicken broth
Minced parsley

1. Use the chicken skin and bones and the onion and celery trimmings to make the broth. Cover the ingredients with water, bring to the boil and then simmer slowly for 1 hour. Strain and reserve.

2. Melt the butter or margarine in a large saucepan and add the onion. Cook slowly to brown and then add the celery, green pepper, and garlic and cook briefly.

3. Add the salt and pepper and the rice, stirring to mix well.

4. Add the chicken, tomatoes, sausage, and broth and mix well. Bring to the boil, then reduce the heat to simmering and cook for about 20-25 minutes, stirring occasionally, until the chicken is done and the rice is tender. The rice should have absorbed most of the liquid by the time it has cooked. Sprinkle with the minced parsley to serve.

TIME: Preparation takes about 1 hour and cooking takes about 30-35 minutes.

PREPARATION: Check the level of liquid occasionally as the rice is cooking and add more water or broth as necessary. If there is a lot of liquid left and the rice is nearly cooked, uncover the pan and boil rapidly.

SERVING IDEAS: Add a green salad to make a complete meal.

CHICKEN IN HOT PEPPER SAUCE

Stir-fried chicken served with peppers in a hot sauce.

SERVES 4

4 boned chicken breasts, skinned
2 tbsps oil
1 tsp chopped garlic
1 green bell pepper, cut into thin strips
1 red bell pepper, cut into thin strips
1 tsp wine vinegar
1 tbsp light soy sauce
1 tsp sugar
1½ cups chicken broth
1 tbsp chili sauce
2 tsps cornstarch
Salt and pepper

1. Cut the chicken breasts crosswise into thin strips.

2. Heat the oil in a wok and stir-fry the garlic, chicken, and the green and red bell peppers for 3-4 minutes.

3. Pour off any excess oil and deglaze the wok with the vinegar. Stir in the soy sauce, sugar, and broth.

4. Gradually stir in the chili sauce, tasting after each addition. Season with a little salt and pepper to taste.

5. Blend the cornstarch with a little water and stir into the wok. Bring to the boil then simmer for 2-3 minutes. Serve piping hot.

TIME: Preparation takes 10 minutes and cooking takes approximately 10 minutes.

COOK'S TIP: Have all your ingredients ready prepared and measured out before you start to cook.

SERVING IDEAS: Serve with boiled or egg fried rice, on its own or as part of a Chinese meal.

CHICKEN IN SWEET-AND-SOUR SAUCE

This is an Italian agrodolce recipe more unusual than the familiar Chinese sweet-and-sauce flavours.

SERVES 4–6

2½ pounds chicken joints
1 large onion, chopped
1 large carrot, chopped
5 tbsps maraschino
5 tbsps white wine vinegar
140ml/¼ pint water
1 bayleaf
15 juniper berries
4 tbsps olive oil
Salt and pepper

1. Marinate the chicken joints for 4–6 hours in the chopped onion, carrot, liqueur, vinegar, water, juniper berries, and bayleaf.

2. Take the joints from the marinade and drain well, reserving the marinade. Sauté the joints in the olive oil until golden.

3. Place the joints in a shallow casserole, add the unstrained marinade, cover and cook at 350°F for a about 1 hour or until the chicken is tender. Place on a warmed serving platter and keep warm.

4. Remove the bayleaf and press the cooking juices through a sieve. Reheat gently and pour the juices over the chicken to serve.

TIME: Allow 4–6 hours for the chicken to marinate. Cooking takes about 1 hour.

SERVING IDEAS: Accompany with pasta and an Italian bread such as Ciabatta.

CHICKEN WITH RED PEPPERS

Easy as this recipe is, it looks and tastes good enough for company.

SERVES 4

4 large red bell peppers
4 skinned and boned chicken breasts
1½ tbsps oil
Salt and pepper
1 clove garlic, finely chopped
3 tbsps white wine vinegar
2 green onions, finely chopped
Sage leaves for garnish

1. Cut the peppers in half and remove the stems, cores, and seeds. Flatten the peppers with the palm of your hand and brush the skin sides lightly with oil.

2. Place the peppers skin side upward on the rack of a preheated broiler and cook about 2 inches away from the heat source until the skins are well blistered and charred.

3. Seal the peppers in a thick plastic bag and allow them to stand until cool. Peel off the skins with a small vegetable knife. Cut peppers into thin strips and set aside.

4. Place the chicken breasts between two sheets of dampened parchment paper and flatten by hitting with a rolling pin or steak hammer.

5. Heat the oil in a large skillet. Season the chicken breasts on both sides and add to the pan. Cook 5 minutes, turn over and cook until tender, lightly browned, and cooked through. Remove the chicken and keep it warm.

6. Add the pepper strips, garlic, vinegar, and green onions to the pan and cook briefly until the vinegar loses its strong aroma.

7. Place the chicken breasts on serving plates. Spoon the pan juices over them.

8. Arrange the pepper mixture over the chicken and garnish with the sage leaves.

TIME: Preparation takes about 35-40 minutes and cooking takes about 10 minutes to char the peppers and about 15 minutes to finish the dish.

VARIATIONS: For convenience, the dish may be prepared with canned pimento instead of red bell peppers. These will be softer so cook the garlic, vinegar and onions to soften, and then add pimento.

SERVING SUGGESTION: If fresh sage is unavailable substitute coriander or parsley leaves as a garnish.

CHICKEN AND PANCETTA ROLLS

These rolls can be prepared in advance and kept chilled until cooking time. They make perfect dinner party fare.

SERVES 4

---

4 large chicken breasts, skinned
⅓ cup butter, softened
1 clove garlic, crushed
1 tbsp fresh oregano leaves or 1 tsp dried
   oregano
Salt and pepper
16 slices pancetta or prosciutto ham
Oil

---

1. Place each chicken breast between two sheets of damp parchment paper and beat out each piece with a rolling pin or steak hammer to flatten.

2. Mix the butter, garlic, oregano, salt, and pepper together. Spread half of the mixture over each chicken scallop, then lay 4 slices of pancetta on top of each. Roll up, tucking in the sides, and secure with cocktail sticks. Spread the remaining butter on the outside of each roll.

3. Cook the rolls under a medium hot preheated broiler for about 15-20 minutes, turning occasionally, until tender. Slice each roll into ½-inch rounds to serve.

TIME: Preparation takes about 20 minutes and cooking takes 15-20 minutes.

VARIATIONS: The chicken rolls can be sautéed in a skillet.

SERVING IDEAS: Serve with a fresh tomato sauce, and accompany with rice or new potatoes, and green beans.

BLUE CHEESE CHICKEN

These chicken parcels make a lovely and unusual dish for a dinner party.

SERVES 4

---

4 ounces blue cheese
⅔ cup butter
2 tbsps heavy cream
1 tbsp parsley, finely chopped
4 chicken breasts, skinned, boned, and
    beaten flat
8 slices bacon
2 tbsps oil
2 tbsps butter
⅔ cup dry white wine
⅔ cup chicken broth
Salt and pepper
2 tsps cornstarch

---

1. In a bowl, cream together the cheese and butter then add the cream to make a spreading consistency. Add the parsley.

2. Spread the cheese mixture on one side only of the chicken breasts, leaving a narrow border. Roll the breasts up, wrap each one in 2 bacon rashers and secure with a cocktail stick or skewer.

3. In a flameproof casserole, heat the oil and butter together and, when sizzling, brown the chicken parcels on each side until golden.

4. Pour in the wine, chicken broth and seasoning (use very little salt because the cheese stuffing will be quite salty). Bring to the boil, cover, and simmer gently for about 40 minutes, turning occasionally.

5. When cooked, transfer the chicken to a hot serving dish and remove the sticks or skewers.

6. Blend the cornstarch in a cup with a little cold water and add to the pan juices. Stir until the sauce thickens, adjust seasoning if necessary, and pour the gravy over the chicken. Serve at once.

TIME: Preparation takes about 25 minutes and cooking takes 45-50 minutes.

PREPARATION: The chicken parcels can be prepared in advance of cooking and refrigerated until required.

SERVING IDEAS: Serve with rice or new potatoes and broccoli.

CHICKEN WITH OLIVES

This is a chicken sauté dish for olive-lovers. Use more or less of them as your own taste dictates.

SERVES 4-6

2 tbsps olive oil

2 tbsps butter or margarine

3 pounds chicken portions

1 clove garlic, crushed

⅔ cup white wine

⅔ cup chicken broth

Salt and pepper

4 zucchini, cut in ½-inch pieces

20 pitted black and green olives

2 tbsps minced parsley

1. Heat the oil in a large skillet and add the butter or margarine. When foaming, add the chicken, skin side down, in one layer. Brown one side of the chicken and turn over to brown the other side. Cook the chicken in two batches if necessary.

2. Turn the chicken skin side up and add the garlic, wine, broth, salt, and pepper. Bring to the boil, cover the pan, and allow to simmer over a gentle heat for about 30-35 minutes.

3. Add the zucchini and cook for 10 minutes. Once the chicken and zucchini are done, add the olives and cook to heat through. Add the parsley and remove to a dish to serve.

TIME: Preparation takes about 25 minutes, cooking takes about 50-55 minutes.

SERVING IDEAS: Serve with rice or pasta and tomato salad.

VARIATIONS: Artichoke hearts may be used in place of the zucchini.

Chicken with Mango

The exotic flavors of mango and spices make a lovely combination in this dish.

SERVES 4

2 tbsps oil
1 tsp grated ginger
½ tsp ground cinnamon
4 chicken breasts, shredded
4 green onions, sliced diagonally
1 tbsp light soy sauce
1 chicken soup cube
⅔ cup water
1 tsp sugar
Salt and pepper
2 ripe mangoes, peeled and sliced, or 1 can
    sliced mangoes, drained
2 tbsps sherry

1. Heat a wok and add the oil. Add the ginger and cinnamon, and sauté for 30 seconds.

2. Add the chicken and green onions, and stir-fry for 5 minutes.

3. Add the light soy sauce, crumbled soup cube, water, and sugar, and bring to the boil.

4. Add salt and pepper to taste, and simmer for 15 minutes.

5. Add the mangoes and sherry, and simmer, uncovered, until the sauce has reduced and thickened.

TIME: Preparation takes about 10 minutes and cooking takes about 30 minutes.

PREPARATION: To cut up a fresh mango, first remove the peel then cut off the two rounded sides either side of the large flat stone.

SERVING IDEAS: Serve with boiled rice and snow-peas.

POULET GRILLÉ AU CITRON VERT

Crisp chicken with a tang of limes makes an elegant yet quickly-made entrée. From the warm regions of southern France, it is perfect for a summer meal.

SERVES 4

2 × 2-pound chickens
1 tsp chopped fresh basil
6 tbsps olive oil
4 limes
Salt, pepper, and sugar

1. Remove the leg ends, neck, and wing tips from the chickens and discard them.

2. Split the chickens in half, cutting away the backbone completely and discarding it.

3. Loosen the ball-and-socket joint in the leg and flatten each half of the chickens by hitting them with the flat side of a cleaver.

4. Season the chickens on both sides with salt and pepper and sprinkle with the basil. Place the chickens in a shallow dish and pour 2 tbsps of olive oil over. Squeeze the juice from 2 of the limes over the chicken.

Cover and leave to marinate in the refrigerator for 4 hours or overnight.

5. Heat the broiler to its highest setting and preheat the oven to 375°F. Remove the chicken from the marinade and place in the broiler pan. Cook one side until golden-brown and turn the pieces over. Sprinkle with 1 tbsp olive oil and brown the other side.

6. Place the chicken in a roasting tin, sprinkle with the remaining oil, and roast in the oven for about 25 minutes. Cut the peel from the remaining limes, removing all the white parts, and slice them thinly. When the chicken is cooked, place the lime slices on top, and sprinkle lightly with sugar. Place under the broiler for a few minutes to caramelize the sugar and cook the limes. Place the chickens in a serving dish and spoon any remaining marinade over them with the cooking juices. Serve immediately.

TIME: Preparation takes about 25 minutes, plus 4 hours marinating, cooking takes about 35 minutes.

WATCHPOINT: Sugar will burn and turn bitter quickly, so watch carefully while broiling.

VARIATIONS: If you can get limes fresh from the tree, use the lime leaves instead of basil, or use fresh lemons and lemon leaves.

357

CHICKEN AND AVOCADO SALAD

The creamy herb dressing complements this easy summer salad.

SERVES 4

8 anchovy fillets, soaked in milk, rinsed,
    and dried
1 green, onion, chopped
2 tbsps chopped fresh tarragon
3 tbsps chopped chives
4 tbsps minced parsley
⅔ cup mayonnaise
⅔ cup plain yogurt
2 tbsps tarragon vinegar
Pinch each sugar and cayenne pepper
1 large head lettuce
4 cups cooked chicken strips or cubes
1 avocado, peeled, and sliced or cubed
    coated with 1 tbsp lemon juice

1. Combine all the ingredients, except the lettuce, chicken and avocado in a food processor. Blend the ingredients until smooth, and well-mixed. Leave in the refrigerator at least 1 hour for the flavors to blend.

2. Shred the lettuce or tear into bite-size pieces and arrange on plates.

3. Top the lettuce with the cooked chicken cut into strips or cubes.

4. Spoon the dressing over the chicken and garnish the salad with the avocado. Serve any remaining dressing separately.

TIME: Preparation takes about 30 minutes plus 1 hour refrigeration for the dressing.

PREPARATION: Dressing may be prepared ahead of time and kept in the refrigerator for a day or two.

POULET FRICASSÉE

This is a white stew, enriched and thickened with an egg-and-cream mixture which is called a liaison.

SERVES 4

4 tbsps butter or margarine
1 × 3-pound chicken, quartered and
    skinned
2 tbsps flour
2½ cups chicken broth
Grated rind and juice of ½ lemon
1 bouquet garni (parsley, bayleaf, thyme)
12-16 pearl onions, peeled
3 cups button mushrooms, whole if small,
    quartered if large
2 egg yolks
6 tbsps heavy cream
3 tbsps milk (optional)
Salt and pepper
2 tbsps minced parsley and thyme
Lemon slices to garnish

1. Melt 3 tbsps of the butter in a large skillet. Add the chicken in one layer and cook over gentle heat for about 5 minutes, or until the chicken is no longer pink. Do not allow the chicken to brown. If necessary, cook the chicken in two batches. When the chicken is sufficiently cooked, remove it from the pan and set aside.

2. Stir the flour into the butter remaining in the pan and cook over very low heat, stirring continuously for about 1 minute, or until pale straw in color. Remove the pan from the heat and gradually beat in the chicken broth. When blended smoothly, add lemon rind and juice, return the pan to the heat, and bring to the boil, whisking constantly. Reduce the heat and allow the sauce to simmer for 1 minute.

3. Return the chicken to the pan with any juices that have accumulated, and add the bouquet garni. The sauce should almost cover the chicken. If it does not, add more broth or water. Bring to the boil, cover the pan, and reduce the heat. Allow the chicken to simmer gently for 30 minutes.

4. Meanwhile, melt the remaining butter in a small skillet, add the onions, cover, and cook very gently for 10 minutes. Do not allow the onions to brown. Remove the onions from the pan with a slotted spoon and add to the chicken. Cook the mushrooms in the remaining butter for 2 minutes. Set the mushrooms aside and add them to the chicken 10 minutes before the end of cooking.

5. Test the chicken by piercing a thigh portion with a sharp knife. If the juices run clear, the chicken is cooked. Transfer chicken and vegetables to a serving plate and discard the bouquet garni. Skim any fat from the sauce and boil it rapidly to reduce by almost half.

6. Blend the egg yolks and cream together and whisk in several spoonfuls of the hot sauce. Return the egg yolk and cream mixture to the remaining sauce and cook gently for 2-3 minutes. Stir the sauce constantly and do not allow it to boil. If very thick, add milk. Adjust the seasoning and stir in the parsley and thyme. Place the chicken in a serving dish and spoon the sauce over it. Garnish with lemon slices.

PECAN CHICKEN

Pecans can be used in both sweet and savory dishes. Here, their rich, sweet taste complements a stuffing for chicken.

SERVES 4

4 boned chicken breasts

3 tbsps butter or margarine

1 small onion, minced

⅓ cup pork sausagemeat

⅔ cup fresh breadcrumbs

1 tsp chopped thyme

1 tsp minced parsley

1 small egg, lightly beaten

½ cup pecan halves

1¼ cups chicken broth

1 tbsp all-purpose flour

2 tbsps sherry

Salt and pepper

Chopped parsley or 1 bunch watercress to
    garnish

1. Cut a small pocket in the thick side of each chicken breast, using a small knife.

2. Melt 1 tbsp of the butter in a small saucepan and add the onion. Cook for a few minutes over gentle heat to soften. Add the sausagemeat and turn up the heat to brown. Break up the sausagemeat with a fork as it cooks.

3. Drain off any excess fat, and add the breadcrumbs, herbs, and a pinch of salt and pepper. Allow to cool slightly and add enough egg to hold the mixture together. Chop the pecans, reserving 8 of them, and add to the stuffing.

4. Using a small teaspoon, fill the pocket in each chicken breast with some of the stuffing.

5. Melt another tbsp of the butter in a casserole and add the chicken breasts, skin side downward. Brown over moderate heat and turn over. Brown the other side quickly to seal.

6. Add the broth, cover the casserole, and cook for about 25-30 minutes in a preheated 350°F oven until tender.

7. When the chicken is cooked, remove it to a serving platter to keep warm. Reserve the cooking liquid.

8. Melt the remaining butter in a small saucepan and stir in the flour. Cook to a pale straw color. Strain the cooking liquid over it and add the sherry. Bring to the boil and stir constantly until thickened. Add the reserved pecans and seasoning.

9. Spoon some of the sauce over the chicken. Garnish with chopped parsley or a bunch of watercress.

TIME: Preparation takes about 30 minutes and cooking takes about 40 minutes.

VARIATIONS: Almonds, butternuts, hicory nuts or macadamias can be used instead. Crush macadamias roughly for the garnish and brown lightly in the butter before adding flour for the sauce.

SERVING IDEAS: Serve with a rice or sauté potatoes.

POULET SAUTÉ VALLÉE D'AUGE

This dish contains all the ingredients that Normandy is famous for – butter, cream, apples, and Calvados.

SERVES 4

4 tbsps butter or margarine

2 tbsps oil

1 × 3-pound chicken, cut into 8 portions

4 tbsps Calvados

6 tbsps chicken broth

2 apples, peeled, cored, and coarsely chopped

1 shallot, minced

2 sticks celery, finely chopped

½ tsp dried thyme, crumbled

2 egg yolks, lightly beaten

6 tbsps heavy cream

Salt and white pepper

Garnish

2 tbsps butter

2 apples, quartered, cored, and cut into cubes

Sugar

1 bunch watercress or small parsley sprigs

1. Heat half the butter and all of the oil in a large skillet over moderate heat. When the foam begins to subside, brown the chicken, a few pieces at a time, skin side downward, then turn it. When all the chicken is browned, pour off most of the fat from the pan and return the chicken to the pan.

2. Pour the Calvados into a small saucepan and warm over gentle heat. Ignite with a match and pour, while still flaming, over the chicken. Shake the skillet gently until the flames subside. If the Calvados should flare up, cover the pan immediately with the lid.

3. Remove the chicken from the pan and reserve it in a warm place. Pour the broth into the skillet and scrape any browned chicken juices from the bottom.

4. Melt the remaining butter in a small saucepan or skillet. Cook the chopped apples, shallot, celery, and the thyme for about 10 minutes or until soft but not browned.

5. Combine the apple mixture with the broth. Place the chicken in a Dutch oven or casserole and pour the sauce over it. Place on high heat. Bring to the boil, then reduce heat, cover the pan and simmer for 50 minutes.

6. When the chicken is cooked, beat the eggs and cream. With a whisk, gradually beat in some of the hot chicken cooking liquid. Pour the mixture back into a saucepan and cook over a low heat for 2-3 minutes, stirring constantly until the sauce thickens and coats the back of a spoon.

7. Season the sauce with salt and white pepper, and set aside.

8. To make the garnish, melt the butter in a small skillet and when foaming, add the apple. Toss over a high heat until beginning to soften. Sprinkle with sugar, and cook until the apple begins to caramelize.

9. To serve, coat the chicken with the sauce and decorate with watercress or parsley. Spoon the caramelized apples over the chicken.

Tarragon Chicken Pancakes

These attractive pancakes look sophisticated enough for a dinner party, but are so easy to make, you can indulge yourself at any time.

SERVES 4

1 cup whole-wheat flour
1 egg
1¼ cups milk
Oil for frying
3 tbsps butter
3 tbsps all-purpose flour
1¼ cups milk
Salt and black pepper, to taste
1 cup chopped, cooked chicken
1 avocado peeled, halved, pitted, and
    chopped
2 tsps lemon juice
1 tbsp chopped fresh tarragon

1. Put the whole-wheat flour into a large bowl, and make a slight well in the center. Break the egg into the well and begin to beat the egg carefully into the flour, incorporating only a little flour at a time.

2. Add the milk gradually to the egg-and-flour mixture, beating well between additions, until all the milk is incorporated and the mixture is smooth.

3. Heat a little oil in a small skillet, or crêpe pan, and cook about 2 tbsps of the mixture at a time, tipping and rotating the pan, so that it spreads evenly over the base to form a pancake. Flip the pancake over, to cook the other side.

4. Repeat this process until all the mixture has been used. Keep the pancakes warm, until required.

5. Melt the butter in a small saucepan, stir in the flour, and cook over a medium heat for 1-2 minutes. Remove from the heat and gradually stir in the milk. Bring to the boil, stirring, then simmer for 1-2 minutes. Season to taste.

6. Stir the chopped chicken, avocado, lemon juice, and tarragon into the sauce.

7. Fold each pancake in half, and then in half again, to form a triangle.

8. Carefully open part of the triangle out to form an envelope, and fill this with the chicken and avocado mixture.

TIME: Preparation takes about 25 minutes, and cooking takes about 25 minutes.

SERVING IDEAS: Serve piping hot, garnished with watercress and accompany with a crisp green salad.

CORNISH GAME HENS IN CURRY SAUCE

Whole roast Cornish game hens served with a spicy sauce makes a nice alternative to the usual curry.

SERVES 4

¼ cup butter

1 tsp oil

4 Cornish game hens

1 medium onion, finely chopped

1 clove garlic, crushed

2 tsps curry powder

⅔ cup chicken broth

Squeeze of lemon juice

2 tsps mango chutney

1 tbsp yellow raisins

2 tsps cornstarch

Cold water

---

1. Put butter and the oil in a roasting pan and place in an oven preheated to 350°F. When sizzling, remove from the oven, add the Cornish game hens and baste well.

Return the pan to the oven and roast the birds for about 35 minutes, basting at regular intervals until they are cooked. Test with a skewer inserted into the thickest part of the leg. If the liquid runs clear, the Cornish game hens are cooked. Remove from the roasting pan and keep them warm.

2. Drain off any excess fat from the pan and place it over a medium heat. Add the chopped onion and garlic, and sauté for a few minutes until softened. Reduce the heat, add the curry powder, and stir well for 2-3 minutes. Add the chicken broth and stir until it is bubbling. Add the squeeze of lemon juice, chutney, and yellow raisins.

3. In a cup, blend the cornstarch with a little cold water and add it to the sauce. Mix well and cook for a few more minutes. Pour over the Cornish game hens or serve separately.

TIME: Preparation takes about 10 minutes and cooking takes about 40 minutes.

VARIATIONS: Substitute other sweet pickles for mango chutney for a different flavor.

SERVING IDEAS: Serve with Indian breads and rice.

Niçoise Chicken

The combination of fresh herbs, tomatoes, and black olives brings the taste of Provence to your table.

SERVES 4

4 boned chicken breasts, unskinned
4 tbsps oil
2 tbsps lemon juice

Tapenade filling

4 cups large black olives, pitted
2 tbsps capers
1 clove garlic, coarsely chopped
4 anchovy fillets
2 tbsps olive oil

Raw tomato sauce

4 cups ripe tomatoes, skinned, de-seeded, and chopped
1 shallot, very finely chopped
2 tbsps minced parsley
2 tbsps chopped basil
2 tbsps white wine vinegar
2 tbsps olive oil
1 tbsp sugar
Salt and pepper
1 tbsp tomato paste (optional)

1. Cut a pocket in the thickest side of the chicken breasts.

2. Combine half the olives, half the capers, and the remaining ingredients for the tapenade in a blender or food processor. Work to a purée.

3. Add the remaining olives and capers and process a few times to chop them coarsely.

4. Fill the chicken breasts with the tapenade. Chill, to help filling to become firm.

5. Combine the oil and lemon juice and baste the skin side. Cook skin side down first for 10 minutes under a pre-heated medium-hot broiler. Turn over, baste again, and broil for another 10 minutes on the other side or until tender.

6. Meanwhile, combine the tomato sauce ingredients, and mix very well. Serve with the chicken.

TIME: Preparation takes about 30 minutes and cooking takes about 20 minutes.

PREPARATION: Both the filling and sauce can be made in advance and kept refrigerated.

SERVING IDEAS: Serve with new potatoes and small green beans.

Chicken
Notes

Chicken
Notes

VITAMIN RICH

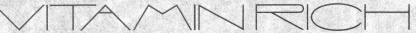

Introduction

Vitamins are substances that are vital to the maintenance of our bodies, yet so much is written concerning these invisible, potent elements in our food that few of us can tell fact from fiction.

There are many different vitamins, but we only need each in very small quantities, and if we maintain a well balanced and varied diet, the food we eat will generally provide us with more than enough vitamins for our daily needs. In certain circumstances, however, such as during pregnancy, illness or in old age, vitamin supplements may be required, and in these cases professional advice should be sought.

Vitamins are mainly identified by letter, but this in no way indicates their order of importance. In the case of vitamin B, there are several complex variations of vitamins within the one heading, and this is called the "B complex". The table below gives general guidance on some of the main vitamins, their source and function.

VITAMIN	SOURCE	FUNCTION
A	Oily fish, fats, offal, carrots, green vegetables, tomatoes, watercress	General growth, good eyesight, healthy skin
B.1	Yeast extract, wheatgerm, peanuts, whole-wheat bread, eggs, pulses	Assists the nervous system and metabolism. Is water soluble and therefore easily lost in cooking
B.2	Milk, dairy products, almonds, mushrooms, pulses, red meat, green vegetables	Assists the metabolism and maintains health of mouth, lips and skin
B.3	Milk, eggs, yeast extract, red meat, dried apricots	Essential to the nervous system
B.6	Yeast, whole cereal products, offal, dairy products, bananas, leaf vegetables	Helps production of new cells and promotes nervous health
B.12	Offal, meat, eggs, cheese, milk	Assists the production of red blood cells
C	Fruit and vegetables	Helps the body resist infection, promotes good skin, helps absorption of iron
D	Oily fish, fats, dairy products, offal, red meat	Helps promote strong bones and teeth. Is produced in the body when there is exposure to sunlight
E	Whole cereal products, eggs, nuts, vegetable oil and whole-wheat flour	Necessary for upkeep of blood cells, tissues and membranes
K	Widely available in many foods such as green vegetables, eggs and cereals	Helps blood to clot and assists in the healing of wounds

SERVES 6-8

COUNTRYSIDE TERRINE

This impressive terrine looks very professional yet is simple to make.

1lb pigs' liver, ground
¾lb lean pork, ground
½lb pork sausagemeat
1 clove garlic, minced
2 shallots, finely chopped
3¾ tbsps Cognac
¾ tsp ground allspice
Salt and freshly ground black pepper
1¼ tsps chopped fresh thyme or sage
½lb bacon, rind and any bones removed
2½ tbsps heavy cream
¼lb smoked tongue or ham, cut into ¼-inch cubes
1 large bay leaf

1. Preheat oven to 350°F.

2. In a large bowl, mix together the ground liver and pork, sausagemeat, garlic, shallots, Cognac, allspice, salt, pepper, and thyme. Stir with a wooden spoon until the ingredients are evenly mixed, but still coarse in texture.

3. Lay the strips of bacon on a flat surface and stretch them with the back of a knife.

4. Line a 2lb loaf pan evenly with the strips of bacon, overlapping each strip slightly to avoid any of the terrine mixture pushing through during cooking.

5. Add the cream, cubed tongue and ham to the liver and pork mixture, blending with your hands to keep the texture coarse.

6. Press the terrine mixture into the bacon-lined loaf pan, spreading it evenly, and pushing down lightly to remove any air bubbles.

7. Place the bay leaf on the top and fold over any over-lapping edges of bacon.

8. Cover the dish with a tight-fitting lid or two layers of aluminum foil.

9. Stand the loaf pan in a roasting pan and pour enough water around it to come halfway up the sides of the dish.

10. Bake the terrine for 2 hours, or until the juices run clear when a knife is inserted into the center.

11. Remove the lid or foil and replace this with some fresh foil.

12. Weigh down the terrine with cans of food or balance scale weights. Allow the terrine to cool at room temperature, then refrigerate it overnight if possible, still weighted, until it is completely chilled and firm.

13. To serve, remove the weights and foil and carefully turn the terrine out onto a serving plate. Scrape away any fat or jelly that may be on the outside of the terrine, and cut into slices just before serving.

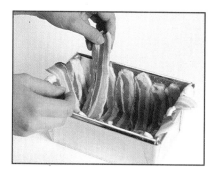

Step 4 Line a 2lb loaf pan evenly with the strips of bacon, overlapping each strip slightly.

Step 12 Cover the terrine with a double thickness of fresh foil and weight it down with cans or scale weights.

Cook's Notes

Time
Preparation takes about 25 minutes, plus refrigeration time. Cooking takes approximately 2 hours.

Freezing
This recipe will freeze well for up to 3 months. It should be packed in plastic wrap and not aluminum or metal foil.

Vitamin Content
This recipe is an extremely good source of all the B complex vitamins.

SERVES 4

TARAMASALATA

This well known, classic Greek appetizer is a delicious way of improving your intake of vitamins B and C.

¼ cup smoked cod roe
6 slices white bread, crusts removed
1 lemon
1 small onion, finely chopped
7½ tbsps olive oil
Black olives and chopped fresh parsley, for garnish

1. Cut the cod roe in half and scrape out the center into a bowl. Discard the skin.

Step 1 Cut the cods roe in half and carefully remove the soft insides using a small spoon. Discard the skin.

2. Put the bread into a bowl along with ⅔ cup warm water. Allow the bread to soak for about 10 minutes, then drain off the water and squeeze the bread until it is almost dry. Add the bread to the bowl containing the cod roe.

3. Squeeze the lemon and add the juice to the bread and roe, stirring it well.

4. Put the cod roe mixture into a blender or food processor, along with the onion. Process until the ingredients form a smooth paste.

Step 2 Squeeze the soaked bread to remove the excess moisture.

Step 5 Gradually add the oil to the fish mixture, beating continuously and very vigorously between additions to prevent curdling.

5. Return the blended cod roe mixture to a bowl and gradually beat in the oil, a little at a time, as if making mayonnaise. Beat the mixture very thoroughly between additions with an eggbeater or wooden spoon.

6. Refrigerate the taramasalata for at least ½ hour to chill thoroughly.

7. Transfer the mixture to a serving bowl and garnish with the black olives and chopped parsley.

Cook's Notes

Time
Preparation takes about 15-25 minutes, plus refrigeration time.

Cook's Tip
Prepare the taramasalata in advance, but remove it from the refrigerator 20 minutes before serving.

Serving Idea
Warm pitta breads and toasts, cut into fingers and used for dipping, make an excellent accompaniment.

Watchpoint
Do not add the oil too quickly or the mixture will curdle. If it does, add a little more soaked bread to draw it back together again.

Vitamin Content
Vitamin B complex and also vitamin C.

SERVES 4

WATERCRESS SOUP

Watercress is packed with vitamins A, C and K, and makes delicious soup.

¼ cup butter
1 leek, cleaned and thinly sliced
½lb potatoes, peeled and sliced thinly
2½ cups chicken stock
Pinch grated nutmeg
Salt and freshly ground black pepper
4 good bunches of watercress, washed and trimmed
3¾ tbsps cream
Few extra sprigs of watercress for garnish

1. Melt the butter in a large saucepan and gently cook the leek until it is just soft, stirring frequently to prevent it from browning.

2. Add the potatoes, stock, nutmeg and seasoning to the saucepan. Bring to the boil, then cover and simmer for 15 minutes.

3. Add the watercress and simmer for a further 10 minutes.

4. Cool the soup slightly, then using a food processor or blender, process until the vegetables are very finely chopped. Rinse the saucepan and stand a fine meshed sieve over the cleaned pan.

5. Push the puréed soup through the sieve using the back of a wooden spoon, working the watercress and vegetables through the mesh until only the tough stalks remain and the soup in the pan is a fine purée.

6. Adjust the seasoning and stir the cream into the soup. Reheat gently, taking care not to boil it. Serve garnished with the reserved watercress sprigs and a little cream if desired.

Step 1 Slowly soften the leek in the melted butter, stirring to prevent it from browning.

Step 4 Blend the soup in a food processor or liquidizer until the vegetables are very finely chopped.

Step 5 Push the soup through a fine meshed sieve using a wooden spoon, work the vegetable pulp through until only the tough stalks remain in the sieve.

Cook's Notes

Time
Preparation takes 15 minutes, cooking takes about 45 minutes.

Serving Idea
Chill the soup, and serve on a bed of crushed ice for a delicious variation.

Vitamin Content
Watercress is an excellent source of vitamins A, C and K.

SERVES 4

GAZPACHO

Gazpacho is a typically Spanish soup which is served well chilled, accompanied by a selection of fresh vegetables.

1lb ripe tomatoes
1 onion, peeled and chopped
1 green pepper, seeded and diced
½ cucumber, chopped
2½ tbsps stale white breadcrumbs
2 cloves garlic, minced
2½ tbsps red wine vinegar
2½ cups tomato juice
Salt and freshly ground black pepper

Accompaniments
½ cucumber, diced
10 green onions, chopped
½lb tomatoes, skinned, seeded and chopped
1 large green pepper, seeded and diced

1. Cut a small cross in the top of each of the ripe tomatoes, and plunge into a bowl of boiling water for a few seconds.

2. Carefully peel the skin away from the blanched tomatoes. Discard the skin and roughly chop the tomatoes, removing the tough stalk as you do.

3. Put the roughly chopped tomatoes into a liquidizer or food processor, along with the onion, pepper and cucumber. Blend until finely chopped.

4. Put the chopped vegetables into a bowl with the breadcrumbs, garlic, vinegar and tomato juice. Mix well to blend evenly and allow to stand for 15 minutes.

5. Season the tomato soup thoroughly, then push through a fine meshed sieve using the back of a wooden spoon and working well to press all the vegetables through, but keeping the pips out of the resulting purée.

6. Chill the soup well before serving, surrounded by bowls containing the accompaniments.

Step 2 Carefully peel the skin away from the blanched tomatoes using a sharp knife.

Step 5 Push the puréed vegetables through a nylon sieve using the back of a wooden spoon, working until all the pulp has been pressed through and the tomato pips remain.

Cook's Notes

Time
Preparation takes approximately 20 minutes, plus chiling time.

Serving Idea
Serve the individual bowls of soup on crushed ice.

Freezing
This soup is ideal for freezing.

Vitamin Content
Extremely high in vitamin C and the tomatoes are a good source of vitamin A.

SERVES 4

MUSSEL SOUP

Shellfish contain a multitude of vitamins and minerals, especially vitamins A, E, D and K, and this soup is, therefore, a delicious way of making sure you have a good supply of all of these.

2 quarts fresh mussels
¼ cup butter
2 onions, peeled and finely chopped
2 cloves garlic, minced
1¼ cups dry white wine
1¼ cups water
2½ tbsps lemon juice
1 cup fresh white breadcrumbs
2½ tbsps freshly chopped parsley
Salt and freshly ground black pepper

1. Scrub the mussels with a stiff brush and remove any barnacle shells or pieces of seaweed that are attached to them.

2. Tap each mussel sharply to make sure that it closes tightly.

3. Melt the butter in a large saucepan and gently fry the onions and garlic until they are soft, but not browned.

4. Add the mussels, wine, water and lemon juice to the pan, and bring to the boil. Season with salt and pepper,

then cover and cook for approximately 10 minutes or until all the mussel shells have completely opened.

5. Discard any mussels which have not opened fully.

6. Strain the mussels through a colander and return the juices and stock to the saucepan. Put the mussels in a serving tureen and keep warm.

7. Add the breadcrumbs and the parsley to the mussel juices and bring them to the boil. Adjust the seasoning, and serve over the mussels in the tureen. Serve immediately.

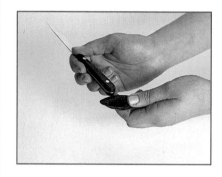

Step 2 Tap each mussel sharply with the handle of a knife to make sure that they shut tightly. Discard any that do not.

Step 1 Scrub the mussels with a stiff brush, removing any barnacles and pieces of seaweed which may be attached to the shells.

Step 4 Cook the mussels until they have all completely opened. Discard any that remain closed.

Cook's Notes

Time
Preparation takes 15 minutes, cooking takes approximately 20 minutes.

Watchpoint
When cooking fresh mussels, great care must be taken to ensure that they are safe to eat. Discard any that do not shut tightly before cooking, or do not open after cooking.

Serving Idea
Serve with warm French bread.

Vitamin Content
This soup contains vitamins A, B, E and K.

SERVES 4-6

SPINACH GNOCCHI

Gnocchi are delicious spinach and cheese dumplings which can be served as a healthy appetizer or snack.

¼lb chopped, frozen spinach
½lb ricotta cheese, crumbled
6 tbsps Parmesan cheese, finely grated
Salt and freshly ground pepper
Pinch freshly grated nutmeg
1 egg, lightly beaten
3½ tbsps butter

1. Defrost the spinach and press it between two plates to extract all the moisture.

Step 1 Press the spinach between two plates to remove excess moisture

2. Mix the spinach with the ricotta cheese, half the Parmesan cheese, the salt, pepper and nutmeg. Gradually add the egg, beating well until the mixture holds together when shaped.

3. With floured hands, shape the mixture into oval shapes. Use about 1 tbsp mixture for each gnocchi.

4. Lower into simmering water 3 or 4 at a time and allow to cook gently until the gnocchi float to the surface (about 1-2 minutes).

5. Remove with a draining spoon and place in a well buttered ovenproof dish.

6. When all the gnocchi are cooked, sprinkle on the re-

Step 3 Shape the gnocchi mixture with well-floured hands into ovals or balls.

Step 4 The gnocchi will float to the surface of the water when cooked. Remove with a draining spoon.

maining Parmesan cheese and dot with the remaining butter.

7. Reheat for 10 minutes in a hot oven and brown under a preheated broiler before serving.

Cook's Notes

Time
Preparation takes 15 minutes, cooking takes about 20 minutes.

Variation
Accompany with a tomato or cheese sauce and a salad for a light meal.

Vitamin Content
Spinach is a good source of vitamin A and the cheese provides vitamin B.

SERVES 4

ZUCCHINI SALAD

Raw vegetables are full of vitamins, and zucchini in particular has a delicious taste and texture.

½lb macaroni
4 tomatoes
4-5 zucchini, sliced thinly
8 stuffed green olives, sliced
7½ tbsps French dressing

1. Put the macaroni into a large saucepan and cover with boiling water. Add a little salt and simmer for 10 minutes, or until tender but still firm. Rinse in cold water and drain well.

2. Cut a small cross in the tops of each tomato and plunge into boiling water for 30 seconds.

3. Carefully remove the skins from the blanched tomatoes, using a sharp knife. Chop the tomatoes coarsely.

4. Mix all the ingredients in a large bowl and chill in the refrigerator for 30 minutes before serving.

Step 1 Rinse the macaroni in lots of cold water, then drain well forking it occasionally to prevent it sticking together.

Step 4 Mix all the ingredients together well, stirring thoroughly to blend the dressing in evenly.

Cook's Notes

Time
Preparation takes 15 minutes, cooking takes approximately 10 minutes.

Variation
Use any other pasta shape of your choice.

Preparation
If you prefer, the zucchini can be blanched in boiling water for 1 minute, then drained and cooled before mixing with the salad ingredients.

V Vitamin Content
This recipe is high in vitamin C from the zucchini and tomatoes, vitamin A from the tomatoes and vitamin B from the pasta.

388

SERVES 4-6

WATERCRESS AND ORANGE SALAD

This colorful salad combination is ideal served with cold meats or fish.

3 large bunches of watercress
4 oranges
7½ tbsps vegetable oil
Juice and rind of 1 orange
Pinch sugar
1¼ tsps lemon juice
Salt and freshly ground black pepper

1. Wash the watercress and carefully cut away any thick stalks. Break the watercress into small sprigs, discarding any yellow leaves.

2. Carefully remove the peel and pith from the oranges using a sharp knife. Catch any juice that spills in a small bowl.

3. Cutting carefully, remove the fleshy segments from between the thin membrane inside the orange. Squeeze any juice from the orange membrane into the bowl with the juice from the peel.

4. Arrange the watercress with the orange segments on a serving dish.

5. Put the remaining ingredients into the bowl with the reserved orange juice, and mix together well.

6. Pour the salad dressing over the oranges and watercress just before serving, to prevent the watercress from going limp.

Step 2 Carefully peel the oranges using a sharp knife, and collecting any juices in a small bowl.

Step 1 Break the watercress into small sprigs, discarding any yellow leaves.

Step 3 Cut the orange segments carefully from between the inner membranes using a sharp knife.

Cook's Notes

Time
Preparation takes approximately 20 minutes.

Serving Idea
Serve this salad on a bed of finely grated carrot.

Variation
Use grapefruit instead of the oranges, and chicory instead of the watercress.

Vitamin Content
This salad is extremely high in vitamin C, and if served with carrot is also a good source of vitamin A.

SERVES 4

CHEESE SALAD

This cheese salad is distinctly Greek in origin, and is ideal as an appetizer as well as being substantial enough to serve as a light lunch.

½ small head of endive or Crisp lettuce
½ small Iceberg lettuce
1 small cucumber
4 large tomatoes
8-10 pitted green or black olives, halved
1 medium-sized Spanish or red onion, peeled and sliced
¼lb feta cheese
6 tbsps olive oil
2½ tbsps red wine vinegar
1¼ tsps chopped fresh oregano
¾ tsp freshly ground sea salt
½ tsp freshly ground black pepper
¾ tsp ready made German mustard

1. Wash the endive and lettuce leaves thoroughly. Pat them dry with paper towels and tear into bite-sized pieces.

2. Thinly slice the cucumber, peeling it if you wish.

3. Cut a small cross into the top of each tomato and plunge into boiling water for 30 seconds.

4. Carefully peel the skins from the blanched tomatoes and slice the flesh crosswise.

5. Put the endive, lettuce, cucumber, tomatoes, olives and onion into a serving bowl and toss them together until well mixed.

6. Cut the feta cheese into ½-inch cubes. Sprinkle these

Step 1 Tear the lettuce and endive into pieces to prevent excessive bruising and destruction of vitamins in the leaves.

Step 4 Using a sharp knife, slice the peeled tomatoes crosswise.

cubes over the salad in the serving bowl.

7. Put all the remaining ingredients into a small bowl and whisk together using a fork or small eggbeater.

8. Pour the dressing over the salad and serve immediately.

Cook's Notes

Time
Preparation takes 10-12 minutes.

Serving Idea
Serve with jacket potatoes or crusty French bread.

Variation
Use Cheddar or Cheshire cheese in place of the feta cheese.

V **Vitamin Content**
Leaf vegetables such as lettuce are an excellent source of vitamin K. The tomatoes and cucumber are high in vitamin C and the cheese is a good source of vitamins B and D.

SERVES 6

ROGNONS À LA DIJONNAISE

This delicious French dish makes good use of vitamin-rich kidneys, an offal which is often underused in cookery.

½lbs lambs' kidneys
¼ cup unsalted butter
1-2 shallots, finely chopped
1¼ cups dry white wine
6 tbsps lightly salted butter, softened
3½ tbsps Dijon mustard
Salt, black pepper and lemon juice, to taste
2½ tbsps chopped parsley

Step 2 Trim away any hard core from the center of each kidney half using a small pair of sharp scissors.

Step 1 Trim the fat from each kidney and cut them in half lengthwise.

Step 8 Whisk the butter, mustard, salt, pepper and lemon juice into the reduced sauce using a fork or eggbeater and beating until it is thick.

1. Trim away any fat from the kidneys and slice them in half lengthwise.

2. Carefully snip out any hard core from the center using a pair of sharp scissors.

3. Melt the unsalted butter in a large frying pan and gently sauté the kidneys, uncovered, until they are light brown on all sides.

4. Remove the kidneys from the frying pan and keep them warm.

5. Add the shallots to the meat juices in the pan and cook

for about 1 minute, stirring frequently until they are just soft.

6. Add the wine and bring to the boil, stirring constantly and scraping the pan to remove any browned juices.

7. Boil this sauce rapidly for 3-4 minutes to reduce by about half. Remove the pan from the heat.

8. Put the softened butter into the pan with the mustard and seasonings. Whisk the mixture into the reduced sauce with an eggbeater or fork.

9. Return the pan to the heat and add the kidneys and the parsley. Heat very gently for 1-2 minutes, taking care not to boil the mixture any further. Serve immediately.

Cook's Notes

Time
Preparation takes approximately 25 minutes, cooking takes 15-17 minutes.

Watchpoint
Do not overcook the kidneys or they will become tough.

Vitamin Content
Kidneys are an excellent source of vitamins A, B and D.

SERVES 6

PORK PROVENÇALE

This hearty casserole of lean pork topped with potatoes is suitable for serving as a family meal, or as part of a dinner party menu.

2lbs pork fillets
¼ cup butter
¾lb onions, peeled and thinly sliced
15oz can tomatoes
Salt and freshly ground black pepper
½ tsp dried mixed herbs
1½lbs potatoes, peeled and thinly sliced
1 tbsp chopped parsley for garnish

1. Trim the pork of any surplus fat and slice into thin strips.

2. Melt half of the butter in a large sauté pan and gently fry

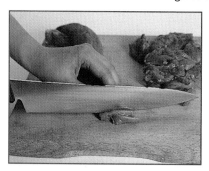

Step 1 Slice the pork into thin strips using a sharp knife.

Step 4 Gently fry the onions in the meat juices until they are just soft.

the slices of meat, stirring continuously to prevent them from burning.

3. Transfer the meat to a plate and set aside.

4. Stir the onions into the meat juices in the sauté pan and cook gently until just soft.

5. Add the tomatoes to the pan along with the salt, pepper and mixed herbs. Bring to the boil, then simmer gently for about 5 minutes, or until the sauce has reduced by about a third.

6. Arrange the meat, sauce and potatoes in layers in an ovenproof serving dish, finishing with a layer of potato.

7. Melt the remaining butter and brush the top layer of potato with this.

8. Cover the dish with a lid or foil, and cook in the oven for 1½ hours at 350°F.

9. Remove the lid from the dish and continue cooking for a further 30 minutes to brown the potatoes. Sprinkle with chopped parsley before serving.

Step 6 Arrange the meat, tomato sauce and potatoes in layers in an ovenproof serving dish.

Cook's Notes

Time
Preparation takes 25 minutes, cooking takes approximately 2 hours.

Freezing
This dish will freeze very well for up to 3 months. Freeze it before the final 30 minutes cooking time, then reheat by thawing and cooking uncovered for 1 hour at 350°F.

V

Vitamin Content
The vegetables are a good source of vitamin C, and the tomatoes also contain vitamin A.

SERVES 4

LENTIL KEDGEREE

This delicious recipe combines spiced rice with lentils and onion to make a substantial vegetarian lunch or supper dish.

1¼ cups basmati rice
1¼ cups red lentils
3¼ cups warm water
½ cup butter, or olive oil
1 medium-sized onion, peeled and chopped
¾ tsp crushed fresh root ginger
¾ tsp minced garlic
1-inch piece cinnamon stick
6 cloves
1 bay leaf
1¼ tsps ground coriander
½ tsp ground turmeric
¾ tsp freshly ground sea salt
2 green chilies, sliced in half lengthwise

Step 5 Stir-fry the rice and lentils together, making sure that they are evenly coated with the fat.

Step 6 Cook the rice and lentils until all the liquid has been absorbed, then fluff up with a fork before serving.

1. Wash the rice and the lentils thoroughly in cold water. Drain well.

2. Put the drained rice and lentils into a large bowl and cover with the warm water. Soak for 30 minutes, then drain very thoroughly, reserving the water.

3. Heat the butter or olive oil in a large saucepan. Stir in the onion and fry gently for 2-3 minutes, stirring to prevent it burning.

4. Add the ginger, garlic, cinnamon stick, cloves and bay leaf to the onion and continue frying for 1 minute.

5. Add the rice and lentils to the fried onion, along with the coriander, turmeric, salt and green chili. Stir over the heat for 2-3 minutes, until the rice and lentils are evenly coated with fat.

6. Pour the reserved water into the rice mixture and bring to the boil. Reduce the heat and cover the pan with a tight fitting lid. Simmer for 8-10 minutes without stirring, or until the water has been completely absorbed.

7. Stir the rice and lentils together, remove and discard the chilies, and serve immediately.

Cook's Notes

 Time
Preparation takes 15 minutes, plus soaking time. Cooking takes approximately 30 minutes.

 Watchpoint
Great care must be taken when using fresh chilies. If any of the juice gets into your mouth or eyes, rinse with lots of cold water.

 Vitamin Content
Lentils and rice are both excellent sources of vitamin B.

SERVES 4

LENTIL AND VEGETABLE CURRY

Lentils are a staple ingredient in Indian cookery. This delicious vegetable curry should be made using fresh spices for the best flavor.

1¼ cups whole green lentils
2½ tbsps vegetable oil
1¼ tsps salt
¾ tsp mustard seed, crushed
1 tsp ground coriander
¾ tsp ground cumin
2 dried red chilies, crushed
1 carrot, peeled and sliced diagonally
1 potato, peeled and cubed
6-8 okra, topped and tailed, then cut into 1-inch pieces
1 small zucchini, sliced diagonally
1 small eggplant, halved and sliced
1¾ cups water
6 curry leaves
1 green chili, slit in half and chopped
1¼ tsps fresh chopped mint
1¼ tbsps fresh chopped coriander
Coriander leaves for garnish

1. Wash the lentils in warm water until it runs clear. Drain well.

2. Put the lentils into a large saucepan and pour over 2½ cups water. Simmer gently for 15-20 minutes.

3. When the lentils are soft, beat with a potato masher or eggbeater until they are puréed.

4. In a large saucepan heat the oil and gently fry the mustard seed, ground coriander, cumin and dried chilies for 1 minute.

5. Add the vegetables to the spices and cook for 2 minutes, stirring all the time, to coat them evenly in the oil and spice mixture.

6. Add the water and the pureed lentils to the vegetable mixture and stir well.

7. Add the curry leaves, chopped chili, mint and fresh coriander, then cook for 15 minutes. Serve hot, garnished with coriander leaves.

Step 3 Using a potato masher or eggbeater, break up the cooked lentils until they are well puréed.

Step 6 Stir the puréed lentils into the vegetable mixture.

Cook's Notes

Time
Preparation takes about 10 minutes, cooking takes 20-30 minutes.

Variation
Use any combination of fresh vegetables to vary this curry.

Serving Idea
Serve with boiled basmati rice.

V **Vitamin Content**
Lentils provide an excellent source of vitamin B and fresh vegetables provide vitamins A and C.

SERVES 4

BEEF WITH PINEAPPLE AND PEPPERS

This delicious sweet and sour main course is distinctly Chinese in origin.

1lb fillet or rump steak
1 small pineapple
1 green pepper
1 red pepper
1¼ tbsps peanut oil
1 onion, peeled and roughly chopped
2 cloves garlic, minced
1-inch fresh root ginger, peeled and thinly sliced
1¼ tsps sesame oil
2½ tbsps light soy sauce
1¼ tbsps dark soy sauce
1¼ tsps sugar
1¼ tbsps brown sauce
5 tbsps water
Salt and freshly ground black pepper

1. Using a sharp knife, cut the steak into thin strips.

2. Carefully peel the pineapple and cut out any eyes using a sharp knife or potato peeler. Cut the pineapple into slices and chop them into bite-sized pieces, removing the hard core.

3. Slice the green and red peppers in half. Remove and discard the cores and seeds. Chop the pepper flesh into thin strips.

4. Heat the peanut oil in a wok or large frying pan, and gently fry the onion, garlic and ginger, stirring continuously until the onion has softened slightly.

5. Add the strips of beef and the strips of pepper, and continue stir-frying for 3 minutes.

6. Add the pineapple and stir-fry again for 2 minutes.

7. Remove the meat, vegetables and fruit from the wok, and put on a plate. Set aside.

8. Stir the sesame oil into the juices in the wok and add the soy sauces, sugar, brown sauce and water. Simmer rapidly for 30 seconds to reduce and thicken.

9. Stir the fruit, vegetables and beef back into the sauce. Season, heat through and serve immediately.

Step 1 Using a sharp knife, cut the steak into thin strips.

Step 5 Stir-fry the beef and peppers with the onions in the wok.

Cook's Notes

Time
Preparation takes 30 minutes, cooking takes about 10 minutes.

Serving Idea
Serve with spring rolls and plain boiled rice.

Watchpoint
Take care not to overcook the meat and vegetables, as this will greatly reduce the vitamin content of this dish.

Vitamin Content
Steak is an excellent source of vitamin B and the vegetables and fruit are high in vitamin C.

SERVES 4

KIDNEYS WITH BACON

Stir-frying is an excellent way of cooking kidneys, as the speedy cooking ensures that they do not become tough.

1lb lambs' kidneys
2½ tbsps vegetable oil
8 strips lean bacon, cut into 1-inch strips
1 onion, peeled and chopped
3 cloves garlic, minced
1¼ tbsps tomato chutney
1¼ tbsps light soy sauce
2½ tbsps water
Salt and freshly ground black pepper
1¼ tbsps cornstarch
3¾ tbsps sherry
2 tbsps fresh chopped parsley

1. Trim the fat from the kidneys and cut each kidney in half with a sharp knife.

2. Carefully trim out the hard core from the center of each kidney with a sharp knife or scissors.

3. Cut a lattice design on the back of each kidney using a sharp knife and taking care not to cut right through.

4. Put the kidneys into a bowl and stir in the sherry. Set aside for 15 minutes to marinate.

5. Heat the oil in a large wok and fry the bacon, onion and garlic for 5 minutes, stirring continuously to prevent burning. Remove from the wok and set aside on a plate.

6. Drain the kidneys and reserve the sherry marinade. Add the kidneys to the wok and stir for 3 minutes only.

7. Stir the tomato chutney, soy sauce and water into the wok with the kidneys, then add the bacon and onion mixture. Season with salt and pepper and stir-fry gently for 5 minutes.

8. Blend the cornstarch with the sherry marinade.

9. Add 1 tbsp parsley to the cornstarch mixture and stir

Step 2 Remove the hard core from each kidney half using a sharp knife or a small pair of scissors.

Step 3 Cut a lattice design on the backs of each kidney, using a sharp knife, and taking care not to cut right through.

Step 6 Stir-fry the kidneys until they are completely browned.

this into the kidneys in the wok, mixing well until the sauce is thickened and smooth. Serve at once, sprinkled with a little extra parsley.

Cook's Notes

Time
Preparation takes 20 minutes, cooking takes 25 minutes.

Serving Idea
Serve with rice or creamed potatoes.

Vitamin Content
All offal is an excellent source of vitamins A, B and D.

SERVES 4

MONKFISH AND PEPPER KEBABS

Monkfish is ideal for making kebabs as it can be cut into firm cubes, which do not disintegrate during cooking.

8 strips of lean bacon, rind removed
1lb monkfish, skinned and cut into 1-inch pieces
1 small green pepper, seeded and cut into 1-inch pieces
1 small red pepper, seeded and cut into 1-inch pieces
12 small mushroom caps
8 bay leaves
3¾ tbsps vegetable oil
½ cup dry white wine
5 tbsps tarragon vinegar
2 shallots, finely chopped
1¼ tbsps chopped fresh tarragon
1¼ tbsps chopped fresh chervil or parsley
1 cup butter, softened
Salt and freshly ground black pepper

Step 2 Wrap each piece of fish in one of the strips of bacon.

Step 8 Add the butter gradually into the simmering wine, whisking briskly to thicken the sauce.

1. Cut the bacon strips in half lengthwise and then again in half crosswise.

2. Put a piece of the fish onto each piece of bacon and roll the bacon around the piece of fish.

3. Thread the bacon and fish rolls onto large skewers, alternating them with slices of pepper, mushroom and the bay leaves.

4. Brush the kebabs with oil and arrange on a broiler pan.

5. Preheat the broiler to hot and cook the kebabs for 10-15 minutes, turning them frequently to prevent the kebabs from burning.

6. Heat the white wine, vinegar and shallots in a small saucepan until boiling. Cook rapidly to reduce by half.

7. Add the herbs and lower the heat.

8. Using a fork or eggbeater beat the butter bit by bit into the hot wine mixture, whisking rapidly until the sauce becomes thick. Season to taste.

9. Arrange the kebabs on a serving plate and serve with a little of the sauce spooned over and the remainder in a separate jug.

Cook's Notes

Time
Preparation takes 30 minutes, cooking will take about 25 minutes.

Preparation
When making the sauce it is important to whisk briskly, or it will not thicken sufficiently.

Vitamin Content
Fish is an excellent source of vitamins A and D. Bacon is a good source of vitamin B, and peppers are high in vitamin C.

SERVES 4

SWORDFISH STEAKS WITH GREEN PEPPERCORNS AND GARLIC SAUCE

Swordfish steaks are delicious and are easily available at most good fishmongers.

2½ tbsps fresh green peppercorns
7½ tbsps lemon juice
5 tbsps olive oil
Freshly ground sea salt
4 swordfish steaks
1 egg
1 clove garlic, roughly chopped
⅔ cup oil
2½ tsps fresh oregano
Salt and freshly ground black pepper

---

1. Crush the green peppercorns lightly using a pestle and mortar.

2. Mix the lemon juice, olive oil and salt into the lightly crushed green peppercorns.

3. Place the swordfish steaks in a shallow ovenproof dish and pour the lemon and oil mixture over each steak. Re-frigerate overnight, turning occasionally until the fish becomes opaque.

4. Using a blender or food processor, mix together the eggs and garlic.

5. With the machine still running, gradually pour the oil through the funnel in a thin steady stream onto the egg and garlic mixture. Continue to blend until the sauce is thick.

6. Remove the leaves from the oregano sprigs and chop them finely.

7. Preheat the broiler to hot and arrange the swordfish on the broiler pan.

8. Sprinkle the chopped oregano over the swordfish steaks and season well. Cook for 15 minutes, turning them frequently and basting with the lemon and pepper marinade.

9. When the steaks are cooked, place on a serving dish and spoon the garlic mayonnaise over.

Step 1 Lightly crush the green pepper-corns using a pestle and mortar.

Step 3 Marinate the swordfish steaks overnight, after such time they should be opaque.

Cook's Notes

Time
Preparation takes 25 minutes, plus overnight soaking.
Cooking takes about 15 minutes.

Variation
Substitute 2½ tbsps well rinsed canned green peppercorns in place of the fresh peppercorns if you cannot get these, and use tuna steaks instead of the swordfish if you prefer.

Serving Idea
Serve with jacket potatoes and fresh salad.

Vitamin Content
The fish contains vitamins B and D.

SERVES 4

TARRAGON GRILLED RED SNAPPER

Red snapper is a very decorative little fish that is now readily available at fishmongers and supermarkets.

4 large or 8 small red snapper, cleaned, scaled, washed and dried
4 or 8 sprigs of fresh tarragon
5 tbsps vegetable oil
2½ tbsps tarragon vinegar
Salt and freshly ground black pepper
1 egg
1¼ tsps Dijon mustard
½ cup sunflower oil
1¼ tbsps wine vinegar
1¼ tsps brandy
1¼ tbsps chopped fresh tarragon
1¼ tbsps chopped fresh parsley
1¼ tbsps heavy cream

1. Rub the inside of each fish with a teaspoonful of salt, scrubbing hard to remove any discolored membranes inside. Rinse thoroughly.

2. Place a sprig of fresh tarragon inside each fish.

3. Using a sharp knife, cut 2 diagonal slits on the side of each fish.

4. Mix together the vegetable oil, tarragon vinegar and a little salt and pepper in a small bowl.

5. Arrange the fish on a shallow dish and pour over the tarragon/vinegar marinade, brushing some of the mixture into the cuts on the side of the fish. Refrigerate for 30 minutes.

6. Put the egg into a blender or food processor along with the mustard and a little salt and pepper. Process for 2-3 seconds to mix.

7 With the machine running, add the oil through the funnel in a thin steady stream. Continue blending the dressing until it is thick and creamy.

8. Add the vinegar, brandy and herbs, and process for a further 30 seconds to mix well.

9. Lightly beat the cream with a small eggbeater until it thickens.

10. Fold the slightly thickened cream carefully into the oil and vinegar dressing. Pour into a serving dish and refrigerate until ready to use.

11. Arrange the fish on a broiler pan and cook under a preheated hot broiler for 5-8 minutes per side, depending on the size of the fish. Baste frequently with the marinade while cooking, then serve with a little of the sauce and some sprigs of fresh tarragon, if you like.

Step 1 Rub the insides of each fish with a teaspoonful of salt, scrubbing briskly to remove any discolored membranes.

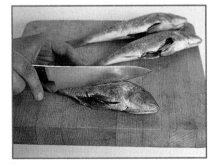

Step 3 Using a sharp knife, cut 2 diagonal slits on the side of each fish, taking great care not to cut right through the flesh.

Cook's Notes

 Time
Preparation takes about 15 minutes, cooking takes 10-16 minutes.

 Variation
Use herrings or mackerel in place of the mullet.

 Vitamin Content
All fish is an excellent source of vitamins A and D.

SERVES 4

DUCK WITH ORANGES

This traditional combination is given extra flavor by cooking the duck in a distinctly oriental manner.

3 oranges
1 duck
1 tbsp butter
1¼ tbsps oil
1¼ cups light chicken stock
⅓ cup red wine
2½ tbsps redcurrant jelly
Salt and freshly ground black pepper
1¼ tsps arrowroot
1¼ tbsps cold water

1. Using a potato peeler carefully pare the rind thinly off 2 of the oranges.

Step 2 Using a sharp knife carefully cut the parred orange rind into very thin strips.

2. Cut the rind into very fine shreds using a sharp knife. Put the shredded orange rind into a small bowl and cover with boiling water. Set aside to blanch for 5 minutes, then drain.

3. Squeeze the juice from the 2 oranges. Set this aside.

4. Cut away the peel and the pith from the remaining orange and then slice the flesh into thin rounds. Set aside.

5. Wash the duck and dry well with paper towels.

6. Put the butter and the oil into a large wok and heat until melted. Add the duck and fry, turning frequently until it is brown all over.

7. Remove the duck from the wok, cool slightly and using poultry shears, cut away the leg and wing ends. Cut the duck in half lengthwise and then cut each half into 1-inch strips.

8. Remove the fat from the wok and return the duck to the wok. Add the stock, red wine, redcurrant jelly, squeezed orange juice, and the well drained strips of rind. Bring to the boil, then season to taste. Reduce the heat, cover the

Step 7 Cut each half of the duck into 1-inch strips using poultry shears or a very sharp knife.

wok and simmer the duck gently for 20 minutes, or until well cooked.

9. Skim away any surface fat and thicken the sauce by mixing the arrowroot with the water and stirring into the wok. Bring the mixture back to the boil and simmer for a further 5 minutes, or until the sauce is thick.

10. Arrange the duck on a serving plate and garnish with the orange slices and some additional watercress if liked.

Cook's Notes

Time
Preparation takes 30 minutes, cooking takes 35 minutes.

Serving Idea
Serve with plain boiled rice or sautéed potatoes.

V **Vitamin Content**
Duck is a good source of vitamin B, and oranges are an excellent source of vitamin C.

SERVES 4-6

LIVER WITH ONIONS

This dish is simple to prepare, but absolutely delicious and highly nutritious.

1lb onions
1lb lambs' liver, thinly sliced
Salt and freshly ground black pepper
⅓ cup all-purpose flour
3¾ tbsps vegetable oil
2 tbsps butter
2½ tbsps fresh chopped parsley

1. Peel the onions and slice thinly, keeping each slice in

Step 2 Trim away any pipes or tubes from the liver slices using a small pair of scissors or a sharp knife

Step 1 Using a sharp knife, thinly slice the peeled onions, keeping them in rings if possible.

Step 3 Coat each liver slice thoroughly with the seasoned flour, pressing it gently onto the surface.

circles if possible.

2. Trim away any large pipes or tubes from the liver using a pair of small scissors or a sharp knife.

3. Mix the seasoning and the flour together on a plate and lay the slices of liver into the flour, turning them and pressing them gently to coat all over evenly.

4. Put the oil and the butter into a large frying pan. Heat

gently until foaming.

5. Add the onion rings and fry until just golden.

6. Add the liver slices and fry for 3-5 minutes on each side until well cooked. Cooking time will depend on the thickness of each slice.

7. Stir the parsley into the liver and onions and serve immediately on hot plates.

Cook's Notes

 Time
Preparation takes 15 minutes, cooking takes about 10 minutes.

 Variation
Add 4 oz shredded bacon to this recipe with the onions.

 Serving Idea
Serve with creamed potatoes and green vegetables.

 Watchpoint
Do not overcook liver or any offal, as it will toughen.

 Freezing
Liver freezes well, but should be frozen before cooking.

 Vitamin Content
Onions are a good source of vitamin C. Liver is an excellent source of vitamins A, B and D.

SERVES 4

'BURNT' CREAM

The gentle cooking of this creamy dessert ensures that the valuable vitamin content in the cream is not decreased in any way.

1¼ cups whole milk
1¼ cups heavy cream
5 egg yolks
⅓ cup superfine sugar
Few drops of vanilla extract
½ cup Barbados sugar
⅔ cup whipped heavy cream (optional)

1. Put the milk and the cream into a heavy-based sauce-pan and heat gently until almost boiling. Remove from the heat and set aside to cool slightly.

2. Put the egg yolks, sugar and vanilla into a bowl and whip vigorously until they become light and creamy.

3. Strain the milk and cream through a sieve into a large jug.

4. Gradually add the strained milk and cream onto the egg yolk mixture, beating vigorously and constantly as you pour.

5. Rinse the saucepan clean and dry it. Return the egg yolk and cream mixture to the saucepan and heat gently, stirring constantly with a wooden spoon, until the mixture becomes a thick and creamy custard.

6. Do not allow the custard to boil or it will curdle.

7. Strain the custard through a sieve into a shallow serving dish. The custard should come almost to the top of the dish.

8. Stand the custard in a refrigerator and chill until set, preferably overnight.

9. Sprinkle the brown sugar thickly over the surface of the set custard

10. Stand the custard under a preheated hot broiler and cook until the sugar melts and caramelizes. Remove the 'burnt cream' from the broiler and chill it until the sugar layer is a hard, crisp caramel.

11. Serve very cold, decorated with piped heavy cream if desired.

Step 2 Whip the egg yolk, sugar and vanilla together until thick and creamy. The mixture is ready when you can leave a trail on the surface as it is lifted with a spoon or eggbeater.

Step 10 Broil the brown sugar on the top of the chilled custard until it melts and caramelizes.

Cook's Notes

Time
Preparation takes about 15 minutes, cooking takes about 30 minutes, plus chiling time.

Preparation
The custard is ready when the mixture coats the back of a wooden spoon.

Watchpoint
Take great care never to boil the mixture at any stage, or it will curdle. If this should happen, blend 2 tbsps cornstarch with a little milk and stir this into the hot curdled mixture, continue stirring until it thickens and becomes smooth.

Serving Idea
Serve with crisp crackers or a fresh fruit salad.

Vitamin Content
Cream and milk contain vitamins A, B and D. Never expose cream or milk to sunlight, as this will destroy the valuable vitamin B.

SERVES 4

RICE PUDDING

Rice pudding has always been a firm family favorite and this recipe adds spices to make it special enough even for dinner parties.

¼ cup unsalted butter
1 bay leaf, crumbled
1-inch piece cinnamon stick, crushed
1 cup pudding rice, washed and drained
5 cups milk
1¾ cups evaporated milk
¾ cup granulated sugar
½ cup chopped blanched almonds
Seeds of 8 small cardamoms, crushed
¼ cup pistachio nuts, chopped or cut into slivers

1. Melt the butter in a saucepan and fry the bay leaf and cinnamon for 1 minute.

2. Add the rice and stir well to coat evenly with the melted fat.

3. Add the milk and bring the mixture to the boil, then reduce the heat and simmer for 40-50 minutes, stirring occasionally to prevent the rice from sticking to the pan.

4. Add the sugar and the evaporated milk to the rice mixture and continue cooking for a further 20-30 minutes, stirring frequently to prevent burning.

5. It is important to keep stirring the mixture during this cooking time to bring up thin layers of light brown skin which form on the base of the saucepan. This is what gives the pudding its rich, reddish tinge and caramel flavor.

6. Add the chopped almonds and the crushed cardamom seeds to the rice puddings. Stir well and pour into a large serving dish.

7. Decorate the top of the rice pudding with the slivered pistachio nuts, and serve hot or cold.

Step 5 Stir the pudding frequently to bring up the thin layers of light brown skin which will form on the base of the saucepan during cooking.

Step 2 Stir the rice into the fried bay leaf and cinnamon, mixing well to coat each grain evenly with the flavored fat.

Step 7 Decorate the pudding with slivered pistachios before serving.

Cook's Notes

Time
Preparation takes 10 minutes, cooking takes 1 hour 30 minutes.

Watchpoint
Frequent stirring is important in this recipe to prevent the sugar from caramelizing too much and giving a bitter flavor to the dessert.

Vitamin Content
Rice contains vitamins from the B group, and milk and evaporated milk contain vitamins A and D.

SERVES 4-6

SUMMER PUDDING

This favorite summer dessert simply oozes vitamins and flavor.

1½lbs fresh soft fruit, e.g. raspberries, strawberries, rhubarb, redcurrants, blackcurrants or any combination of these fruits
¾ cup granulated sugar
10 thick slices of white bread, crusts removed
1¾ cups fresh cream
1lb fresh whole raspberries

1. Put the 1½lbs of mixed fruit into a large saucepan and stir in the sugar.

2. Heat the fruit gently, shaking the pan vigorously so that the sugar dissolves but the fruit stays as intact as possible. Remove from the heat and cool completely.

3. Cut the slices of bread into thick fingers and use them to line the base and sides of a medium-sized mixing bowl. Press the slices of bread together as firmly as possible to avoid leaving any gaps between them.

4. Pour the cooled fruit and the juice into the center of the pudding, and cover the top completely with the remaining bread. Press down firmly.

5. Place a saucer or small plate over the top of the pudding and weigh this down with cans of food or balance scale weights.

6. Chill the pudding overnight in the refrigerator.

7. Remove the weights and the small plate or saucer. Loosen the sides of the pudding carefully with a round bladed knife, and invert a serving plate over the top of the bowl.

8. Carefully turn both the serving plate and the bowl over, and shake gently. The pudding should drop onto the serving plate.

9. Whip the cream until it is thick, then spread approximately half of the cream over the summer pudding.

Step 2 Shake the fruit and sugar together gently over a low heat until the sugar dissolves, but the fruit remains mainly intact.

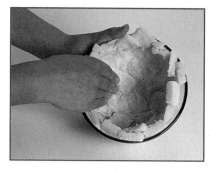

Step 3 Press the slices of bread together well around the sides and the base of the mixing bowl, trying to make sure that there are no gaps in between each slice.

Step 10 Press the whole raspberries into the cream layer covering the summer pudding.

10. Press the fresh raspberries onto the cream in a thick layer all over the pudding, and pipe the remaining cream in small rosettes between the gaps.

11. Chill well, before serving.

Cook's Notes

Time
Preparation takes approximately 30 minutes, plus overnight chiling.

Freezing
This pudding freezes extremely well, but should be decorated with the fruit and cream after it has been thawed.

Vitamin Content
The bread contains vitamin B, the fruit contains vitamin C, and the cream contains vitamin D.

SERVES 4-6

CARROTELLA

Carrots have a natural sweetness which lends itself to sweet as well as savory dishes. Carrotella is a sweet and spicy dessert which should be served very cold.

5 cups milk
1lb carrots, peeled and finely grated
1 cup evaporated milk
½ cup granulated sugar
⅓ cup golden raisins
Seeds of 8 small cardamoms, crushed
2 drops vanilla extract
¼ cup chopped blanched almonds
¼ cup chopped pistachio nuts

1. Put the milk into a saucepan and simmer over a low heat until reduced to about 3½ cups.

2. Add the carrots. Cover and cook over a medium heat for approximately 15 minutes, or until the carrots have begun to soften.

3. Stir in the evaporated milk, sugar and golden raisins, re-cover and simmer gently for about another 5 minutes.

4. Remove the saucepan from the heat, then stir in the crushed cardamom seed and vanilla essence.

5. Beat the carrotella briskly to break up the carrots, then turn into a serving dish and cool slightly.

6. Sprinkle the nuts on top and chill very well before serving.

Step 2 Cook the carrots over a medium heat for 15 minutes, or until they have softened and are breaking up.

Step 6 Sprinkle the partially chilled carrotella with the chopped nuts.

Cook's Notes

Time
Preparation takes 15 minutes. Cooking takes 40 minutes, plus chiling time.

Serving Idea
Serve with a spoonful of chilled fromage frais.

Variation
Use rosewater instead of the vanilla extract, and finely chopped hazelnuts instead of the pistachio nuts.

Vitamin Content
Milk and evaporated milk contain vitamins D and E. Carrots are an excellent source of vitamins A and C.

SERVES 4

BROWN BREAD ICE CREAM

This unusual ice cream is easy to make and is an ideal standby dessert to keep in the freezer.

2 egg yolks
⅓ cup superfine sugar
2 cups heavy or whipping cream
Few drops of vanilla extract
½ cup water
½ cup Barbados sugar
7 tbsps fresh brown breadcrumbs
1¼ tsps ground cinnamon

1. Put the egg yolks and the superfine sugar into a bowl, and whisk vigorously with an electric beater until thick, pale and creamy.

2. Pour in the heavy cream and continue whisking until thick and creamy.

3. Beat in the vanilla extract, then pour the cream mixture into a freezer-proof container and freeze for 1 hour, or until beginning to set around the edges.

4. Break the ice cream away from the edges and whisk with the electric beater until the ice crystals have broken. Return to the freezer and chill for a further hour. Repeat this procedure 2 more times, then freeze completely.

5. Put the water and the brown sugar into a small saucepan and heat gently, stirring until the sugar has dissolved. Bring the mixture to the boil and boil rapidly until the sugar caramelizes.

6. Remove the caramel sugar from the heat and stir in the breadcrumbs and the cinnamon.

7. Spread the caramel mixture onto a cookie sheet lined with oiled wax paper, and allow to set.

8. Break up the caramelized breadcrumbs by placing

Step 1 Whisk the eggs and superfine sugar together until they are pale, thick and creamy.

Step 7 When cooled, the caramelized breadcrumbs should set completely hard.

them in plastic food bags and crushing with a rolling pin.

9. Turn the frozen ice cream into a large bowl and break it up with a fork.

10. Allow the ice cream to soften slightly, then stir in the caramelized breadcrumbs, mixing thoroughly to blend evenly.

11. Return the brown bread ice cream to the freezer tray and freeze completely.

12. Allow the mixture to soften for 10 minutes before serving in scoops.

Cook's Notes

Time
Preparation takes approximately 40 minutes, plus freezing time.

Preparation
Be very careful when making the caramel sugar as it can burn very easily.

Vitamin Content
Wholemeal bread contains vitamins B and E. Fresh cream contains vitamins A, B and D.

SERVES 4-6

FRUITY BREAD PUDDING

This traditional family pudding is made extra nutritious by using whole-wheat bread and a rich assortment of dried fruits.

¾ cup raisins
¾ cup currants
¾ cup golden raisins
¾ cup prunes, stoned and chopped
Finely grated rind and juice of 1 orange
8 thick slices whole-wheat bread, crusts removed
¼ cup butter, softened
½ cup Barbados sugar
1¼ cups whole milk
2 eggs, lightly beaten
½ tsp ground nutmeg
½ tsp ground cinnamon

1. Put all the dried fruit, orange rind and orange juice into a large bowl and mix well.

2. Put about half of the mixed fruit into the base of a lightly buttered ovenproof serving dish.

3. Spread the bread with the butter and cut it into small squares.

4. Arrange half of the bread squares over the fruit in the base of the serving dish.

5. Sprinkle with half of the brown sugar, then repeat the layers once again, finishing with a layer of sugar.

6. Whisk together the milk, eggs, nutmeg and cinnamon. Pour the mixture over the bread pudding and allow to stand for 1 hour.

7. Bake the pudding in a preheated oven, 375°F, for about 35-40 minutes, or until crisp on top but still soft at the bottom. Serve very hot.

Step 5 Arrange the fruit, bread and sugar in layers in an ovenproof dish.

Step 3 Cut the buttered bread into squares approximately 2 inches.

Step 6 Pour the egg and milk mixture over the bread and fruit, taking care not to dislodge the pieces of bread.

Cook's Notes

Time
Preparation takes 15 minutes, plus 1 hour soaking. Cooking takes 40 minutes.

Freezing
This pudding will freeze well and should be reheated for 20 minutes in a hot oven, 375°F. Cover the top with foil to prevent it from burning or browning further.

Vitamin Content
Dried fruit is an excellent source of vitamin C, and milk and eggs are good sources of vitamins A, B, D and E. Whole-wheat bread is an excellent source of vitamins B and E.

Vitamin Rich
Notes

Vitamin Rich
Notes

FISH &
SEAFOOD
COOKING

Introduction

Fish and seafood are among our most valuable natural assets. They are high in easily digestible protein, low in fat, offer endless variety and are quick and easy to cook: The popularity of fish and seafood has waned in the recent past due to its unjustified reputation for being difficult to prepare. Today, however, people acknowledge that although it needs a little preparation, this is mostly very straightforward and is well worth the effort. And, of course, if you don't want to put in any effort, the selection of ready-prepared fresh and frozen fish in the supermarket grows larger every year.

Better refrigeration techniques have meant more and more consumers can now enjoy varieties of fish and seafood that once would have been considered very exotic. And unusual fish, that would once have been impossible to find, are now regularly available at supermarkets. The most important thing to bear in mind when buying fish and seafood is freshness. Buy the freshest produce you possibly can and you will not go wrong. Find a source that has a very high turnover and examine the produce carefully before you buy it. If it is fish, it should not smell "fishy" as this means it is past its best. It should be moist, the flesh firm and the eyes bright. Seafood, too, should be firm, have a good color and look moist and fresh.

Cooking fish and seafood is much more simple than many people imagine and it has the added advantage of being quick to cook. The essential point to remember is never to overcook fish and seafood as it quickly loses its lovely tasty juiciness. The best way to treat it, therefore, is to combine it with ingredients and sauces that enhance, rather than mask, this fresh flavor. It is for this reason that stuffed fish dishes are so popular – all the flavor of the fish is to the fore with a little stuffing to add extra "bite." Mixing fish and seafood in chowders is also wonderful as a whole variety of flavors such as crab, shrimp and mussels can be blended with your own favorite flavorings to create a dish that is completely original!

The recipes in this book highlight some of the tastiest recipes for fish and seafood, whether for a simple lunch dish or a family meal, but they should also inspire the cook to experiment with the expanded range of fish and seafood now available.

Contents

HOT AND SOUR SEAFOOD SOUP

This interesting combination of flavors and ingredients makes a sophisticated beginning to an informal meal.

SERVES 4

3 dried Chinese mushrooms
1 tbsp vegetable oil
¾ cup shrimp, shelled and deveined
1 red chili, seeded and finely sliced
1 green chili, seeded and finely sliced
½ tsp lemon rind, cut into thin slivers
2 green onions, sliced
2½ cups fish stock
1 tbsp Worcestershire sauce
1 tbsp light soy sauce
2 oz whitefish fillets
1 cake of fresh bean curd, diced
1 tbsp lemon juice
1 tsp sesame seeds
Salt and pepper
1 tsp fresh coriander, finely chopped
   (optional)

1. Soak the mushrooms in enough hot water to cover for 20 minutes, or until completely reconstituted.

2. Heat the vegetable oil in a large wok or frying pan, and add the shrimp, chilies, lemon rind and green onions. Stir-fry quickly for 1 minute.

3. Add the stock, the Worcestershire sauce and the soy sauce. Bring this mixture to a boil, reduce the heat and simmer for 5 minutes. Season to taste.

4. Remove the hard stalks from the mushrooms and discard them. Slice the caps very finely.

5. Cut the whitefish fillets into small dice, and add them to the soup, together with the bean curd and Chinese mushrooms. Simmer for a further 5 minutes.

6. Stir in the lemon juice and sesame seeds. Adjust the seasoning and serve sprinkled with chopped fresh coriander leaves, if desired.

TIME Preparation takes about 20 minutes, cooking takes about 20 minutes.

COOK'S TIP If you cannot buy coriander use parsley instead.

CHILLED SHRIMP, AVOCADO AND CUCUMBER SOUP

Avocado and cucumber give this soup its pretty color.

SERVES 4

---

8 oz unpeeled shrimp
1 large ripe avocado
1 cucumber
1 small bunch dill
Juice of half a lemon
1¼ cups chicken stock
2½ cups plain yogurt
Salt and pepper

---

1. Peel all the shrimp, reserving the shells. Add shells to chicken stock and bring to a boil. Allow to simmer for about 15 minutes. Cool and strain.

2. Peel the avocado and cut it into pieces. Cut 8 thin slices from the cucumber and peel the rest. Remove seeds and chop the cucumber coarsely.

3. Put the avocado and cucumber into a food processor or blender and process until smooth. Add a squeeze of lemon juice, and pour on the cold chicken stock.

4. Reserve a sprig of dill for garnish, and add the rest to the mixture in the processor and blend again.

5. Add about 1½ cups of yogurt to the processor and blend until smooth. Add salt and pepper. Stir in the peeled shrimp by hand, reserving a few as garnish.

6. Chill the soup well. Serve in individual bowls, garnished with a spoonful of yogurt, a sprig of dill, and thinly sliced rounds of cucumber.

TIME Preparation takes 15 minutes, cooking takes 15 minutes.

CRABMEAT BALLS

*Delicious an appetizer or a cocktail snack, crabmeat balls can be made ahead,
then coated and fried at the last minute.*

SERVES 6-8

1 lb fresh or frozen crabmeat, chopped
   finely
4 slices white bread, crusts removed and
   made into crumbs
1 tbsp butter or margarine
1 tbsp flour
½ cub milk
½ red or green chili, seeded and finely
   chopped
1 green onion, finely chopped
1 tbsp chopped parsley
Salt
Flour
2 eggs, beaten
Dry bread crumbs
Oil for frying

1. Combine the crabmeat with the fresh
bread crumbs and set aside.

2. Melt the butter and add the flour off the
heat. Stir in the milk and return to moderate
heat. Bring to a boil, stirring constantly.

3. Stir the white sauce into the crabmeat
and bread crumbs, adding the chili, onion
and parsley. Season with salt to taste, cover
and allow to cool completely.

4. Shape the cold mixture into 1 inch balls
with floured hands.

5. Coat with beaten egg using a fork to turn
balls in the mixture or use a pastry brush to
coat with egg.

6. Coat with the dry bread crumbs.

7. Fry in oil in a deep frying pan, saucepan
or deep-fat fryer at 350°F until golden
brown and crisp, about 3 minutes per batch
of 6. Turn occasionally while frying.

8. Drain on paper towels and sprinkle
lightly with salt.

TIME Preparation takes about 40-50 minutes, including time for the mixture
to cool. A batch of 6 balls takes about 3 minutes to cook.

MUSSELS MARINIÈRE

*Brittany and Normandy are famous for mussels and for cream and
so cooks combined the two in one perfect seafood dish.*

SERVES 4

---

3 quarts mussels
1½ cups white wine
4 shallots, finely chopped
1 clove garlic, crushed
1 bouquet garni
½ cup heavy cream
3 tbsps butter, cut into small pieces
2 tbsps fresh parsley, finely chopped
Salt and pepper

---

1. Scrub the mussels well and remove the beards and any barnacles from the shells. Discard any mussels that have cracked shells and do not close when tapped. Put the mussels into a large bowl and soak in cold water for at least 1 hour. Meanwhile, chop the parsley very finely.

2. Bring the wine to the boil in a large saucepan and add the shallots, garlic and bouquet garni. Add the mussels, cover the pan and cook for 5 minutes. Shake the pan or stir the mussels around frequently until the shells open. Lift out the mussels into a large soup tureen or individual serving bowls. Discard any mussels that have not opened.

3. Reduce the cooking liquid by about half and strain into another saucepan. Add the cream and bring to the boil to thicken slightly. Beat in the butter, a few pieces at a time. Season to taste, add the parsley and pour the sauce over the mussels to serve.

TIME Preparation takes about 30 minutes, cooking takes about 15 minutes.

SERVING IDEAS Serve as a first course with French bread, or double the quantity of mussels to serve for a light main course.

FISH TEMPURA

This is a traditional Japanese dish, which can be served as an unusual appetizer.

SERVES 4

12 uncooked large shrimp

2 whitefish fillets, skinned and cut into
   2 ¾-inch strips

Small whole fish, e.g. smelt or whitebait

2 squid, cleaned and cut into 3-inch strips

2 tbsps all-purpose flour

1 egg yolk

½ cup iced water

1 cup all-purpose flour

Oil for frying

6 tbsps soy sauce

Juice and finely grated rind of 2 limes

4 tbsps dry sherry

1. Shell the shrimp, leaving the tails intact. Wash the fish and the squid and pat dry. Sprinkle them all with the 2 tbsps flour.

2. Make a batter by beating together the egg yolk and water. Sieve in the 1 cup of flour and mix in well with a knife.

3. Dip each piece of fish into the batter, shaking off any excess.

4. In a wok or deep-fat fryer, heat the oil to 350°F. Lower in the fish pieces a few at a time and cook for 2-3 minutes. Lift them out carefully and drain on paper towels, keeping warm until required.

5. Mix together the soy sauce, lime juice, rind and sherry and serve as a dip with the cooked fish.

TIME Preparation takes about 30 minutes, cooking time varies from 2 to 3 minutes depending on the type of fish.

VARIATIONS Use a few vegetables, as well as fish, for an interesting change. Whole mushrooms are especially good.

SALMON PÂTÉ

This highly nutritious, elegant pâté is low in fat and very quick to prepare.

SERVES 4

8 oz can red or pink salmon, drained
½ cup low fat cottage cheese
Few drops lemon juice
Pinch ground mace, or ground nutmeg
¼ tsp Tabasco sauce
Freshly ground sea salt and black pepper
2 tbsps low fat plain yogurt
4 small pickles

1. Remove any bones and skin from the salmon. In a bowl, work the fish into a smooth paste with the back of a spoon.

2. Beat the cottage cheese until it is smooth.

3. Add the salmon, lemon juice, seasonings, and yogurt to the cheese and mix well, until thoroughly incorporated.

4. Divide the mixture equally among 4 individual ramekins. Smooth the surfaces carefully.

5. Slice each pickle lengthways, 4 or 5 times, making sure that you do not cut completely through the pickle at the narrow end. Splay the cut ends into a fan, and use these to decorate the tops of the pâtés in the ramekins.

TIME Preparation takes about 15 minutes.

PREPARATION If you have a food processor or blender you can work the cheese and salmon together in this, instead of beating them in a bowl.

445

DRESSED CRAB

*No book on fish cookery would be complete without instructions on how to dress
a crab. Crabs should have rough shells, large claws and feel heavy for their size.
Do not buy a crab that sounds to have water in when shaken.*

SERVES 2-3

1 large cooked crab (see note)
Chopped fresh parsley, to garnish

1. Pull off the crab claws, and crack these
with a small hammer or nutcrackers. Pull
out the meat and put into a bowl for light
meat.

2. Turn the crab onto its back or uppermost
shell, and pull the underbody firmly away
from the main shell.

3. Remove and discard the stomach bag
and gray, feathered gills, or fingers, as these
must not be eaten. Scoop out the dark meat
from the shell with a spoon and put into a
bowl.

4. Crack open the underbody and remove
all the white meat with a skewer or fork. Put
into the appropriate bowl.

5. Remove enough of the top shell to make
a flat case, in which to serve the meat.
Scrub the shell thoroughly.

6. Arrange layers of dark and light meat
alternately in the shell, and garnish with the
parsley.

TIME Preparation takes about 35-45 minutes.

SERVING IDEAS Serve with new potatoes and a simple, mixed lettuce
salad.

PREPARATION To cook a hard-shell crab, place crab in a saucepan of
boiling, salted water, reduce heat and simmer for 20-25 minutes.

MATELOTE

A tasty, impressive dish perfect for entertaining.

SERVES 4

1 lb lemon sole
1 lb monkfish
1 small wing of skate
4 cups mussels
8 oz unpeeled shrimp
3 onions
⅓ cup butter
2 cups white wine
¼ cup flour
2 tbsps parsley, chopped
Salt
Freshly ground black pepper
Lemon juice

1. Fillet and skin the lemon sole. Cut the sole fillets and monkfish into large pieces. Chop the skate wing into 4 large pieces.

2. Peel the shrimp and set aside. Scrub the mussels well, discarding any with broken shells.

3. Chop the onion finely. Melt half the butter in a saucepan and soften the onion in a large saucepan.

4. Add the mussels and about 3-4 tbsps water. Cover the pan and shake over a high heat until all the mussels have opened, discarding any that have not.

5. Strain the liquid into a bowl, allow mussels to cool, and then shell them.

6. Return the cooking liquid to the saucepan. Place the pieces of fish in the liquid. Add the wine until it just covers the fish. Simmer gently for about 8 minutes or until fish is just cooked.

7. Mix together the flour and the remaining butter to make a paste.

8. Remove the cooked fish from the liquid and put into a serving dish to keep warm. Bring liquid to a boil. Add the flour and butter paste, a little at a time, whisking it in and allowing liquid to boil after each addition, until liquid is thickened.

9. Add the parsley, shelled shrimp, shelled mussels, a little lemon juice, and seasoning. Heat for a few minutes to warm the shellfish through. Pour over the fish in the serving dish and sprinkle with more chopped parsley if desired.

TIME Preparation takes 20 minutes, cooking takes 20 minutes.

449

MUSSELS ALLA GENOVESE

Mussels Italian style – the perfect start to any meal.

SERVES 4

3 lbs mussels
Juice of 1 lemon
1 shallot
1 handful fresh basil leaves, or 1 tsp dried
    basil
1 small bunch parsley
¼ cup walnut halves
1 clove garlic
2 tbsps freshly grated Parmesan cheese
3-6 tbsps olive oil
2 tbsps butter
Salt and pepper
Flour or oatmeal

Garnish
Fresh basil leaves

1. Scrub the mussels well and discard any with broken shells or those that do not close when tapped. Put the mussels into a bowl of clean water with a handful of flour or oatmeal. Leave for ½ hour, then rinse under clear water.

2. Chop the shallot finely and put into a large saucepan with lemon juice. Cook until shallot softens.

3. Add the mussels and a pinch of salt and pepper. Cover the pan and cook the mussels quickly, shaking the pan. When mussel shells have opened, take mussels out of the pan, set aside and keep warm. Discard any that do not open. Strain the cooking liquid for possible use later.

4. To prepare Genovese sauce, wash the basil leaves, if fresh, and parsley, peel the garlic clove and chop coarsely, and chop the walnuts coarsely.

5. Put the herbs, garlic, nuts, 1 tbsp grated cheese and salt and pepper into a food processor and work to chop coarsely. Add butter and work again. Turn machine on and add oil gradually through the feed tube. If the sauce is still too thick, add the reserved liquid from cooking the mussels.

6. Remove the top shells from mussels and discard. Arrange mussels evenly in 4 shallow dishes, spoon some of the sauce into each, and sprinkle the top lightly with remaining Parmesan cheese.

7. Garnish with basil leaves and serve.

TIME Preparation takes 15 minutes, cooking takes 5-8 minutes.

CRAB AND CITRUS SALAD

This delicious salad is perfect for a summer lunch.

SERVES 4

8 oz crabmeat, or 1 large crab

2 oranges

2 lemons

2 limes

1 pink grapefruit

1 small iceberg lettuce

½ cup plain yogurt

6 tbsps heavy cream

1 tbsp chili sauce

½ tbsp brandy

Pinch of cayenne pepper

Salt

2 tbsps salad oil

1. Separate the body from the shell of the whole crab, and remove and discard the lungs and stomach sac. Chop body into 3 or 4 pieces with a very sharp knife and pick out the meat. Scrape brown meat from inside shell and add to body meat.

2. Break off large claws and remove meat from legs; then crack the claws and remove claw meat.

3. Mix all the meat together and reserve legs for garnish. If using canned or frozen crabmeat, pick over the meat to remove any bits of shell or cartilage.

4. Mix together yogurt, chili sauce, cream, brandy, cayenne pepper and a pinch of salt, and toss with the crabmeat.

5. Take a thin strip of peel from each of the citrus fruits, scraping off the bitter white pith. Cut each strip of peel into thin slivers. Put into boiling water and allow to boil for about 1 minute. Drain, refresh under cold water, and set aside.

6. Peel each of the citrus fruits and cut into segments; do all this over a bowl to reserve juices.

7. Add 2 tbsps salad oil to the juice in the bowl, and toss with citrus segments. Shred iceberg lettuce and arrange on plates. Put the crabmeat in its dressing on top of lettuce.

8. Arrange citrus segments over and around crabmeat and sprinkle citrus peel over the top.

TIME Preparation takes about 20 minutes.

SOUR FRIED SEAFOOD

A fragrant sour fried curry from the Far East. This can be served on its own, or as one of a combination of dishes.

SERVES 4

1 lb mixed fish and seafood, to include any of the following: large shrimp; scallops; squid, cleaned and cut into rings; oysters, shelled; clams, shelled; crab claws, shelled; small whole fish, e.g. whitebait or smelt.

½ cup oil

1 tbsp fresh ginger, grated

4 shallots, finely chopped

3 cloves garlic, crushed

4 red chili peppers, seeded and finely chopped

1 tsp ground mace

½ tsp shrimp paste

1 piece tamarind, soaked in 4 tbsps hot water (see variation)

Pinch soft brown sugar

Salt

1. Heat the oil in a frying pan over a high heat. Fry the fish in several batches for 2-3 minutes per batch, or until lightly browned and cooked through. Drain on paper towels and keep warm.

2. Grind the shallots, ginger, garlic, chilies and mace to a smooth paste in a mortar and pestle. Add the shrimp paste and blend together well.

3. Put 1 tbsp of oil into a wok and add the spice paste. Cook gently for 2-3 minutes. Strain in the tamarind and water or lemon juice. The sauce should be of a thin coating consistency; add a little more water, if it is too thick.

4. Stir in the sugar, the cooked fish and salt to taste. Cook for 2-3 minutes, or until the fish is heated through.

TIME Preparation takes about 20 minutes, cooking takes about 12-15 minutes.

COOK'S TIP Great care should be taken when preparing fresh chilies. Always wash hands thoroughly afterwards, and avoid getting any neat juice in the eyes or mouth. Rinse with copious amounts of clear water if this happens.

VARIATION If tamarind is not available, substitute 2 tbsps of lemon juice.

455

SALMON AND VEGETABLE SALAD

The fish in this salad "cooks" in the refrigerator in its vinegar marinade. Insist on very fresh fish for this recipe.

SERVES 4

12 oz salmon fillets
2 carrots, peeled and diced
1 large zucchini, peeled and diced
1 large turnip, peeled and diced
Chopped fresh coriander or pinch of dried
3 tbsps tarragon or wine vinegar
Salt and pepper
Pinch cayenne pepper
3 tbsps olive oil
Whole coriander leaves to garnish

1. Skin the salmon fillet and cut the fish into 1 inch pieces. Place in a bowl and add the vinegar, stirring well. Leave to stand for at least 2 hours.

2. Cut the vegetables into ½ inch dice and place the carrots in a saucepan of boiling water for about 5 minutes. Add the zucchini and turnip during the last minute of cooking time. Drain well.

3. Add the coriander, oil, salt and pepper and pinch cayenne pepper to the fish. Combine with the vegetables, mixing carefully so the fish does not break up. Chill briefly before serving and garnish with fresh coriander if available.

TIME Preparation takes about 30 minutes, with 2 hours for the salmon to marinate.

COOK'S TIP Fish allowed to marinate in vinegar, lemon or lime juice will appear opaque and "cooked" after standing for about 2 hours.

457

FISHERMAN'S STEW

This quick, economical and satisfying fish dish will please any fish lover for lunch or a light supper.

SERVES 4-6

6 tbsps olive oil
2 large onions, sliced
1 red pepper, seeded and sliced
1½ cups mushrooms, sliced
16oz can tomatoes
Pinch salt and pepper
Pinch dried thyme
1¾ cups water
2 lbs cod or other whitefish fillets, skinned
¾ cup white wine
2 tbsps parsley, chopped

1. Heat the oil in a large saucepan and add the onions. Cook until beginning to look transluscent. Add the red pepper and cook until the vegetables are softened.

2. Add the mushrooms and the tomatoes and bring the mixture to a boil.

3. Add thyme, salt, pepper and water and simmer for about 30 minutes.

4. Add the fish and wine and cook until the fish flakes easily, about 15 minutes. Stir in parsley.

5. To serve, place a piece of toasted French bread in the bottom of the soup bowl and spoon over the fish stew.

TIME Preparation takes about 20 minutes, cooking takes about 45 minutes.

VARIATIONS Shellfish may be added with the fish, if desired. Substitute green peppers for red peppers.

SERVING IDEAS The stew may also be served over rice. Accompany with a green salad.

SALADE NIÇOISE

This classic French salad is a meal in itself when served with a green salad and some crusty bread.

SERVES 4

2 large, or 6 small, new potatoes, cooked and cut into ½ inch dice

6 oz green beans, trimmed and cooked

3 oz black olives, halved and stoned

1 small cucumber, diced

4 tomatoes, cut into eight

6 oz can tuna, in water

¾ cup peeled shrimp

4 hard-cooked eggs, shelled and quartered lengthwise

2 oz can anchovies, drained and chopped

6 tbsps olive oil

2 tbsps white wine vinegar

3 tbsps chopped fresh mixed herbs or 1 tbsp dried

2 tsps Dijon mustard

Salt and pepper

1. In a large bowl, mix together the potatoes, beans, olives, cucumber and tomatoes.

2. Drain the tuna and flake it with a fork. Mix this, along with the shrimp, eggs and anchovies into the salad mixture.

3. In a small bowl, mix together the oil, vinegar, herbs and mustard. Whisk with a fork until thick.

4. Pour the dressing over the salad ingredients and stir gently to coat evenly. Season to taste.

TIME Preparation takes about 20 minutes, cooking takes about 20 minutes.

PREPARATION If you have a screw top jar, the dressing ingredients can be put into this and shaken vigorously, until they have thickened.

COOK'S TIP The dressing used in this recipe is delicious and will keep for up to 2 weeks in a refrigerator. So make double quantities and keep some to enliven other salad meals.

VARIATION If fresh herbs are not available substitute 1 tbsp dried mixed herbs.

461

Coconut Fried Fish with Chilies

A real treat for lovers of spicy food.

SERVES 4

Oil for frying
1 lb sole or other white fish fillets, skinned,
    boned and cut into 1 inch strips
Seasoned flour
1 egg, beaten
¾ cup shredded coconut
1 tbsp vegetable oil
1 tsp fresh ginger, grated
¼ tsp chili powder
1 red chili, seeded and finely chopped
1 tsp ground coriander
½ tsp ground nutmeg
1 clove garlic, crushed
2 tbsps tomato paste
2 tbsps tomato chutney
2 tbsps dark soy sauce
2 tbsps lemon juice
2 tbsps water
1 tsp light brown sugar
Salt and pepper

1. In a frying pan, heat about 2 inches of oil to 375°F. Toss the fish strips in the seasoned flour and then dip them into the beaten egg. Roll them in the shredded coconut and shake off the excess.

2. Fry the fish, a few pieces at a time, in the hot oil and drain them on paper towels. Keep warm.

3. Heat the 1 tbsp oil in a wok or frying pan and fry the ginger, red chili, spices and garlic, for about 2 minutes.

4. Add the remaining ingredients and simmer for about 3 minutes. Serve the fish, with the sauce served separately.

TIME Preparation takes about 30 minutes, cooking takes about 30 minutes.

SERVING IDEAS Serve with plain boiled rice, a cucumber relish and plenty of salad.

Swordfish Kebabs

Swordfish won't fall apart during cooking – a bonus when making kebabs.

SERVES 4-6

2¼ lbs swordfish steaks

6 tbsps olive oil

1 tsp chopped fresh oregano or ½ tsp dried

1 tsp chopped fresh marjoram or ½ tsp dried

Juice and rind of ½ lemon

4 tomatoes, cut in thick slices, or cherry tomatoes

2 lemons, cut in thin slices

Salt and freshly ground pepper

Lemon slices and Italian flat leaf parsley for garnish

1. Cut the swordfish steaks into 2 inch pieces.

2. Mix the olive oil, herbs, lemon juice and rind, and seasoning together and set it aside. Thread the swordfish, tomato slices or cherry tomatoes and lemon slices on skewers, alternating the ingredients. Brush the skewers with the oil and lemon juice mixture and cook under a preheated broiler for about 10 minutes, basting frequently with the lemon and oil. Serve garnished with lemons and parsley.

TIME Preparation takes about 15 minutes, cooking takes about 10 minutes.

VARIATIONS Fresh tuna may be used instead of swordfish.

SERVING IDEAS Accompany the kebabs with risotto and a green salad.

465

VINEGARED CRAB

An unusual way of serving fresh crab. You should be able to buy the rice vinegar from a supermarket or health food store. If not, substitute white wine vinegar.

SERVES 4

1 cucumber, grated
Salt, for sprinkling
1 large cooked crab
1 small piece fresh ginger, grated
Chinese cabbage, for serving
3 tbsps rice vinegar
2 tbsps dry sherry
2 tbsps soy sauce

1. Sprinkle the cucumber with salt and leave for 30 minutes.

2. Crack the legs and claws off the crab. Remove the meat from the claws and legs, but leave four thin legs whole as a garnish.

3. Separate the underbody from the shell. Remove and discard the stomach sac and the gray, feathered gills.

4. Scrape the brown meat from the shell and crack open the underbody. Use a skewer to pick out the meat.

5. Rinse the cucumber, drain well and squeeze out excess moisture. Mix together the cucumber, crab meat and ginger.

6. Arrange the Chinese cabbage on serving plates, to represent crab shells. Pile equal quantities of crab mixture onto the Chinese cabbage, leaving some of the leaf showing. Garnish with a whole crab leg and some grated, pickled ginger, if you can get it.

7. Mix together the vinegar, sherry and soy sauce. Serve in little bowls with the crab.

TIME Preparation takes about 30 minutes.

SERVING IDEAS A rice or pasta salad would be excellent with this dish.

Shrimp and Cashews in Pineapple with Tarragon Dressing

Served in the pineapple shells, this impressive salad is ideal for a summer lunch.

SERVES 4

2 small fresh pineapples, with green tops
1¼ cups cooked, peeled shrimp
1 cup roasted, unsalted cashew nuts
2 celery stalks, thinly sliced
4 tbsps lemon juice
1 egg
2 tbsps superfine sugar
1 tbsp tarragon vinegar
2 tsps chopped fresh tarragon or 1 tsp dried
½ cup heavy cream

1. Cut the pineapples carefully in half lengthwise, leaving their green tops attached.

2. Cut out the pineapple flesh carefully, leaving a ¼ inch border of flesh on the inside of the shell. Remove the cores and cut the flesh into bite-sized pieces.

3. Put the chopped pineapple into a bowl, along with the shrimp, cashew nuts and celery. Pour in the lemon juice and mix well. Divide the mixture equally between the pineapple shells, and chill them in the refrigerator.

4. In a heat-proof bowl, whisk together the egg and sugar. Stand the bowl over a pan of simmering water, and whisk in the vinegar and tarragon. Continue whisking until the mixture has thickened.

5. Remove the bowl from the heat and allow to cool completely, whisking occasionally.

6. When completely cold, whip the cream until it is just beginning to thicken, then fold it into the dressing mixture.

7. Pour the cream dressing over the salad in the pineapple shells and serve.

Time Preparation takes about 30 minutes, cooking takes about 10-15 minutes.

469

SPANISH RICE AND SOLE SALAD

A complete meal in itself, this salad is ideal for a summer lunch.

SERVES 4

2 large lemon sole, each filleted into 4
    pieces
4-6 peppercorns
Slice of onion
1 tbsp lemon juice
¾ cup long grain rice
1 small eggplant
2 tbsps olive oil
1 red pepper, seeded and chopped into ¼
    inch dice
1 shallot, finely chopped
1 green pepper, seeded and chopped into
    ¼ inch dice
3 tbsps Italian dressing
1 tbsp chopped fresh mixed herbs or ½ tsp
    dried
1 cup mayonnaise
1 clove garlic, crushed
1 tsp tomato paste
1 tsp paprika
Salt and pepper
2 bunches watercress, to garnish

1. Lay the sole fillets in an ovenproof dish, together with the peppercorns, slice of onion, lemon juice and just enough water to cover. Sprinkle with a little salt and cover the dish with foil or a lid. Poach in a preheated oven, 350°F, for 8-10 minutes. Allow the fish to cool in the liquid, then cut each fillet into 1 inch pieces.

2. Cook the rice in boiling water until soft. Rinse in cold water and separate the grains with a fork.

3. Cut the eggplant in half and sprinkle with 2 tsps salt. Allow to stand for half an hour, then rinse very thoroughly. Pat dry and cut into ½ inch dice.

4. Heat the oil in a large frying pan, and fry the eggplant, until it is soft. Allow the eggplant to cool, then mix it into the rice along with the shallot, peppers, half the chopped herbs and the Italian dressing.

5. Mix together the mayonnaise, garlic, tomato paste, paprika, remaining herbs and seasoning.

6. Arrange the rice on one side of a serving dish and the sole pieces on the other. Spoon the mayonnaise over the sole and garnish the dish with watercress.

TIME Preparation will take about 20 minutes, cooking takes about 15-20 minutes.

SOLE AND MUSHROOM TURNOVERS

These delicious individual pies make a warming family lunch or supper dish.

SERVES 4

4 sole fillets, skinned
Salt and pepper
½ cup milk
1 cup mushrooms, trimmed and thinly
　　sliced
2 tbsps butter
Juice of 1 lemon
5 tbsps white bread crumbs mixed with
　　1 tbsp crushed hazelnuts
3 tbsps hazelnut, or lemon stuffing mix
12 oz puff pastry
Beaten egg, for glazing
Poppy seeds, for sprinkling

1. Season the sole fillets and roll them up jelly roll fashion. Secure each roll with a wooden pick and poach gently in the milk for about 10 minutes in a preheated oven, 350°F.

2. Drain the fish and allow it to cool. Remove the wooden picks.

3. Put the mushrooms and butter in a saucepan with the lemon juice. Cook over a moderate heat for about 5 minutes.

4. Allow the mushrooms to cool and then stir in the bread crumb mix.

5. Roll out the pastry, quite thinly, into 4 circles, each 6 inches in diameter. Brush the edges with beaten egg.

6. Put a fish roll into the center of each circle and top with a quarter of the mushroom mixture. Pull the pastry edges up and over the fish and pinch together to seal.

7. Preheat the oven to 400°F. Place the turnovers on a greased cookie sheet and glaze with the beaten egg. Sprinkle with a few poppy seeds.

8. Bake in the pre-heated oven for about 25 minutes, or until well risen, puffed and golden. Serve piping hot.

TIME Preparation will take about 25 minutes, plus the cooling time, cooking will take about 35 minutes.

Pizza Marinara

Seafood pizzas are wonderful – this one is especially tasty.

SERVES 4

¾ cup all-purpose flour, sifted

1 tsp baking powder

½ tsp salt

⅓ cup milk

2 tbsps salad oil

4 oz canned tomatoes

1 tsp tomato paste

1 clove crushed garlic

½ tsp dried oregano

½ tsp dried basil

Pinch of fennel seeds

Salt and pepper

¾ cup shrimp

4 anchovy fillets

8-10 mussels

1 tsp capers

2-3 black olives

4 oz sliced mozzarella cheese

1. Sift the flour, baking powder and salt into a bowl and add milk and oil. Stir vigorously until mixture leaves the sides of the bowl.

2. Press it into a ball and knead it in the bowl for about 2 minutes until smooth. Cover, and leave it to sit while preparing sauce.

3. Put the tomatoes, paste, herbs, seasoning and garlic together in a small saucepan. Bring to a boil and reduce to thicken. Leave to cool.

4. Roll out the pizza dough into a 12-inch circle. Spread the sauce evenly leaving a ½ inch border around the edge. Scatter over the shellfish, anchovy fillets, olives and capers.

5. Slice the cheese thinly and place it on top of the fish.

6. Bake in a 425°F oven for 10-15 minutes until cheese browns lightly and the crust is crisp.

TIME Preparation takes 15 minutes, cooking takes 25-30 minutes.

BROILED HERRING WITH DILL AND MUSTARD

Mustard and dill enhance the fish perfectly in this dish.

SERVES 4

---

4 tbsps fresh dill, chopped

6 tbsps mild mustard

2 tbsps lemon juice, or white wine

4-8 fresh herrings, cleaned but heads and
    tails left on

2 tbsps butter or margarine, melted

Salt and pepper

---

1. Mix the dill, mustard and lemon juice or wine together thoroughly.

2. Cut three slits, just piercing the skin, on both sides of each herring and lay them on a broiler pan.

3. Spread half the mustard mixture equally over the exposed side of each fish, pushing some into the cuts.

4. Preheat the broiler. Spoon a little of the melted butter over each herring, and broil the fish 3-5 inches from the heat for 5-6 minutes.

5. Turn the fish over and spread the remaining mustard and dill mixture over them. Spoon over the remaining melted butter and broil for another 5-6 minutes.

6. Sprinkle the fish with a little salt and pepper before serving.

TIME Preparation takes about 10 minutes, cooking takes 12-15 minutes, although this may be longer if the herring are large.

SERVING IDEAS Arrange the fish on a serving dish, garnished with lemon wedges and sprigs of fresh dill. Serve with new potatoes, if available.

MONKFISH IN PAPRIKA SAUCE

Monkfish is a firm, succulent fish, which should be used more often than it is. It is ideal for use in kebabs or fish casseroles, and in this recipe it is complemented magnificently by the creamy paprika sauce.

SERVES 4

1 lb monkfish fillets
Lemon juice
1 bay leaf
Slice of onion
6 peppercorns
2 tbsps butter
1 cup mushrooms, trimmed and sliced
1 small red pepper, seeded and sliced
1 shallot, finely chopped
2 tsps paprika
1 clove garlic, crushed
¼ cup all-purpose flour
1¼ cups milk
1 tbsp fresh parsley, chopped or ½ tbsp dried
1 tsp fresh thyme, chopped or ½ tsp dried
1 tsp tomato paste
Salt and pepper
8 oz fresh pasta, cooked
2 tbsps sour cream, or plain yogurt

1. Cut the monkfish into 1 inch chunks. Put these into an ovenproof dish with the lemon juice, bay leaf, onion, peppercorns and just enough water to cover. Cover with a lid and poach for about 10 minutes in a preheated oven at 350°F.

2. Melt the butter in a saucepan and stir in the mushrooms, pepper, shallot, paprika and garlic. Cook gently, until the pepper begins to soften.

3. Stir the flour into the mushrooms and pepper. Gradually add the milk, stirring until the sauce has thickened.

4. Remove the fish from the dish and strain off the liquid. Stir enough of this liquid into the sauce to make it of coating consistency. Add the parsley, thyme and tomato paste to the sauce and simmer for 2-3 minutes. Season to taste.

5. Arrange the hot, cooked pasta on a serving plate and place the fish on top. Coat with the paprika sauce, and spoon over the sour cream, or yogurt, to serve.

TIME Preparation takes about 20 minutes, and cooking takes about 16 minutes.

VARIATIONS Use any other firm-fleshed white fish instead of the monkfish.

SERVING IDEAS A mixed salad would be ideal to serve with this dish.

479

RED SNAPPER WITH HERB & MUSHROOM SAUCE

This fish has a slight taste of shrimp. It is often cooked with the liver left in – a delicacy.

SERVES 4

---

1 lb small mushrooms, left whole

1 clove garlic, finely chopped

3 tbsps olive oil

Juice of 1 lemon

1 tbsp fresh parsley, finely chopped or 1 tbsp dried

2 tsps fresh basil, finely chopped or ½ tsp dried

1 tsp fresh marjoram or sage, finely chopped or ½ tsp dried

4 tbsps dry white wine mixed with ½ tsp cornstarch

Anchovy paste

4 red snapper, each weighing about 8 oz

2 tsps white bread crumbs

2 tsps freshly grated Parmesan cheese

1. Heat the olive oil in a small frying pan and add the mushrooms and garlic. Cook over moderate heat for about 1 minute, until the garlic and mushrooms are slightly softened. Add all the herbs, lemon juice and white wine and cornstarch mixture. Bring to a boil and cook until thickened. Add anchovy essence to taste. Set aside while preparing the fish.

2. To clean the fish, cut along the stomach from the gills to the vent, the small hole near the tail. Clean out the cavity of the fish, leaving the liver, if desired.

3. To remove the gills, lift the flap and snip them out with a sharp pair of scissors. Rinse the fish well and pat dry.

4. Place the fish head to tail in a shallow ovenproof dish that can be used for serving. The fish should fit snugly into the dish.

5. Pour the prepared sauce over the fish and sprinkle with the bread crumbs and Parmesan cheese.

6. Cover the dish loosely with foil and bake in a preheated oven, 375°F, for about 20 minutes. Uncover for the last 5 minutes, if desired, and raise the oven temperature slightly. This will lightly brown the fish.

TIME Preparation takes about 30 minutes, cooking takes about 5 minutes for the sauce and 20 minutes for the fish.

COOK'S TIP If you don't want to clean the fish yourself, buy them ready-cleaned.

481

STUFFED SOLE

This traditional German dish is elegant enough for a formal dinner party.

SERVES 6

4 tbsps butter or margarine

2 tbsps flour

1½ cups fish or vegetable stock

1 cup button mushrooms, sliced

6 oz peeled, cooked shrimp

4 oz canned, frozen or fresh cooked crabmeat

4 tbsps heavy cream

2 tbsps brandy

1 oz fresh bread crumbs

Salt and pepper

6-12 sole fillets, depending upon size

4 tbsps melted butter

1. Preheat the oven to 350°F. Melt 4 tbsps butter and add the flour. Cook for about 3 minutes over gentle heat or until pale straw colored. Add the stock and bring to a boil. Add the mushrooms and allow to cook until the sauce thickens.

2. Add the cream and re-boil the sauce. Remove the sauce from the heat and add the brandy, shrimp, crab and bread crumbs.

3. Skin the sole fillets and spread the filling on the skinned side. Roll up and arrange in a buttered baking dish. Spoon melted butter over the top and cook in the pre-heated oven for 20-30 minutes, until the fish is just firm.

TIME Preparation takes about 30 minutes, cooking takes 20-30 minutes.

VARIATIONS For special occasions, substitute lobster for the crabmeat.

SERVING IDEAS Serve with a green vegetable such as broccoli, asparagus or spinach. Accompany with new potatoes tossed in parsley butter.

SARDINE AND TOMATO GRATIN

Fresh sardines are becoming more widely available and this recipe makes the most of these delicious fish.

SERVES 4

3 tbsps olive oil

2 lbs large fresh sardines, descaled and cleaned

2 leeks, cleaned and sliced

½ cup dry white wine

6-8 tomatoes, skinned and quartered

Salt and pepper

2 tbsps fresh basil, chopped, or 1 tbsp dried basil

2 tbsps fresh parsley, chopped

½ cup Parmesan cheese, grated

½ cup dry bread crumbs

1. Heat the oil in a frying pan and fry the sardines until they are brown on both sides. It may be necessary to do this in several batches, to prevent the fish from breaking up.

2. When all the sardines are cooked, set them aside and cook the leeks gently in the sardine oil. When the leeks are soft, pour in the wine and boil rapidly, until it is reduced by about two thirds.

3. Add the tomatoes, seasoning and herbs to the leeks and cook for about 1 minute. Pour the vegetables into an ovenproof dish and lay the sardines on top.

4. Sprinkle the cheese and bread crumbs evenly over the sardines and bake in a preheated oven, 425°F, for about 5 minutes.

TIME Preparation takes about 20-25 minutes, cooking takes about 15 minutes.

VARIATIONS Try substituting herrings or mackerel for the sardines. They will take a little longer to fry.

SERVING IDEAS Cut a few anchovy fillets in half lengthwise and arrange them in a lattice on top of the gratinée, before serving with hot garlic bread.

SWEET-SOUR FISH

In China this dish is almost always prepared with freshwater fish, but sea bass is also an excellent choice.

SERVES 2

---

1 sea bass, snapper or carp, weighing about
    2 lbs, cleaned
1 tbsp dry sherry
Few slices fresh ginger
½ cup sugar
6 tbsps cider vinegar
1 tbsp soy sauce
2 tbsps cornstarch
1 clove garlic, crushed
2 green onions, shredded
1 small carrot, peeled and finely shredded
½ cup bamboo shoots, shredded

---

1. Rinse the fish well inside and out. Make three diagonal cuts on each side of the fish with a sharp knife.

2. Trim off the fins, leaving the dorsal fin on top.

3. Trim the tail to two neat points.

4. In a wok, bring enough water to a boil to cover the fish. Gently lower the fish into the boiling water and add the sherry and ginger. Cover the wok tightly and remove at once from the heat. Allow to stand 15-20 minutes to let the fish cook in the residual heat.

5. To test if the fish is cooked, pull the dorsal fin – if it comes off easily the fish is done. If not, return the wok to the heat and bring to a boil. Remove from the heat and leave the fish to stand a further 5 minutes. Transfer the fish to a heated serving dish and keep it warm. Take all but 4 tbsps of the fish cooking liquid from the wok. Add the remaining ingredients including the vegetables and cook, stirring constantly, until the sauce thickens. Spoon some of the sauce over the fish to serve and serve the rest separately.

TIME Preparation takes about 25 minutes, cooking takes about 15-25 minutes.

COOK'S TIP The diagonal cuts in the side of the fish ensure even cooking.

SWORDFISH FLORENTINE

*Swordfish has an almost "meaty" texture. Here it has a distinctly
Mediterranean flavor.*

SERVES 4

4 swordfish steaks, about 6-8 oz each in
   weight
Salt, pepper and lemon juice
Olive oil
2 lbs fresh spinach, stems removed and
   leaves well washed

Garlic Mayonnaise
2 egg yolks
1-2 cloves garlic
Salt, pepper and dry mustard
Pinch cayenne pepper
1 cup olive oil
Lemon juice or white wine vinegar

1. Sprinkle fish with pepper, lemon juice
and olive oil. Place under a preheated
broiler and broil for about 3-4 minutes per
side. Fish may aso be cooked on an
outdoor barbecue grill.

2. Meanwhile, use a sharp knife to shred
the spinach finely. Place in a large
saucepan and add a pinch of salt. Cover
and cook over moderate heat with only the
water that clings to the leaves after
washing. Cook about 2 minutes, or until
leaves are just slightly wilted. Set aside.

3. Place egg yolks in a food processor or
blender. Add the garlic. Process several
times to mix eggs and purée garlic. Add
salt, pepper, mustard and cayenne pepper.
With the machine running, pour oil through
the funnel in a thin, steady stream.

4. When the sauce becomes very thick, add
enough lemon juice or vinegar to thin
slightly.

5. To serve, place a bed of spinach on a
plate and top with the swordfish. Spoon
some of the garlic mayonnaise on top of the
fish and serve the rest separately.

TIME Preparation takes about 25 minutes, cooking takes about 6-8 minutes.

PREPARATION The garlic mayonnaise may be prepared in advance and will
keep for 5-7 days in the refrigerator. It is also delicious served with poached
shellfish, chicken or vegetables. If too thick, thin the sauce with hot water.

HALIBUT AND CRAB HOLLANDAISE

Rich and creamy, the hollandaise sauce adds an air of sophistication to this lovely dish.

SERVES 4

---

4 large fillets of halibut
1 bay leaf
Slice of onion
5 tbsps white wine
2 egg yolks
1 tbsp lemon juice
Pinch cayenne pepper
Pinch paprika
½ cup butter, melted
1 tbsp butter
2 tbsps flour
2 tbsps heavy cream
Salt and pepper
8 oz crab meat

---

1. Put the fish with the bay leaf, onion slice, wine and just enough water to cover the fish, into a baking dish. Cover and cook in a preheated oven, 325°F, for 10 minutes.

2. Put the egg yolks, lemon juice, cayenne and paprika into a blender, or food processor. Turn the machine on and gradually pour in the melted butter. Continue processing, until the hollandaise sauce is thick. Set aside.

3. Put the 1 tbsp unmelted butter into a saucepan, melt over a gentle heat and stir in the flour. Cook gently for 1 minute.

4. Remove the fish from the baking dish and strain the cooking liquid onto the flour and butter in the saucepan, stirring well to prevent lumps from forming. Cook this sauce gently, until it is smooth and has thickened. Stir in the cream, but do not allow to boil. Season to taste.

5. Stir the crab meat into the fish stock sauce and pour this mixture into a flameproof dish. Lay the halibut fillets on top and cover these with the hollandaise sauce.

6. Brown the sauce under the broiler before serving.

TIME Preparation will take about 15 minutes and cooking takes about 20 minutes.

SERVING IDEAS Serve with new potatoes and broccoli.

491

Trout Meunière aux Herbes

The miller (meunier) caught trout fresh from the mill stream and his wife used the flour that was on hand to dredge them with, or so the story goes.

SERVES 4

---

4 even-sized trout, clean and trimmed
Flour
Salt and pepper
½ cup butter
Juice of 1 lemon
2 tbsps chopped fresh herbs such as
    parsley, chervil, tarragon, thyme or
    marjoram
Lemon wedges to garnish

---

1. Trim the trout tails to make them more pointed. Rinse the trout well.

2. Dredge the trout with flour and shake off the excess. Season with salt and pepper. Heat half the butter in a very large frying pan and, when foaming, place in the trout. It may be necessary to cook the trout in two batches to avoid overcrowding the pan.

3. Cook over fairly high heat on both sides to brown evenly. Depending on size, the trout should take 5-8 minutes per side to cook. The dorsal fins will pull out easily when the trout are cooked. Remove the trout to a serving dish and keep them warm.

4. Wipe out the pan and add the remaining butter. Cook over moderate heat until beginning to brown, then add the lemon juice and herbs. When the lemon juice is added, the butter will bubble up and sizzle. Pour immediately over the fish and serve with lemon wedges.

TIME Preparation takes 15-20 minutes, cooking takes 5-8 minutes per side for the fish and about 5 minutes to brown the butter.

SERVING IDEAS Serve with new potatoes and peeled, cubed cucumber quickly sautéed in butter and chopped dill.

SINGAPORE FISH

The cuisine of Singapore was much influenced by that of China. In turn, the Chinese welcomed ingredients from Singapore like curry powder into their own cuisine.

SERVES 6

1 lb whitefish fillets

1 egg white

1 tbsp cornstarch

2 tsps white wine

Salt and pepper

Oil for frying

1 large onion, cut into ½ inch thick wedges

1 tbsp mild curry powder

1 small can pineapple chunks, drained and juice reserved, or ½ fresh pineapple, peeled and cubed

1 small can mandarin orange segments, drained and juice reserved

1 small can sliced water chestnuts, drained

1 tbsp cornstarch mixed with juice of 1 lime

2 tsps sugar (optional)

1. Starting at the tail end of the fillets, skin them using a sharp knife.

2. Slide the knife back and forth along the length of each fillet, pushing the fish flesh along as you go.

3. Cut the fish into even-sized pieces, about 2 inches.

4. Mix together the egg white, cornstarch, wine, salt and pepper. Place the fish in the mixture and leave to stand while heating the oil in a wok.

5. When the oil is hot, fry a few pieces of fish at a time until light golden brown and crisp. Remove the fish and put on paper towels to drain. Continue until all the fish is cooked.

6. Remove all but 1 tbsp of the oil from the wok and add the onion. Stir-fry the onion for 1-2 minutes and add the curry powder. Cook the onion and curry powder for another 1-2 minutes. Add the juice from the pineapple and mandarin oranges and bring to a boil.

7. Combine the cornstarch and lime juice and add a tablespoon of the boiling fruit juice. Return the mixture to the wok and cook until thickened, about 2 minutes. Taste and add sugar if desired. Add the fruit, water chestnuts and fried fish to the wok and stir to coat. Heat through 1 minute and serve immediately.

TIME Preparation takes about 25 minutes, cooking takes about 10 minutes.

KUNG PAO SHRIMP WITH CASHEW NUTS

It is said that Kung Pao invented this dish, but to this day no one knows who he was!

SERVES 6

½ tsp fresh ginger, chopped

1 tsp garlic, chopped

1½ tbsps cornstarch

¼ tsp baking soda

Salt and pepper

¼ tsp sugar

1 lb uncooked shrimp

4 tbsps oil

1 small onion, diced

1 large or 2 small zucchini, cut into ½ inch cubes

1 small red pepper, cut into ½ inch cubes

½ cup cashew nuts

Sauce

¾ cup chicken stock

1 tbsp cornstarch

2 tsps chili sauce

2 tsps bean paste (optional)

2 tsps sesame oil

1 tbsp dry sherry or rice wine

1. Mix together the ginger, garlic, cornstarch, baking soda, salt, pepper and sugar.

2. If the shrimp are unpeeled, remove the peels and the dark vein running along the rounded side. If large, cut in half. Place in the dry ingredients and leave to stand for 20 minutes.

3. Heat the oil in a wok and when hot add the shrimp. Cook, stirring over high heat for about 20 seconds, or just until the shrimp change color. Transfer to a plate.

4. Add the onion to the same oil in the wok and cook for about 1 minute. Add the zucchini and red pepper and cook for about 30 seconds.

5. Mix the sauce ingredients together and add to the wok. Cook, stirring constantly, until the sauce is slightly thickened. Add the shrimp and the cashew nuts and heat through completely.

TIME Preparation takes about 20 minutes, cooking takes about 3 minutes.

STUFFED FISH

A whole baked fish makes an impressive main course for a dinner party. The stuffing makes the fish go further and with no bones it's easy to serve and eat.

SERVES 4-6

2-3 lb whole fish such as carp or sea bass
Salt and pepper
2 tbsps melted butter

Stuffing

1 tbsp butter or margarine
1 small onion, finely chopped
1½ cups mushrooms, coarsely chopped
1 hard-cooked egg, peeled and coarsely
　　chopped
¾ cup fresh bread crumbs, white or whole-
　　wheat
Pinch salt and pepper
2 tsps fresh dill, chopped
2 tsps fresh parsley, chopped
Pinch nutmeg

Sauce

½ cup sour cream
Pinch sugar
Grated rind and juice of ½ lemon
Pinch salt and white pepper
Lemon slices and parsley sprigs to garnish

1. Ask the assistant to gut and bone the fish for you, leaving on the head and tail. Sprinkle the cavity of the fish with salt and pepper and set it aside while preparing the stuffing.

2. To chop the onion finely, peel it and cut it in half lengthwise. Place the onion cut side down on a chopping board. Using a large, sharp knife, make four cuts into the onion, parallel to the chopping board, but not completely through to the root end. Using the pointed tip of the knife, make four or five cuts into the onion lengthwise, following the natural lines in the onion and not cutting through to the root end. Next, cut the onion crosswise into thin or thick slices as desired and the onion should fall apart into individual dice. Keep fingers well out of the way when slicing.

3. Melt the butter or margarine in a medium-sized saucepan and add the chopped onion and mushrooms. Cook briefly to soften the vegetables and take off the heat. Stir in the remaining stuffing ingredients.

4. Spread the stuffing evenly into the cavity of the fish, sprinkle the top with melted butter and place the fish in lightly buttered foil in a large baking dish. Bake in a preheated 350°F oven for about 40 minutes, basting frequently.

5. When the fish is cooked, combine the sauce ingredients and pour over the fish. Cook another 5 minutes to heat the sauce, but do not allow it to bubble. Remove the fish to a serving dish and garnish with lemon and parsley.

TIME Preparation takes about 20 minutes. If boning the fish yourself, add a further 30 minutes. Cooking takes approximately 45 minutes.

COOK'S TIP Cover the head and tail of the fish with lightly greased foil about halfway through cooking time. This will prevent the fish from drying out and improve the appearance of the finished dish.

PAELLA

This dish has as many variations as Spain has cooks! Fish, meat and poultry combine with vegetables and rice to make a complete meal.

SERVES 6

12 mussels in their shells

6 clams

Flour

6 oz cod, skinned and cut into 2 inch pieces

12 large shrimp

3 chorizos or other spicy sausage

3 tbsps oil

2 lb chicken, cut in 12 serving-size pieces

1 small onion, chopped

1 clove garlic, crushed

2 small peppers, red and green, seeded and shredded

3 cups long grain rice

Large pinch saffron

Salt and pepper

4 cups boiling water

4 oz frozen peas

3 tomatoes, peeled, seeded and chopped or shredded

1. Scrub the clams and mussels well to remove beards and barnacles. Discard any with broken shells or those that do not close when tapped. Leave the mussels and clams to soak in water with a handful of flour for 30 minutes.

2. Remove the heads and legs from the shrimp, if desired, but leave on the tail shells.

3. Place the sausage in a saucepan and cover with water. Bring to a boil and then simmer for 5 minutes. Drain and slice into ¼ inch rounds. Set aside.

4. Heat the oil and fry the chicken pieces, browning evenly on both sides. Remove and drain on paper towels.

5. Add the sausage, onions, garlic and peppers to the oil in the frying pan and fry briskly for about 3 minutes.

6. Combine the sausage mixture with uncooked rice and saffron and place in a special paella dish or a large oven- and flame-proof casserole. Pour on the water, season with salt and pepper and bring to a boil. Stir occasionally and allow to boil for about 2 minutes.

7. Add the chicken pieces and place in a preheated 400°F oven for about 15 minutes.

8. Add the clams, mussels, shrimp, cod and peas and bake another 10-15 minutes or until the rice is tender, chicken is cooked and mussels and clams open. Discard any that do not open. Add the tomatoes 5 minutes before the end of cooking time and serve immediately.

TIME Preparation takes about 30-40 minutes, cooking takes about 35-40 minutes.

SOLE WITH SPICY TOMATO SAUCE

This delicious recipe mixes white fish with a spicy Mexican sauce.

SERVES 4

3 oz cream cheese
1 tsp dried oregano
Pinch cayenne pepper
4 whole fillets of sole
Lime slices and dill to garnish

Tomato Sauce
1 tbsp oil
1 small onion, chopped
1 celery stalk, chopped
1 chili pepper, seeded and chopped
¼ tsp each ground cumin, coriander and
    ginger
½ red and ½ green pepper, seeded and
    chopped
14 oz can tomatoes
1 tbsp tomato paste
Salt, pepper and a pinch sugar

1. Heat the oil in a heavy-based pan and cook the onion, celery, chili pepper and spices for about 5 minutes over very low heat.

2. Add red and green peppers and the remaining ingredients and bring to a boil. Reduce heat and simmer for 15-20 minutes, stirring occasionally. Set aside while preparing the fish.

3. Mix the cream cheese, oregano and cayenne pepper together and set aside.

4. Skin the fillets using a filleting knife. Start at the tail end and hold the knife at a slight angle to the skin.

5. Push the knife along using a sawing motion, with the blade against the skin. Dip fingers in salt to make it easier to hold onto the fish skin. Gradually separate the fish from the skin.

6. Spread the cheese filling on all 4 fillets and roll each up. Secure with wooden picks.

7. Place the fillets in a lightly greased baking dish, cover and bake for 10 minutes in a preheated 350°F oven.

8. Pour over the tomato sauce and bake another 10-15 minutes. Fish is cooked when it feels firm and looks opaque. Garnish with lime slices and dill.

TIME Preparation takes about 30 minutes and cooking takes 20-25 minutes.

SERVING IDEAS Add rice and an avocado salad.

503

SMOKED HADDOCK AND EGG QUICHE

This classic quiche is a firm favorite for lunches and suppers alike.

SERVES 6

8 oz ready-made whole-wheat dough
12 oz smoked haddock fillet
½ cup chicken stock
2 hard-cooked eggs, chopped
1 tbsp fresh chives, chopped
¾ cup Cheddar cheese, grated
3 eggs
1 cup milk
Salt and pepper

1. Roll out the pastry to fit a 9 inch deep fluted pie pan. Press the edges up well and push the base well down. Prick the base with a fork and bake for 15 minutes in a preheated oven, 375°F.

2. Place the fish in a saucepan and poach gently in the chicken stock for about 8 minutes, or until just tender. Drain the fish and flake it into a bowl, discarding any skin or bones.

3. Mix the chopped eggs, chives and cheese into the fish, and spread this mixture evenly into the part-baked pastry shell.

4. Beat together the eggs and milk, and season to taste. Pour over the fish mixture in the pastry shell.

5. Bake at 375°F for 25-30 minutes, or until the filling is set.

TIME Preparation will take about 25 minutes, and cooking takes about 40 minutes.

505

CHILLED FISH CURRY

This sophisticated, mild curry will serve four as a refreshing summer lunch, or eight as an elegant appetizer.

SERVES 4-8

8 oz fresh salmon fillet
12 oz whitefish fillet
Chicken stock
Salt and pepper
½ cup mayonnaise
1½ cups plain yogurt
2 tsps curry powder
Juice and grated rind of ½ lemon
¾ cup peeled shrimp

Garnish
Kiwi fruit, peeled and sliced
Sprigs fresh mint
Shredded coconut

1. Put the salmon and whitefish fillets into a shallow pan and add just enough chicken stock to cover.

2. Season to taste and simmer gently, until the fish is just tender.

3. Remove the fish carefully from the cooking liquid and leave to cool slightly.

4. In a medium-sized bowl, mix together the mayonnaise and the yogurt. Blend in the curry powder and the lemon juice and rind.

5. Flake the cooked fish, removing any bones and skin. Mix the flaked fish and the shrimp into the curry sauce.

6. Arrange the fish curry on serving plates and garnish with slices of kiwi fruit, sprigs of fresh mint and coconut.

TIME Preparation takes about 20 minutes, and cooking takes about 6 minutes.

VARIATIONS If you prefer, use slices of peeled cucumber instead of the kiwi fruit.

SZECHUAN FISH

The piquant spiciness of Szechuan pepper is quite different from that of black or white pepper. Beware, though, too much can numb the mouth temporarily!

SERVES 6

Whole chili peppers
1 lb whitefish fillets
Pinch salt and pepper
1 egg
5 tbsps flour
6 tbsps white wine
Flour for dredging
Oil for frying
2 oz cooked ham, cut in small dice
1 inch piece fresh ginger, finely diced
½-1 red or green chili pepper, cored, seeded and finely diced
6 water chestnuts, finely diced
4 green onions, finely chopped
3 tbsps light soy sauce
1 tsp cider vinegar or rice wine vinegar
½ tsp ground Szechuan pepper (optional)
1¼ cups light fish stock
1 tbsp cornstarch dissolved with 2 tbsps water
2 tsps sugar

1. To prepare the garnish, choose unblemished chili peppers with the stems on. Using a small, sharp knife, cut the peppers in strips, starting from the pointed end.

2. Cut down to within ½ inch of the stem end. Rinse out the seeds under cold running water and place the peppers in iced water.

3. Leave the peppers to soak for at least 4 hours or overnight until they open up like flowers.

4. Cut the fish fillets into 2 inch pieces and season with salt and pepper. Beat the egg well and add flour and wine to make a batter. Dredge the fish lightly with flour and then dip into the batter. Mix the fish well.

5. Heat a wok and when hot, add enough oil to deep-fry the fish. When the oil is hot, fry a few pieces of fish at a time, until golden brown. Drain and proceed until all the fish is cooked.

6. Remove all but 1 tbsp of oil from the wok and add the ham, ginger, diced chili pepper, water chestnuts and green onions. Cook for about 1 minute and add the soy sauce and vinegar. If using Szechuan pepper, add at this point. Stir well and cook for another 1 minute. Remove the vegetables from the pan and set them aside.

7. Add the stock to the wok and bring to a boil. When boiling, add 1 spoonful of the hot stock to the cornstarch mixture. Add the mixture back to the stock and reboil, stirring constantly until thickened.

8. Stir in the sugar and return the fish and vegetables to the sauce. Heat through for 30 seconds and serve at once.

TIME Preparation takes about 30 minutes. Chili pepper garnish takes at least 4 hours to soak. Cooking takes about 10 minutes.

FISH MILANESE

These fish, cooked in the style of Milan, have a crispy crumb coating and the fresh tang of lemon juice.

SERVES 4

---

8 sole fillets
2 tbsps dry vermouth
1 bay leaf
6 tbsps olive oil
Seasoned flour for dredging
2 eggs, lightly beaten
Dry bread crumbs
Oil for shallow frying
6 tbsps butter
1 clove garlic, crushed
2 tsps parsley, chopped
2 tbsps capers
1 tsp fresh oregano, chopped
Juice of 1 lemon
Lemon wedges and parsley to garnish

1. Skin the fillets with a sharp filleting knife. Remove any small bones and place the fillets in a large, shallow dish. Combine the vermouth, oil and bay leaf in a small saucepan and heat gently. Allow to cool completely and pour over the fish. Leave the fish to marinate for about 1 hour turning them occasionally.

2. Remove the fish from the marinade and dredge lightly with the seasoned flour.

3. Dip the fillets into the beaten eggs to coat, or use a pastry brush to brush the eggs onto the fillets. Dip the egg-coated fillet into the bread crumbs, pressing the crumbs on firmly.

4. Heat the oil in a large frying pan. Add the fillets and cook slowly, about 3 minutes, on both sides until golden brown. Remove and drain on paper towels.

5. Pour the oil out of the frying pan and wipe it clean. Add the butter and the garlic and cook until both turn a light brown. Add the herbs, capers and lemon juice and pour immediately over the fish. Garnish with lemon wedges and sprigs of parsley.

TIME Preparation takes 1 hour for the fish to marinate, cooking takes about 6 minutes. It may be necessary to cook the fish in several batches, depending upon the size of the frying pan.

SEA BASS WITH VEGETABLES

A delicious lemon sauce perfectly enhances the fish in this impressive dish.

SERVES 4

1 sea bass, weighing 2-2½ lbs
8 oz broccoli or green beans
1 lb new potatoes
4 zucchini
4 very small turnips
1 small bunch green onions
2 carrots
¼ cup butter
¼ cup flour
1¼ cups milk
1 small bunch fresh thyme or 1 tbsp dried
3 lemons
Paprika
Fresh parsley, chopped
Salt and pepper

1. Clean the bass, trim the fins, but leave the head and tail on. Put salt and pepper and half thyme inside the fish. Put the fish in the center of a large square of buttered foil. Add the juice of 1 lemon, wrap fish loosely, and bake at 350°F for 40-60 minutes, depending on weight.

2. Cut the broccoli into small florets (or trim the beans, but leave whole). Scrub potatoes and turnips but do not peel. Cut the zucchini into 2-inch strips. Trim the green onions, leaving some of the green. Peel the carrots, and cut to the same size as the zucchini.

3. Keeping the vegetables in separate piles, steam the potatoes and turnips for 15-20 minutes, the carrots, broccoli or beans for 6 minutes, and the zucchini and green onions for 3 minutes. Arrange on a serving dish and keep warm.

4. Remove the fish from its wrapping and place in the middle of the vegetables; keep them warm while preparing the sauce.

5. Melt the butter, add the flour and cook gently for 1-2 minutes until pale brown. Stir in the milk, add the flour gradually, stirring constantly. Bring the sauce to boil for 1-2 minutes until thick. Strain in the cooking liquid from the fish.

6. Peel and segment the remaining lemons, working over a bowl to collect any juice. Chop the remaining thyme and add to the sauce along with lemon segments and juice.

7. Sprinkle paprika on the potatoes, and chopped parsley on the carrots. Coat the fish with lemon sauce and serve.

TIME Preparation takes 30 minutes, cooking takes 40-60 minutes.

Fish & Seafood
Notes

Fish & Seafood
Notes

HEALTHY COOKING

LOW
CHOLESTEROL

FOR YOUR HEART'S SAKE

Introduction

Health and diet are inextricably linked to such a degree that none of us can afford to regard healthy eating simply as a fad. Heart disease in particular, is one of the most common fatal conditions in the Western world, and one of the most crucial factors which causes this is a high cholesterol diet.

Cholesterol is a fatty substance found in all animal tissue and it is also produced in the body by the liver. Essentially, cholesterol is needed to carry fats through the bloodstream. Problems occur when too much fat builds up and is left on the walls of arteries, narrowing them and restricting the blood flow around the body. If this flow becomes completely blocked, a heart attack will occur.

In order to reduce excess cholesterol we must change our eating habits by reducing the amount of animal tissue and animal fat which we eat.

Research has shown that by eating non-animal fats the blood levels of cholesterol can actually be reduced. The reason being that vegetable fats are mainly polyunsaturated and these help to regulate the blood flow and keep the arteries clear of fatty deposits. Polyunsaturated fats from vegetables can therefore be included freely in a low cholesterol diet but high fat animal products such as red meat, pork and dairy foods must be restricted. Fish contains a type of fat called mono-unsaturated, which has no effect on cholesterol levels and can therefore be included in your diet without any detrimental effect. Shellfish, however, are very high in cholesterol and should be avoided completely.

One point to watch out for is that some products, such as margarines, are not always as "healthy" as their packaging suggests. A production method called hydrogenation actually changes polyunsaturated fats into saturates, so look on labels and do not buy items which contain "hydrogenated vegetable oils" or "hydrogenated unsaturated fats."

These low cholesterol recipes have been developed to offer a wide choice of favorite items which combine healthy eating with flavor and variety. So delve inside and you will realize that as well as protecting your health, nutritious food can also tickle your taste buds.

SERVES 4-6

ONION SOUP

This delicious recipe demonstrates that food which is good for your heart need be neither bland nor boring.

¼ cup polyunsaturated margarine
2lbs onions, peeled and thinly sliced
3 tsps sugar
½ cup all-purpose flour
7½ cups chicken stock or water
Salt and freshly ground black pepper
1½ tsps dried thyme
½ cup dry white wine or dry sherry
12 x 1-inch slices French bread
3 tbsps olive oil
½ cup grated Cheddar cheese, optional
Fresh parsley for garnish

Step 1 Brown the onions in a large saucepan with the margarine and sugar.

Step 6 Lightly brush the slices of bread with the olive oil.

1. Melt the margarine in a large saucepan. Stir in the onions and add the sugar. Cook uncovered over a low heat, stirring occasionally, for 15-20 minutes or until the onions become golden brown.

2. Stir the flour into the onions and cook for 1 minute.

3. Gradually pour the stock into the onions, mixing well with each addition to blend smoothly.

4. Season with the salt, pepper and thyme, and add the wine or sherry. Return the soup to a low heat and bring to the boil.

5. Partially cover the saucepan, then simmer the soup for 20-30 minutes.

6. Brush each side of the slices of bread lightly with the olive oil and arrange them on a metal rack in a broiler pan.

7. Lightly toast one side of the bread under a hot broiler until it turns pale gold.

8. Turn the slices of bread over and sprinkle with the grated cheese, if used.

9. Return the slices of bread to the broiler and cook until the cheese has melted and is golden brown, or if the cheese is not being used, until the other side of the bread has been lightly toasted.

10. Serve the soup in individual bowls with 2 or 3 of the croutons floating on the top. Garnish with fresh parsley.

Cook's Notes

Time
Preparation takes about 20 minutes, cooking takes about 45 minutes-1 hour.

Freezing
This soup freezes very well, but the croutons should be prepared fresh each time.

Cook's Tip
The addition of sugar will help the onion to brown. For a paler soup, omit the sugar and gently fry the onions until they are just soft and not browned.

Fat Type
Chicken stock contains fairly small amounts of saturated fat. The cheese contains a higher amount, but is used in such small quantities that this should not matter. Use vegetable stock and omit the cheese if desired.

SERVES 4

CELERY AND APPLE SOUP

This interesting combination of flavors produces a tasty soup that is also suitable for vegetarians.

2 tbsps polyunsaturated margarine
1 large onion, peeled and finely chopped
3 cooking apples, peeled, cored and sliced
5 cups vegetable stock
1 bay leaf
Salt and freshly ground black pepper
3 sticks of celery, finely chopped
Finely sliced celery for garnish

celery. Bring to the boil, then cover and simmer for 30 minutes.

5. Using a liquidizer or food processor, blend the onion and apple mixture until it is smooth.

6. Beat the puréed onion and apple mixture into the pan containing the stock and celery.

7. Return the pan to the heat and bring back to the boil. Garnish with the celery sticks and serve immediately

Step 2 Gently cook the apples with the onion until it begins to soften.

Step 4 Cook the celery in half of the stock, simmering until it is tender.

1. Melt the margarine in a large pan and stir in the onions. Fry gently for 5 minutes, or until the onions are soft but not browned.

2. Add the apple to the onion mixture and cook for a further 3 minutes, or until the apple begins to soften.

3. Stir half the stock into the onion and apple, along with the bay leaf and seasoning. Bring the mixture to the boil, cover and simmer for half an hour. Remove the bay leaf.

4. Put the remaining stock into another pan along with the

Step 6 Beat the puréed onion and apples into the stock and celery, mixing well to blend evenly.

Cook's Notes

Time
Preparation takes about 15 minutes, cooking takes about 45 minutes.

Serving Idea
Serve with whole-wheat rolls or a French stick.

Freezing
This recipe freezes well.

Fat Type
This recipe contains no saturated fat at all.

SERVES 6

MINESTRONE SOUP

There are numerous different recipes for minestrone. This one is high in fiber, which helps to reduce cholesterol levels in the blood, and it has hardly any saturated fats at all.

½ cup dried white cannellini beans
5 cups vegetable stock
3 tbsps olive oil
1 large onion, peeled and finely chopped
1 clove garlic, minced
1 stick celery, thinly sliced
2 carrots, peeled and diced
¼lb spring greens, finely shredded
½ cup cut green beans
1 large zucchini, trimmed and diced
¼lb tomatoes, peeled, seeded and diced
1 bay leaf
⅓ cup whole-wheat pasta
1½ tbsps fresh chopped basil
1½ tbsps fresh chopped parsley
Salt and freshly ground black pepper

1. Put the beans into a large bowl and cover with the vegetable stock. Leave to soak overnight. During this time the beans will double in volume.

2. Heat the oil in a large saucepan and gently fry the onion and garlic until they have softened, but not browned.

3. Stir in the celery, carrots, spring greens, green beans and zucchini. Fry gently, stirring until they have just began to soften.

4. Add the beans with the stock to the pan of vegetables, along with the tomatoes, bay leaf, pasta and seasoning. Bring to the boil, then cover and simmer for about 1 hour, or until the beans are very tender. Stir occasionally during this time to prevent the ingredients from sticking.

5. Stir in the basil and parsley, heat through for 5 minutes and serve immediately.

Step 1 Soak the beans overnight in the vegetable stock. They will double in volume during this time.

Step 4 Add the beans and stock to the partially cooked vegetables.

Cook's Notes

Time
Preparation takes about 20 minutes, plus overnight soaking for the beans. Cooking takes about 1½ hours.

Serving Idea
Serve with crusty whole-wheat rolls.

Watchpoint
It is most important to cook any dried beans very thoroughly as they can be dangerous if eaten before they are sufficiently cooked.

Variation
Use red kidney beans instead of the white cannellini beans in this recipe.

Fat Type
Olive oil contains polyunsaturated fat and the pasta contains negligible amounts of saturated fat.

SERVES 4

VICHYSSOISE

Although this French soup is usually eaten cold, it also delicious served hot.

3 large leeks
2 tbsps polyunsaturated margarine
1 medium-sized onion, peeled and sliced
2 medium-sized potatoes, peeled and thinly sliced
2½ cups vegetable stock
Salt and ground white pepper
1¼ cups skim milk
Finely chopped parsley or chives, for garnish

1. Trim the top and bottom from the leeks and peel away the outer leaf.

2. Slit the leeks lengthwise down one side cutting right into the center of the vegetable.

3. Hold the leek under running cold water, allowing it to wash any bits of soil or grit from in between the leaves.

4. Slice the leeks very thinly using a sharp knife.

5. Melt the margarine in a saucepan and add the leek and sliced onion. Cover and allow to sweat gently over a low heat for about 10 minutes.

6. Add the potatoes to the leek mixture, and pour in the stock.

7. Season with the salt and pepper, cover and cook gently for 15 minutes, or until the potatoes are soft.

8. Using a liquidizer or food processor, purée the soup until it is smooth.

9. Return the puréed soup to the saucepan and stir in the milk. Adjust the seasoning and reheat very gently until it is almost boiling. Remove from heat.

10. Either serve the soup immediately or allow to cool, then chill in a refrigerator for at least 2 hours.

Step 2 Slit the leeks lengthwise down one side, cutting into the center of each vegetable.

Step 3 Hold the slit leeks under cold running water, allowing it to penetrate between the leaves to wash out any soil or grit.

Step 8 Purée the leek and potato mixture in a liquidizer or food processor, until it is very smooth.

11. Serve garnished with the finely chopped parsley or chives.

Cook's Notes

Time
Preparation takes about 15 minutes, plus chilling time.
Cooking takes about 30 minutes.

Serving Idea
Serve with lightly toasted slices of whole-wheat bread.

Freezing
This soup freezes very well.

Fat Type
This soup contains a minimal amount of saturated fat in the milk.

SERVES 4

CHICKEN SATAY

This typical Indonesian dish is very spicy, but uses ingredients which are all low in fat, making it an excellent appetizer for four.

3 tbsps soy sauce
3 tbsps sesame oil
3 tbsps lime juice
1½ tsps ground cumin
1½ tsps turmeric powder
3 tsps ground coriander
1lb chicken breast, cut into 1-inch cubes
3 tbsps peanut oil
1 small onion, very finely chopped or minced
1½ tsps chili powder
½ cup crunchy peanut butter
1½ tsps brown sugar
Lime wedges and coriander leaves, for garnish

1. Put the soy sauce, sesame oil, lime juice, cumin, turmeric and coriander into a large bowl and mix well.

2. Add the cubed chicken to the soy sauce marinade and stir well to coat the meat evenly.

3. Cover with plastic wrap or a damp cloth and allow to stand in a refrigerator for at least 1 hour, but preferably overnight.

4. Drain the meat, reserving the marinade.

5. Thread the meat onto 4 large or 8 small skewers and set aside.

6. Heat the peanut oil in a small saucepan and add the onion and chili powder. Cook gently until the onion is slightly softened.

7. Stir the reserved marinade into the oil and onion mixture, along with the peanut butter and brown sugar. Heat gently, stirring constantly, until all the ingredients are well blended.

Step 5 Thread the marinated meat onto 4 large, or 8 small, kebab skewers.

Step 9 Brush the partially broiled chicken with a little of the peanut sauce to baste.

8. If the sauce is too thick, stir in 2-4 tbsps boiling water.

9. Arrange the skewers of meat on a broiler pan and cook under a preheated moderate broiler for 10-15 minutes. After the first 5 minutes of cooking, brush the skewered meat with a little of the peanut sauce to baste.

10. During the cooking time turn the meat frequently to cook it on all sides and prevent it browning.

11. Serve the skewered meat garnished with the lime and coriander leaves, and the remaining sauce separately.

Cook's Notes

Time
Preparation takes about 25 minutes, cooking takes about 15 minutes.

Serving Idea
Serve with a mixed salad.

Variation
Use a selection of fresh vegetables instead of the chicken to make a vegetarian alternative, which would contain no saturated fat at all.

Fat Type
Chicken contains low amounts of saturated fat. The remaining ingredients contain unsaturated fats.

SERVES 4-6

SPICY VEGETABLE FRITTERS WITH TOMATO SAUCE

This delicious dish makes a ideal appetizer or interesting snack. Use any favorite vegetables or those that are in season.

1 cup all-purpose flour
1 cup whole-wheat flour
1½ tsps salt
1 tsp chili powder
1½ tsps ground cumin
1¼ cups water
1½ tbsps lemon juice
1 small cauliflower, broken into small flowerets
1 eggplant, cut into 1-inch cubes
3 zucchini, trimmed and cut into 1-inch pieces
2 cups button mushrooms
1 red pepper, seeded and cut into ¼-inch thick rounds
1 green pepper, seeded and cut into ¼-inch thick rounds
1 large potato, peeled and cut into 1-inch cubes
1⅔ cups canned plum tomatoes, drained
1 red chili, seeded and chopped
1 clove garlic, minced
1 small onion, peeled and finely chopped
1½ tbsps white wine vinegar
1½ tbsps soft brown sugar
Salt the freshly ground black pepper, to taste
1 sliced green chili for garnish
1 sliced red chili for garnish

1. Put the flours, salt, chili powder and cumin into a large bowl. Make a slight well in the center.

2. Gradually add the water and lemon juice to the flour, beating well until a smooth batter is formed.

3. Wash the fresh vegetables and allow them to drain completely on paper towels or a clean cloth.

4. Put the tomatoes, fresh chili, garlic, onions, vinegar and sugar into a food processor or liquidizer and blend until the sauce is smooth.

5. Pour the sauce mixture into a small pan and heat gently, stirring until it is completely warmed through. Season with salt and transfer to a small serving dish and garnish with slices of red and green chilies.

6. Heat some vegetable oil in a deep fat fryer until it is warm enough to brown a 1-inch cube of bread in just under 1 minute.

7. Make sure the vegetables are completely dry, patting any moisture off them with paper towels if necessary.

8. Using a slotted spoon drop the vegetables, a few at a time, into the batter and dip them to coat thoroughly.

9. Remove the vegetables from the batter, again using the slotted spoon, and allow some of the batter to drain back into the bowl.

10. Drop the vegetables into the hot oil, and fry quickly until they are golden brown and the batter puffy.

11. Remove the fried vegetables from the oil and drain completely on paper towels, keeping them warm until all the remaining vegetables have been prepared in this manner.

12. Serve immediately, providing small forks with which to dip the vegetables into the spicy tomato sauce.

Cook's Notes

Time
Preparation takes about 20 minutes, cooking takes about ½ hour.

Watchpoint
It is important to ensure that the vegetables are completely dry before coating with the batter, or it will not cover them.

Fat Type
There is no saturated fat in this dish, but it is important to check that the oil used in the deep fat frying is polyunsaturated and that it is fresh.

SERVES 6

TUNA, BEAN AND TOMATO SALAD

Fish is of great value in a low cholesterol diet as it contains mono-unsaturated fats which do not affect the cholesterol level in the blood.

1 cup dried flageolet beans
6oz canned tuna in brine
Juice of 1 lemon
⅔ cup olive oil
1½ tsps chopped fresh herbs, e.g. parsley, basil or
   marjoram
Salt and freshly ground black pepper
8 firm tomatoes

1. Put the beans into a bowl and pour over enough cold water to just cover. Allow to soak overnight.

2. Drain the beans and put them into a saucepan. Cover with boiling water, then simmer for at least 1 hour. Drain thoroughly and cool.

3. Drain the can of tuna and flake it into a bowl.

4. Put the lemon juice, olive oil, herbs and seasoning into a small bowl and beat together with a fork.

5. Stir the beans into the tuna fish and mix in the dressing, tossing the salad together carefully so that the tuna does not break up too much, but the dressing is thoroughly incorporated.

6. Adjust the seasoning and arrange the salad in a mound on a shallow serving dish.

7. Cut a small cross into the skins of the tomato and plunge them into boiling water for 30 seconds.

8. Using a sharp knife carefully peel away the skins from the tomatoes.

9. Slice the tomatoes thinly and arrange them around the edge of the bean and tuna salad. Serve immediately.

Step 5 Mix the dressing into the salad by tossing it carefully, to ensure that the tuna does not break up too much.

Step 8 When blanched, the skins on the tomatoes should peel away very easily if you use a sharp knife.

Cook's Notes

Time
Preparation takes about 25 minutes, plus overnight soaking.

Variation
Use any type of bean of your choice.

Watchpoint
Great care must be taken with cooking beans, as any that are under cooked could be dangerous when eaten.

Fat Type
This recipe contains mono-unsaturated and polyunsaturated fats.

Serving Idea
Serve with a simple lettuce salad.

SERVES 4

SMOKED MACKEREL PÂTÉ

Smoked fish has a wonderful flavor and is ideal for making pâté.

8oz smoked mackerel fillets, skin and bones removed
¼ cup polyunsaturated margarine
Juice of half an orange
1½ tsps tomato paste
1½ tsps white wine vinegar
Salt and freshly ground black pepper, optional
1 x 3½ oz can pimento peppers, drained
1¼ cups clear vegetable stock
3 tsps powdered gelatin
3 tbsps dry sherry
3 tbsps cold water

1. Put the mackerel, margarine, orange juice, paste, vinegar and seasonings into a liquidizer or food processor and blend until smooth.

2. Put the pâté into a serving dish and smooth the top evenly.

3. Cut the pimentos into thin strips and arrange in a lattice over the top of the pâté.

4. Bring the stock to the boil in a small pan. Remove from the heat and cool for 1 minute.

5. Sprinkle over the gelatin and allow to stand, stirring occasionally until it has completely dissolved.

6. When the gelatin has dissolved the liquid should be

Step 3 Arrange the strips of pimento in a lattice pattern over the top of the pâté.

Step 5 Sprinkle the gelatine over the hot stock and allow it to stand, to dissolve completely.

clear. At this point stir in the sherry and cold water.

7. Very carefully spoon the aspic over the top of the mackerel pâté and the pimentos, taking great care not to dislodge the lattice pattern.

8. Chill the pâté in a refrigerator until the aspic has completely set.

Cook's Notes

Time
Preparation takes about 30 minutes, plus chilling time. Cooking takes about 2 minutes.

Variation
Use any type of smoked fish in place of the mackerel in this recipe.

Preparation
If you do not have a food processor or blender, this pâté can be made by mashing with a fork, but it will not have such a smooth texture.

Fat Type
Fish contains mono-unsaturated fat which does not affect the cholesterol level in the blood.

Serving Idea
Serve with crusty whole-wheat bread or French toast.

SERVES 4-6

TOMATO AND PEPPER ICE

Similar to frozen gazpacho, this appetizer is ideal for serving on warm summer days. It could also be used, in smaller quantities, as a palate freshener between courses in place of a conventional sweet sorbet.

6 ice cubes
½ cup canned tomato juice
Juice 1 lemon
1½ tsps Worcestershire sauce
½ small green pepper, seeded and roughly chopped
½ small red pepper, seeded and roughly chopped

1. Break the ice into small pieces using a small hammer.

2. Put the broken ice into a blender or food processor, along with the tomato juice, lemon juice and Worcestershire sauce. Blend the mixture until it becomes slushy.

3. Pour the tomato mixture into ice trays and freeze for ½ hour, or until it is just half frozen.

4. Using a sharp knife, chop the peppers into very small pieces.

5. Remove the tomato ice from the freezer trays and put it into a bowl.

6. Mash the tomato ice with the back of a fork until the crystals are well broken up.

7. Mix in the chopped peppers and return the tomato ice to the freezer trays.

8. Re-freeze for a further 1½ hours, stirring occasionally to prevent the mixture from solidifying completely.

9. To serve, allow the tomato ice to defrost for about 5 minutes, then mash with the back of a fork to roughly break up the ice crystals. Serve in small glass dishes which have been chilled beforehand.

Step 2 Blend the ice, tomato juice, lemon juice and Worcestershire sauce until it becomes a smooth slush.

Step 6 Mash the semi-frozen tomato ice with the back of a fork to break up the ice crystals finely.

Step 8 During the freezing time, keep stirring the tomato and pepper ice with a fork, to prevent the mixture from becoming a solid block.

Cook's Notes

 Time
Preparation takes about 15 minutes, plus freezing time.

 Freezing
This recipe will freeze for up to 2 months.

 Watchpoint
Take care not to allow the tomato ice to freeze into a solid block, or it will be too hard to break into rough crystals.

 Serving Idea
Scoop out the tomatoes and serve this ice in the shells, instead of glass dishes.

 Fat Type
There is no fat in this recipe.

SERVES 4

SUMMER PASTA SALAD

Lightly cooked summer vegetables and whole-wheat pasta are combined to create this delicious wholesome salad.

1 eggplant
1 zucchini
1 red pepper
1 green pepper
1 medium-sized onion
2 large tomatoes
6 tbsps olive oil
1 clove garlic, minced
Salt and freshly ground black pepper
1⅓ cups whole-wheat pasta spirals
1½ tbsps vinegar
¾ tsp dry English mustard

Step 1 Sprinkle the eggplant slices liberally with salt and allow them to de-gorge for 30 minutes to remove their bitterness.

1. Cut the eggplant into ½-inch slices. Sprinkle the slices liberally with salt and allow to stand for 30 minutes.

2. Using a sharp knife, trim the zucchini and cut into ¼-inch slices.

3. Cut the peppers in half and carefully remove the cores and seeds. Using a sharp knife, cut the pepper into thin strips.

4. Peel and finely chop the onion.

5. Cut a small cross in the skins of the tomatoes and plunge them into boiling water for 30 seconds. After this time remove the tomatoes and carefully peel away the skins.

6. Cut the peeled tomatoes into 8. Remove and discard the pips from each tomato slice.

7. Put 3 tbsps of the olive oil in a frying pan and stir in the onion. Fry gently until it is transparent, but not colored.

8. Thoroughly rinse the salt from the eggplant slices and pat them dry on absorbent paper towels. Roughly chop the slices.

9. Add the chopped eggplant, zucchini, peppers, tomatoes and garlic to the cooked onion and fry very

Step 9 Gently fry all the vegetables together, stirring frequently to prevent them from browning.

gently for 20 minutes, or until just soft. Season with salt and pepper and allow to cool.

10. Put the pasta spirals in a large saucepan and cover with boiling water. Sprinkle in a little salt and simmer for 10 minutes or until tender but still firm.

11. Rinse the pasta in cold water and drain very well.

12. Beat together the remaining olive oil, the vinegar and mustard in a small bowl. Season with salt and pepper.

13. Put the pasta and cooled vegetables into a serving dish and pour over the dressing, tossing the ingredients together to coat them evenly. Serve well chilled.

Cook's Notes

Time
Preparation takes approximately 40 minutes, cooking takes 30 minutes.

Preparation
Make sure that the eggplant is rinsed very thoroughly or the salad will be much too salty.

Fat Type
Olive oil contains polyunsaturated fat and is therefore beneficial to those on a low cholesterol diet.

SERVES 4

MUSHROOM PASTA SALAD

Mushrooms are always delicious in a salad and this recipe, which combines them with whole-wheat pasta shapes, is no exception.

7½ tbsps olive oil
Juice of 2 lemons
1½ tsps fresh chopped basil
1½ tsps fresh chopped parsley
Salt and freshly ground black pepper
2 cups mushrooms
1⅓ cups whole-wheat pasta shapes of your choice

boiling water. Season with a little salt and simmer for 10 minutes, or until just tender.

5. Rinse the pasta in cold water and drain well.

6. Add the pasta to the marinated mushrooms and lemon dressing, mixing well to coat evenly.

7. Adjust the seasoning if necessary, then chill well before serving.

Step 1 Beat the lemon juice, herbs and seasoning together in a large bowl using a fork.

Step 2 Use a sharp knife to slice the mushrooms thinly.

1. In a large bowl mix together the olive oil, lemon juice, herbs and seasoning.

2. Finely slice the mushrooms and add these to the lemon dressing in the bowl, stirring well to coat the mushrooms evenly.

3. Cover the bowl with plastic wrap and allow to stand in a cool place for at least 1 hour.

4. Put the pasta into a large saucepan and cover with

Step 6 Stir the cooled pasta into the marinated mushrooms, mixing well to coat evenly.

Cook's Notes

 Time
Preparation takes approximately 10 minutes, plus 1 hour at least for the mushrooms to marinate. Cooking takes about 15 minutes.

 Variation
Use a mixture of button and wild mushrooms for a delicious variation in flavor.

 Serving Idea
Serve mushroom pasta salad on a bed of mixed lettuce.

 Fat Type
Olive oil contains polyunsaturated fat and is beneficial for those on a low cholesterol diet.

SERVES 4-6

STIR-FRY TOFU SALAD

Ideal for vegetarians, but so delicious that it will be enjoyed by everyone.

1 cake of tofu
¼lb snow peas
½ cup mushrooms
2 carrots, peeled
2 sticks celery
½ cup broccoli flowerets
⅔ cup vegetable oil
4½ tbsps lemon juice
3 tsps honey
1½ tsps grated fresh ginger
4½ tbsps soy sauce
Dash of sesame oil
4 green onions
½ cup unsalted roasted peanuts
1 cup bean sprouts
½ head Chinese cabbage

1. Drain the tofu well and press gently to remove any excess moisture. Cut into ½-inch cubes.

2. Trim the tops and tails from the snow peas.

3. Thinly slice the mushrooms with a sharp knife.

4. Cut the carrots and celery into thin slices, angling your knife so that each slice is cut on the diagonal.

5. Trim the green onions and slice them in the same way as the carrots and celery.

6. Heat 3 tbsps of the vegetable oil in a wok or large frying pan. Stir in the snow peas, mushrooms, celery, carrots and broccoli, and cook for 2 minutes, stirring constantly.

7. Remove the vegetables from the wok and set them aside to cool.

8. Put the remaining oil into a small bowl and beat in the lemon juice, honey, ginger, soy sauce and sesame oil.

9. Stir the sliced green onions, peanuts and bean sprouts into the cooled vegetables.

10. Mix the dressing into the salad vegetables, then add the tofu. Toss the tofu into the salad very carefully so that it does not break up.

11. Shred the Chinese cabbage and arrange them on a serving platter. Pile the salad ingredients over the top and serve well chilled.

Step 4 Slice the carrots and celery thinly, cutting with your knife at an angle to produce diagonal pieces

Step 10 Toss the tofu very carefully into the salad ingredients taking care not the break it up.

Cook's Notes

 Time
Preparation takes approximately 25 minutes, cooking takes 2-4 minutes.

 Preparation
Make sure that the stir-fried vegetables are completely cool before adding the remaining salad ingredients, or they will lose their crispness.

 Variation
Shredded cooked chicken can be used in place of the tofu in this recipe.

 Fat Type
All the fat in this recipe is polyunsaturated.

SERVES 6-8

MIXED PEPPER SALAD

It is now possible to buy sweet peppers in a variety of colors, so include as many as you wish in this eye-catching salad.

3 red peppers
3 green peppers
3 yellow peppers
3 tbsps vegetable oil
9 tbsps sunflower oil
3 tbsps lemon juice
3 tbsps white wine vinegar
1 small clove garlic, minced
Pinch salt
Pinch cayenne pepper
Pinch sugar
3 hard-cooked eggs
⅓ cup black olives, pitted
3 tbsps finely chopped fresh coriander leaves, optional

Step 2 Put the cored pepper halves cut side down on a flat surface and gently press them with the palm of your hand to flatten them out.

Step 4 Cook the oiled peppers under the broiler until the skin begins to char and split.

1. Cut all the peppers in half and remove the seeds and cores.

2. With the palm of your hand lightly press the halved peppers down onto a flat surface, to flatten them out.

3. Brush the skin side of each pepper with a little of the vegetable oil and place under a preheated hot broiler.

4. Cook until the skins begin to char and split.

5. Remove the peppers from the broiler and wrap them in a clean dishtowel. Allow to stand for 10-15 minutes.

6. Put the sunflower oil, lemon juice, vinegar, garlic, salt, pepper and sugar into a small bowl and beat together well.

7. Shell the eggs and cut each one into four.

8. Unwrap the peppers and carefully peel away the burnt skin. Cut the pepper flesh into thick strips about 1-inch wide.

9. Arrange the pepper strips in a circle, alternating the colors all the way round.

10. Arrange the olives and quartered eggs in the center.

11. Sprinkle with the coriander leaves, and spoon over all the dressing.

12. Chill the salad for at least 1 hour before serving.

Cook's Notes

 Time
Preparation takes 20 minutes, cooking takes about 5 minutes.

 Serving Idea
Serve this salad with crusty French bread or rolls.

 Cook's Tip
Peeled peppers will keep in a refrigerator for up to 5 days if they are covered with a little oil.

 Fat Type
This recipe is high in polyunsaturated fats. The eggs contain saturated fats, but can be omitted if desired.

SERVES 4

CHEESY STUFFED TOMATOES

Although cheese should be avoided on a low fat diet, soft cheeses such as Brie and Camembert do have a lower fat content than Cheddar and in small amounts can provide welcome variety in a restricted diet.

4 beefsteak tomatoes
4 anchovy fillets
3 tsps capers, drained
2 green onions
1 cup Camembert or Brie cheese, rind removed
3 tsps caraway seeds
Salt and freshly ground black pepper
Lettuce to garnish

1. Cut a slice from the rounded end of each tomato and carefully scoop out the pulp and seeds. Strain out the seeds and reserve the pulp and juice for the filling.

Step 1 Strain the seeds out of the tomato pulp, keeping only the pulp and juice for use in the recipe.

2. Put the anchovies in a bowl and cover with a little milk. Allow to soak for 5 minutes to remove the saltiness.

3. Drain and rinse the anchovies, then pat them dry. Chop the anchovies finely.

4. Put the capers and green onions onto a board and chop them finely also.

5. Put the cheese into a bowl and mash it with a fork.

6. Stir in the capers, anchovies, onions, caraway seeds, tomato juice and pulp. Mix together thoroughly, then season with a little salt and pepper.

7. Carefully spoon the cheese filling into the hollowed out tomatoes and arrange them on a serving plate.

Step 7 Carefully pile the cheese filling back into the hollowed out tomatoes.

8. Replace the sliced tops and serve them well chilled on a bed of lettuce.

Cook's Notes

Time
Preparation takes 15 minutes, plus chilling time of at least 1 hour.

Preparation
Use a grapefruit knife or serrated teaspoon to remove the centers of the tomatoes.

Variation
Use cottage or curd cheese instead of the Camembert or Brie.

Serving Idea
Serve with a vinaigrette dressing and whole-wheat bread or rolls.

Fat Type
The cheese contains saturated fat, so should only be eaten in moderation.

SERVES 4

MEDITERRANEAN EGGPLANTS

These delicious stuffed eggplants can be served as an accompaniment to a main meal for four or as a lunch dish for two.

2 small eggplants
2 tbsps polyunsaturated margarine
1 small onion, finely chopped
1 clove garlic, minced
¼lb tomatoes
⅔ cup long grain rice, cooked
3 tsps fresh chopped marjoram
Pinch cinnamon
Salt and freshly ground black pepper

1. Preheat an oven to 350°F. Wrap the eggplants in aluminum foil and bake for 20 minutes to soften. Allow to cool.

2. Cut the eggplants in half, then using a serrated teaspoon or grapefruit knife, carefully scoop out the pulp leaving a ½-inch border to form a shell.

3. Melt the margarine in a frying pan and gently sauté the onion and garlic until they are just soft.

4. Chop the eggplant pulp roughly and stir into the pan along with the onions. Cover and cook for about 5 minutes.

5. Cut a small cross in the skins of the tomatoes and plunge them into boiling water for 30 seconds.

6. Remove the tomatoes from the water and carefully peel away the skin using a sharp knife.

7. Quarter the tomatoes and remove and discard the pips. Chop the tomato flesh roughly and stir into the cooked eggplant and onion mixture, along with the rice, marjoram and cinnamon. Season with salt and pepper.

8. Carefully pile the rice filling back into the eggplant shells and arrange them on an ovenproof dish or cookie sheet. Cover with aluminum foil.

9. Return to the oven and bake for 20 minutes. Serve hot, garnished with a little finely chopped parsley if desired.

Step 2 Carefully scoop the pulp out of each eggplant half with a serrated spoon or grapefruit knife, leaving a thin border on the inside to form a shell.

Step 7 Remove and discard the seeds from the peeled tomatoes.

Cook's Notes

 Time
Preparation takes 25 minutes, cooking takes about 40 minutes.

 Preparation
Take care not to split the eggplant shells when scooping out the pulp.

 Variation
½ cup mature Cheddar cheese can be added to the filling if desired or allowed!

 Fat Type
This recipe contains only polyunsaturated fats.

SERVES 4

CHICKEN WITH "BURNT" PEPPERS AND CORIANDER

"Burning" peppers is a technique for removing the skins which also imparts a delicious flavor to this favorite vegetable.

2 red peppers, halved and seeded
1 green pepper, halved and seeded
6 tbsps vegetable oil, for brushing
1½ tbsps olive oil
3 tsps paprika
Pinch ground cumin
Pinch cayenne pepper
2 cloves garlic, minced
1lb canned tomatoes, drained and chopped
4½ tbsps fresh chopped coriander
4½ tbsps fresh chopped parsley
Salt, for seasoning
4 large chicken breasts, boned
1 large onion, sliced
⅓ cup slivered almonds

1. Put the peppers, cut side down, on a flat surface and gently press them with the palm of your hand to flatten them out.

2. Brush the skin side with 3 tbsps of the vegetable oil and cook them under a hot broiler until the skin chars and splits.

3. Wrap the peppers in a clean towel for 10 minutes to cool.

4. Unwrap the peppers and carefully peel off the charred skin. Chop the pepper flesh into thin strips.

5. Heat the olive oil in a frying pan and gently fry the paprika, cumin, cayenne pepper and garlic for 2 minutes, stirring to prevent the garlic from browning.

6. Stir in the tomatoes, coriander, parsley and season with a little salt. Simmer for 15-20 minutes, or until thick. Set aside.

7. Heat the remaining vegetable oil in an ovenproof casserole dish, and sauté the chicken breasts, turning them frequently until they are golden brown on both sides.

8. Remove the chicken and set aside. Gently fry the onions in the oil for about 5 minutes, or until softened but not overcooked.

9. Return the chicken to the casserole with the onions and pour on about 1¼ cups of water. Bring to the boil.

10. Cover the casserole and simmer for about 30 minutes, turning the chicken occasionally to prevent it from burning.

11. Remove the chicken from the casserole and boil the remaining liquid rapidly to reduce to about ⅓ cup of stock.

12. Add the peppers and the tomato sauce to the chicken stock and stir well.

13. Return the chicken to the casserole, cover and simmer very gently for a further 30 minutes, or until the chicken is tender.

14. Arrange the chicken on a serving dish with a little of the sauce spooned over. Sprinkle with the almonds and serve any remaining sauce separately.

Cook's Notes

Time
Preparation takes 30 minutes, cooking takes about 1 hour 30 minutes.

Preparation
Take care not to cook this dish too rapidly or the peppers will disintegrate.

Fat Type
The chicken contains saturated fats, but only in small quantities, the rest of the dish contains only polyunsaturated fat.

SERVES 4

HERRINGS WITH APPLES

The addition of fresh tasting apples beautifully complements the delicious and wholesome flavor of herring.

4 herrings, cleaned
2 large dessert apples
1 large onion
4 large potatoes, peeled and sliced
Salt and freshly ground black pepper
½ cup dry cider
1 cup dried breadcrumbs
¼ cup polyunsaturated margarine
1½ tbsps fresh chopped parsley

1. Cut the heads and tails from the herrings and split them open from the underside.

2. Put the herrings, belly side down, on a flat surface and carefully press along the back of each fish with the palm of your hand, pushing the backbone down towards the surface.

3. Turn the herrings over and with a sharp knife, carefully prise away the backbone, pulling out any loose bones as you go. Do not cut the fish into separate fillets. Wash and dry them well.

4. Peel, quarter, core and slice one of the apples. Peel and slice the onion thinly.

5. Lightly grease a shallow baking pan and layer with the potatoes, apple and onions, seasoning well with salt and pepper between layers.

6. Pour the cider over the potato layers and cover the dish with foil. Bake in a preheated oven 350°F for 40 minutes.

7. Remove the dish from the oven and arrange the herring fillets over the top.

8. Sprinkle the breadcrumbs over the herrings and dot

Step 2 Press down the backbone of the herrings with the palm of your hand, pushing the spine towards the work surface as you go.

Step 3 Carefully lift the backbone away from the fish with a sharp knife, pulling any loose bones out at the same time. Do not cut the fish into separate fillets.

with half of the margarine.

9. Increase the oven temperature to 400°F and return the dish to the oven for about 10–15 minutes, or until the herrings are cooked and brown.

10. Core the remaining apples and slice into rounds, leaving the peel on.

11. Melt the remaining margarine in a frying pan and gently fry the apple slices.

12. Remove the herrings from the oven and garnish with the fried apple slices and chopped parsley. Serve at once.

Cook's Notes

Time
Preparation takes 15-20 minutes, cooking takes about 50 minutes.

Variation
Use small mackerel instead of herrings in this recipe.

Serving Idea
Serve with a carrot, orange and watercress salad.

Fat Type
Fish contains mono-unsaturated fats which do not affect the cholesterol levels in the blood.

SERVES 6-8

SALMON TROUT WITH SPINACH AND WALNUT STUFFING

1 fresh whole salmon trout, weighing 2½lbs, cleaned
2lbs fresh spinach
1 small onion
¼ cup polyunsaturated margarine
½ cup walnuts, roughly chopped
2 cups fresh white breadcrumbs
1½ tbsps fresh chopped parsley
1½ tbsps fresh chopped thyme
Pinch grated nutmeg
Salt and freshly ground black pepper
Juice 2 lemons
Watercress sprigs and lemon slices, to garnish

1. Carefully cut the underside of the fish from the end of the slit made when the fish was cleaned, to the tip of the tail.

2. Place the fish, belly side down, on a flat work surface, spreading the cut underside out to balance the fish more easily.

3. Using the palm of your hand press down along the backbone of the fish, pushing the spine downwards towards the work surface.

4. Turn the fish over and using a sharp knife, carefully pull the backbone away from the fish, cutting it away with scissors at the base of the head and tail.

5. Remove the backbone completely and pull out any loose bones you may find with a pair of tweezers. Lay the boned fish in the center of a large square of lightly oiled aluminum foil and set aside.

6. Wash the spinach leaves well and tear off any coarse stalks. Put the spinach into a large saucepan and sprinkle with salt. Do not add any extra water. Cover and cook over a moderate heat for about 3 minutes.

7. Turn the spinach into a colander and drain well, pressing with the back of a wooden spoon to remove all the excess moisture.

8. Chop the cooked spinach very finely using a sharp knife.

9. Peel and chop the onion finely and fry gently in about 1 tbsp of the margarine until soft, but not colored.

10. Stir the cooked onion into the chopped spinach along with the walnuts, breadcrumbs, herbs, nutmeg, salt, pepper and half of the lemon juice. Mix well to blend evenly.

11. Use the spinach stuffing to fill the cavity inside the trout. Push the stuffing in firmly, re-shaping the fish as you do so. Allow a little of the stuffing to show between the cut edge of the fish.

12. Seal the foil over the top of the fish, but do not wrap it too tightly.

13. Place the fish in a roasting pan and bake in a preheated oven at 350°F for 35 minutes.

14. Carefully unwrap the fish and transfer it to a large serving dish.

15. Using a sharp knife, peel away the skin from all exposed sides of the fish. If possible remove some skin from the underside also.

16. Whilst the fish is still hot, dot with the remaining margarine, sprinkle with the remaining lemon juice, then serve garnished with the watercress and sliced lemon.

Cook's Notes

Time
Preparation takes 35-40 minutes, cooking takes about 40 minutes.

Cook's Tip
If you feel that you cannot bone the fish yourself, ask your fishmonger to do it for you, but explain that you wish the bone to be removed from the underside of the fish.

Fat Type
Fish contains mono-unsaturated fats and the remainder of fats used in this recipe are all polyunsaturated.

SERVES 4

SPANISH GUINEA FOWL

The olive oil in this recipe gives a wonderful flavor to the sauce without loading it with saturated fat.

4 small guinea fowl
Salt and freshly ground black pepper
Olive oil, to brush
4 small wedges of lime or lemon
4 bay leaves
3 tbsps olive oil
1 small onion, thinly sliced
1 clove garlic, peeled and minced
1lb tomatoes
⅔ cup red wine
⅔ cup chicken or vegetable stock
1½ tbsps tomato paste
1 green chilies, seeded and thinly sliced
1 small red pepper, seeded and cut into thin strips
1 small green pepper, seeded and cut into thin strips
3 tbsps chopped blanched almonds
1½ tbsps pine kernels
12 small black olives, pitted
1½ tbsps raisins

1. Rub the guinea fowl inside and out with salt and pepper. Brush the skins with olive oil and push a wedge of lemon or lime, and a bay leaf into the center of each one.

2. Roast the guinea fowl, uncovered, in a preheated oven 375°F for 45 minutes, or until just tender.

3. Heat the 3 tbsps olive oil in a large frying pan and gently cook the onion and the garlic until they are soft, but not colored.

4. Cut a slit into the skins of each tomato and plunge into boiling water for 30 seconds.

5. Using a sharp knife carefully peel away the skins from the blanched tomatoes.

6. Chop the tomatoes roughly. Remove and discard the seeds and cores.

7. Add the chopped tomatoes to the cooked onion and garlic, and fry gently for a further 2 minutes.

8. Add all the remaining ingredients and simmer for 10-15 minutes, or until the tomatoes have completely softened and the sauce has thickened slightly.

9. Arrange the guinea fowl on a serving dish and spoon a little of the sauce over each one.

10. Serve hot with the remaining sauce in a separate jug.

Step 3 Fry the onion and garlic gently in the olive oil until they are soft but not colored.

Step 5 Using a sharp knife carefully peel away the loosened skins from the blanched tomatoes.

Cook's Notes

Time
Preparation takes 15 minutes, cooking takes about 1 hour.

Serving Idea
Serve with rice and a mixed green salad.

Cook's Tip
If the guinea fowl start to get too brown during the cooking time, cover them with aluminum foil.

Fat Type
Chicken contains only small amounts of saturated fats, and the remaining ingredients in this recipe contain only unsaturated fats.

SERVES 4

SAFFRON CHICKEN

The delicate color and flavor of saffron enhances the taste of chicken and gives this dish a Mediterranean flavor.

2-3lb chicken
3 tbsps olive oil
Salt and freshly ground black pepper
1 small onion, peeled and finely chopped
1 clove garlic, minced
3 tsps paprika
8 tomatoes
1½ cups long grain white rice
2½ cups boiling water
Large pinch saffron strands or ¼ tsp ground saffron
1 cup frozen peas
3 tbsps chopped fresh parsley

Step 4 Remove the skin from the chicken joints by pulling and cutting with a sharp knife.

1. Cut the chicken into 8 pieces with a sharp knife or cook's cleaver, cutting lengthwise down the breast bone and through the backbone, to halve it completely.

2. Cut the chicken halves in half again, slitting between the leg joint diagonally up and around the breast joint.

3. Finally cut each chicken quarter in half by cutting away the drumsticks from the leg thigh joint, and the wings from the breast joints.

4. Remove the skin from the chicken joints by pulling and cutting with a sharp knife.

5. Heat the oil in a large casserole dish or sauté pan,and fry the chicken, turning it frequently to brown evenly. Season with a little salt and pepper, then remove it from the pan and set aside.

6. Add the onions and garlic to the juices in the sauté pan and cook slowly until softened but not colored.

7. Add the paprika to the onions and fry quickly for about

30 seconds to just burn.

8. Cut a small cross into the skins of the tomatoes and plunge them into boiling water.

9. Using a sharp knife peel away the loosened skin from each tomato.

10. Cut the tomatoes into quarters and remove the cores and seeds. Chop the tomato flesh finely and add this to the sauté pan with the paprika and the onions.

11. Cook for about 5-10 minutes to draw off the liquid from the tomatoes. The sauce mixture should be of a dropping consistency when this has been done.

12. Stir the rice, water and saffron into the tomato purée along with the browned chicken portions. Bring to the boil, reduce the heat to simmering, then cover the casserole tightly and cook for about 20 minutes.

13. Add the peas and the parsley to the casserole, stir well and continue cooking for a further 5-10 minutes, or until the rice is tender and all the liquids have been absorbed.

14. Serve very hot.

Cook's Notes

Time
Preparation takes about 25 minutes, cooking takes 30-35 minutes.

Watchpoint
Stir the casserole frequently after step 12 to prevent the rice from sticking.

Fat Type
Chicken contains small amounts of saturated fat, but the remainder in this recipe is polyunsaturated.

SERVES 4

CHICKEN LIVER STIR-FRY

Chicken livers are very low in fat and high in flavor. They also require very little cooking so are perfect for stir-fry recipes.

1lb chicken livers
4½ tbsps sesame oil
⅓ cup split blanched almonds
1 clove garlic, peeled
⅓ cup snow peas, trimmed
8-10 Chinese cabbage leaves, shredded
3 tsps cornstarch
1½ tbsps cold water
3 tbsps soy sauce
⅔ cup chicken or vegetable stock

1. Trim the chicken livers, removing any discolored areas or fatty tubes.

2. Cut the chicken livers into even-sized pieces.

3. Heat a wok and pour in the oil. When the oil is hot, reduce the heat and stir-fry the almonds until they are pale golden brown. Remove the almonds, draining any oil back into the wok, and set them aside on kitchen towels.

4. Add the garlic clove to the wok and cook for 1-2 minutes to flavor the oil only. Remove the clove of garlic and discard.

5. Stir the chicken livers into the flavored oil and cook for 2-3 minutes, stirring frequently to brown evenly. Remove the chicken livers from the wok and set them aside.

6. Add the snow peas to the hot oil and stir-fry for 1 minute. Then stir in the Chinese cabbage leaves and cook for 1 minute further. Remove the vegetables and set aside.

7. Mix together the cornstarch and water, then blend in the soy sauce and stock.

8. Pour the cornstarch mixture into the wok and bring to the boil, stirring until the sauce has thickened and cleared.

Step 1 Trim the chicken livers, cutting away any discolored areas or bits of fat or tubes using a sharp knife.

Step 3 Stir-fry the almonds in the hot oil until they are a pale golden brown.

Step 8 Cook the sauce in the wok, stirring all the time until it has thickened and cleared.

9. Return all other ingredients to the wok and heat through for 1 minute. Serve immediately.

Cook's Notes

Time
Preparation takes 25 minutes, cooking takes 5-6 minutes.

Variation
Use finely sliced lamb or calves' liver in place of the chicken livers.

Serving Idea
Serve with fried rice or noodles.

Fat Type
Liver contains saturated fat, but in very small quantities.

SERVES 4-6

CHICKEN WITH LEMON JULIENNE

Lean chicken served with a tangy julienne of fresh vegetables makes a delicious main course – ideal for those on a low cholesterol diet.

1 x 3lb chicken
3 tbsps olive oil
3 tbsps polyunsaturated margarine
2 sticks celery
2 carrots
1 small onion, peeled and thinly sliced
1½ tbsps chopped fresh basil
1 bay leaf
Juice and grated rind of 2 small lemons
⅔ cup water
Salt and freshly ground black pepper
Pinch sugar, optional
Lemon slices for garnish

1. Cut the chicken into 8 pieces with a sharp knife or a cook's cleaver, cutting the chicken lengthwise down the breastbone and through the backbone to halve it completely.

2. Cut the chicken halves in half again, slitting between the leg joint diagonally up and around the breast joint.

3. Finally cut each chicken quarter in half by cutting away the drumsticks from the leg thigh joint, and the wings from the breast joints.

4. Remove the skin from the chicken joints by pulling and cutting with a sharp knife.

5. Heat the oil in a large sauté pan along with the margarine. Gently fry the chicken pieces, turning them frequently to brown evenly.

6. Remove the chicken pieces to a plate and set aside.

7. Using a sharp knife cut the celery into pieces 1½-inches long. Cut these pieces into long thin matchsticks lengthwise.

8. Cut the carrots into similar length pieces, then cut each piece in half lengthwise. Continue cutting each carrot half into the same sized pieces as the celery.

9. Stir the carrots and celery into the chicken juices, along with the onion. Cook over a gentle heat for about 3 minutes or until just beginning to soften but not brown.

10. Stir the basil, bay leaf, lemon juice and rind, the water, salt and pepper into the vegetables, mix well and cook for 2-3 minutes.

11. Return the chicken portions to the casserole and bring the mixture to the boil.

12. Cover the pan and reduce the heat. Allow the casserole to simmer for about 35-45 minutes, or until the chicken is tender and the juices will run clear when the meat is pierced with a sharp knife.

13. Remove the chicken and vegetables to a serving dish and discard the bay leaf.

14. Heat the sauce quickly to thicken if necessary. Adjust the flavor of the sauce with the sugar if desired.

15. Spoon the sauce over the chicken and garnish with the lemon slices.

Cook's Notes

Time
Preparation takes 40 minutes, cooking will take about 55 minutes.

Serving Idea
Serve with rice and a green salad.

Watchpoint
Make sure that the chicken pieces are patted dry with paper towels before you fry them or the oil will spit.

Fat Type
The chicken contains saturated fats in small amounts, the remainder is polyunsaturated fat.

SERVES 4

TROUT IN ASPIC

This attractive main course is ideal for serving as a part of a summer's meal.

7½ cups water
Pinch salt
6 black peppercorns
2 bay leaves
2 sprigs fresh parsley
1 small onion, quartered
1¼ cups dry white wine
4 even-sized rainbow trout, cleaned and well washed
2 egg whites, softly beaten
3 tbsps powdered gelatin
Lemon slices, capers and sprigs of fresh dill, to garnish

1. Put the water, salt, peppercorns, bay leaves, parsley, onion and wine into a large saucepan or fish kettle. Bring to the boil and simmer for about 30 minutes.

2. Cool slightly, then lay the fish into the hot stock. Cover the pan and bring back to simmering point.

3. Cook the fish gently for 5 minutes, then remove from the heat.

4. Allow the fish to cool in the covered pan before removing and draining on paper towels.

5. Reserve the stock.

6. Using a sharp knife, carefully peel away the skin from the cooked fish.

7. Using a palette knife, lift the fillets from the top of each fish, taking great care that they do not break, and lay them on a large serving dish that has a slight well in the center.

8. Lift the backbone away from the lower fillets and discard.

9. Arrange the lower fish fillets on the serving dish along with the others.

10. Strain the reserved fish stock into a large saucepan through a nylon sieve to remove the spices, herbs and vegetables.

11. Add the egg whites to the fish stock and heat gently, whipping constantly with an eggbeater.

12. While you are whipping, the egg whites should form a thick frosty crust on top which removes all particles from the stock.

13. Bring the mixture to the boil then stop whipping and allow the egg whites and liquid to rise up the sides of the pan. Remove from the heat and allow to subside. Repeat this process twice more, then allow to settle completely.

14. Line a colander with several thicknesses of paper towels or cheesecloth and stand the colander over a large bowl. Pour the fish stock into the colander along with the egg whites and allow to drain slowly. Do not allow the egg whites to fall into the clarified liquid.

15. When the liquid has drained through, remove about ½ cup and heat it gently. Sprinkle over the gelatin and allow to stand until the gelatin has dissolved completely.

16. Mix the gelatin mixture into the remaining stock and allow to cool in a refrigerator until just beginning to set.

17. Decorate the trout and the base of the dish with the lemon slices, capers and dill.

18. When the aspic has become syrupy and slightly thickened, spoon it carefully over the fish fillets for decoration.

19. Place the serving plate into a refrigerator and chill until set (about 1-2 hours).

Cook's Notes

Time
Preparation takes 45 minutes to 1 hour. Total cooking time is about 50 minutes plus at least 1 hour to chill the dish.

Watchpoint
Do not stir or whip the aspic or bubbles will form and these will spoil the appearance. For speed you can use powdered aspic, available from most delicatessens.

Fat Type
Fish contains mono-unsaturated fats, and there are no other fats in this recipe.

SERVES 6

TURKEY KEBABS

For this low fat dish, use the ready-prepared turkey joints which are now easily available from supermarkets or butchers.

3lbs lean turkey meat
3 tsps fresh chopped sage
1 sprig rosemary, chopped
Juice 1 lemon
3 tbsps olive oil
Salt and freshly ground black pepper
¼lb lean back bacon, rind removed
Whole sage leaves

1. Remove any bone from the turkey and cut the meat into even-sized cubes.

2. Put the chopped sage, rosemary, lemon juice, oil, salt and pepper into a large bowl and stir in the turkey meat, mixing well to coat evenly. Cover and leave in the refrigerator overnight.

3. Cut the bacon strips into half lengthwise and then again crosswise.

4. Wrap these pieces around as many of the cubes of marinated turkey meat as possible.

5. Thread the turkey and bacon rolls alternately with the sage leaves and any unwrapped turkey cubes onto kebab skewers.

6. Heat the broiler to moderate, and cook the kebabs under the heat for 30 minutes, turning frequently and basting with the marinade whilst cooking. Serve immediately.

Step 3 Cut the bacon slices in half lengthwise and then again crosswise.

Step 2 Stir the cubed turkey pieces into the marinade, mixing well to coat evenly.

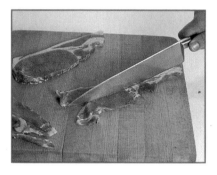

Step 4 Carefully roll each piece of marinated turkey in a strip of bacon.

Cook's Notes

Time
Preparation takes 20 minutes, plus overnight soaking.
Cooking takes about 30 minutes.

Variation
Use chicken if preferred.

Serving Idea
Serve with pitta bread and salad, or on a bed of rice.

Fat Type
Both chicken and turkey contain low amounts of saturated fat. The bacon contains saturated fat, but this will be reduced whilst broiling.

SERVES 6

GREEN GRAPE SHORTCAKE

Plenty of fiber in the diet will help to reduce the amount of cholesterol found in the blood, and the whole-wheat flour and grape skins in this recipe are a good source of fiber.

¼ cup polyunsaturated margarine
2 tbsps soft brown sugar
½ cup whole-wheat flour
¼ cup ground almonds
½lb green grapes, halved and pitted
2½ cups water
Thinly pared rind of 2 lemons
1½ tbsps honey
1 tbsp powdered gelatin
Few drops yellow food coloring, optional

1. Put the margarine, sugar, flour and almonds into a large bowl.

2. Work the margarine into the dry ingredients using your fingertips, and pressing the mixture together gently to form a soft dough.

3. Knead the dough lightly until it is smooth.

4. Line the base of a 8-inch loose-bottomed cake pan with silicone paper. Press the shortcake dough evenly over the base of the lined pan, making sure that it is pushed well into the sides.

5. Bake in a preheated oven 375°F for 15 minutes, or until the shortcake is firm and golden brown. Remove from the oven and allow to cool in the pan.

6. Lightly oil the inside of the cake pan above the shortcake with a little vegetable oil.

7. Arrange the grape halves on top of the shortcake.

8. Put the pint of water and lemon rind into a small pan and bring to the boil. Allow to simmer for 5 minutes, then remove the pan from the heat and allow the liquid to cool completely.

9. Strain the lemon liquid through a nylon sieve to remove the rinds. Measure off 2 cups of the strained liquid and stir in the honey.

10. Put the remaining lemon liquid into a small saucepan and heat gently until it is very hot, but not boiling.

11. Sprinkle over the gelatin and allow to stand until it has completely dissolved.

Step 7 Arrange the grape halves over the cooked shortcake whilst it is still in the pan.

12. At this stage the food coloring can be added to the liquid if desired.

13. Stir the gelatin mixture into the lemon and honey mixture and stand in a cool place until it is beginning to set.

14. Spoon the partially set jelly carefully over the grapes making sure that they remain evenly spread.

15. Stand the shortcake in a refrigerator until the jelly has set completely. Serve in wedges.

Cook's Notes

Time
Preparation takes 45 minutes, plus cooling and chilling. Cooking takes about 20 minutes.

Preparation
It is important never to boil gelatin or it will not dissolve completely.

Fat Type
The fat in this recipe is polyunsaturated.

SERVES 4

SPICED ORANGES WITH HONEY AND MINT

An unusual combination of flavors blend to create this light and very refreshing dessert.

1¼ cups clear honey
1½ cups water
2 large sprigs of fresh mint
12 whole cloves
4 large oranges
4 small sprigs of mint, to garnish

1. Put the honey and the water into a heavy-based saucepan. Add the mint and cloves, and slowly bring to the boil.

2. Stir the mixture to dissolve the honey and boil rapidly for 5 minutes, or until the liquid is very syrupy.

3. Cool the mixture completely, then strain the syrup through a nylon sieve into a jug or bowl to remove the sprigs of mint and cloves.

4. Using a potato peeler, carefully pare the rind very thinly from one orange.

5. Cut the pared orange rind into very fine shreds with a sharp knife.

6. Put the shreds of orange peel into a small bowl and cover with boiling water. Allow to stand until cold then drain completely, reserving only the strips of peel.

7. Stir the strips of peel into the honey syrup and chill well.

8. Peel the oranges completely, removing all the skin and especially the white pith.

Step 3 Strain the syrup through a nylon sieve into a jug or bowl to remove the sprigs of mint and cloves.

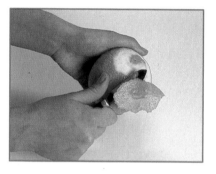

Step 4 Carefully pare the rind from one of the oranges, using a potato peeler and making sure that no white pith comes away with the rind.

9. Slice the oranges into thin rounds using a sharp knife. Arrange the orange rounds onto four individual serving plates.

10. Pour the chilled syrup over the oranges on the plates and garnish with the small sprigs of mint just before serving.

Cook's Notes

Time
Preparation takes 20 minutes, cooking takes about 5 minutes.

Fat Type
There is no fat in this recipe.

Preparation
It is important that all the white pith is removed from the oranges, otherwise this will give a bitter flavor to the dessert.

Variation
Use ruby grapefruits in place of the oranges in this recipe. Allow half a grapefruit per person, and cut it into segments rather than slices to serve.

Low Cholesterol
Notes

Low Cholesterol
Notes

My Favorite Recipes

My Favorite Recipes

My Favorite Recipes

My Favorite Recipes

CONVERSION TABLE

VOLUME MEASUREMENT (dry)

1/8 teaspoon = .5 mL
1/4 teaspoon = 1 mL
1/2 teaspoon = 2 mL
3/4 teaspoon = 4 mL
1 teaspoon = 5 mL
1 tablespoon = 15 mL
2 tablespoons = 25 mL
1/4 cup = 50 mL
1/3 cup = 75 mL
2/3 cup = 150 mL
3/4 cup = 175 mL
1 cup = 250 mL
2 cup = 1 pint = 500 mL
3 cups = 750 mL
4 cups = (1 quart) = 1 L

VOLUME MEASUREMENT (fluid)

1 fluid ounce (2 tablespoons) = 30 mL
4 fluid ounces (1/2 cup) = 125 mL
8 fluid ounces (1 cup) = 250 mL
12 fluid ounces (1 1/2 cups) = 375 mL
16 fluid ounces (2 cups) = 500 mL

DIMENSION

1/16 inch = 2 mm
1/8 inch = 3 mm
1/4 inch = 6 mm
1/2 inch = 1.5 cm
3/4 inch = 2 cm
1 inch = 2.5 cm

TEMPERATURES

250° F = 120° C
275° F = 140° C
300° F = 150° C
325° F = 160° C
350° F = 180° C
375° F = 190° C
400° F = 200° C
425° F = 220° C
450° F = 230° C

WEIGHT

1/2 ounce = 15 g
1 ounce = 30 g
3 ounces = 85 g
3.75 ounces = 100 g
4 ounces = 115 g
8 ounces = 225 g
12 ounces = 340 g
16 ounces = (1 pound) = 450 g

SUGAR

1 teaspoon = 4 g
1 tablespoon = 12 g
4 tablespoons (1/4 cup) = 50 g
5 1/3 tablespoons (1/3 cup) = 70 g
1/2 cup = 100 g
2/3 cup = 135 g
3/4 cup = 150 g
1 cup = 200 g